BLACK WRITERS
ON WHAT IT MEANS
TO BE WHITE

EDITED AND WITH AN

INTRODUCTION BY

DAVID R. ROEDIGER

SCHOCKEN BOOKS NEW YORK

Introduction, commentary, and compilation copyright © 1998
by David R. Roediger

All rights reserved under International and Pan-American Copyright
Conventions. Published in the United States by Schocken Books Inc., New York,
and simultaneously in Canada by Random House of Canada Limited, Toronto.
Distributed by Pantheon Books, a division of Random House, Inc., New York.

SCHOCKEN and colophon are trademarks of Schocken Books Inc.

Permissions Acknowledgments appear on pages 351–353.

Library of Congress Cataloging-in-Publication Data
Black on white : Black writers on what it means to be white / edited and with an
introduction by David R. Roediger.
p.   cm.
ISBN 0-8052-4146-9
1. Whites—United States.   2. Race awareness—United States.
3. United States—Race relations.   4. Afro-Americans—Attitudes
5. American literature—Afro-American authors.   6. Whites in literature.
7. Race relations in literature.   I. Roediger, David R.
E185.61.B586   1998

305.8'00973—dc21   97-31361
                                                          CIP

Random House Web Address: http://www.randomhouse.com

Book design by Maura Fadden Rosenthal/Mspace

Printed in the United States of America
First Edition
2   4   6   8   9   7   5   3   1

TO JEAN

CONTENTS

Preface   xi

Introduction   1

PART II
WHITENESS AS PROPERTY: THE WORKINGS OF RACE

PART III
THE WHITE WORLD AND WHITER AMERICA

PART VI
WHITE TERRORS

PREFACE

This book is dedicated to Sterling Stuckey. With George Fredrickson, Stuckey taught me African-American history two decades ago. Insistent on broad training in literature and folklore as well as in social and political history, Stuckey also taught by example the value of rereading classic works. When I began to write more on the history of white workers, and less on the African-American past, Stuckey continued to refer to me as an African Americanist. Only gradually, as I came to research the racial identity of those white workers, did I come to realize how right he was. Rereading African-American studies of white people, especially those by W.E.B. Du Bois and James Baldwin, became my consistent source of insight and inspiration. The tendency of many writers to believe that "whiteness studies" is a recent creation in which white scholars have pioneered thus runs directly counter to my experience. This volume attempts to show that such studies are part of the long, rich, varied, and unsurpassed tradition of Black thought about white people and whiteness.

In addition to uncommon generosity with regard to permissions to republish material, I have also benefited from the excellent advice and the support of other scholars. Particular thanks in those connections go to Stuckey, Angela Dillard, Toni Morrison, John Wright, Sundiata Cha-Jua, George Lipsitz, Robin D. G. Kelley, Troy Duster, Martha Hodes, Walter Johnson, Brendan Roediger, Franklin Rosemont, Peter Rachleff, Mia Bay, Wahneema Lubiano, Michael Gomez, Vron Ware, and Tiffany Patterson. The cover illustration, of Black puppeteers in the Buffalo Historical Marionettes performing *The Life of Stephen Foster*, was unearthed by the historian of theater Beth Cleary. The research assistance of Tiya Miles and Deirdre Murphy made possible the timely completion of this book and enriched it with new discoveries, measured opinions, and fresh insights. Vital too were opportunities to speak about the book as it went through various stages of evolution. In that connection I especially thank the Lefler Lecture Fund at Carleton College, the Kaplan Lecture Fund of the University of Pennsylvania, the Committee on Social Theory at the University of Kentucky, the Black Student Union at the State University of New York, Binghamton, the Ethnic Studies Program at the University of California, Berkeley, the Black History Month Lecture Series at Spelman College, the Haven Center at the University of Wisconsin, the University of Minnesota's Immigration History Research Center in Saint Paul, the American Studies Association, and the History Departments at New York University and at Southern Illinois University, Edwardsville. Research funding has come from the McKnight Summer Fellowship and from the College of Liberal Arts at the University of Minnesota. Cecelia Cancellaro has been a model editor, contributing not only sound editorial advice but also great intellectual energy and subtlety. My wife, Jean Allman, titled the book and sharpened my thinking about it in a host of ways.

The book's structure assumes that the powerful pieces of art, poetry, and prose it contains stand on their own, without extensive editorial commentary. The selections are grouped under general subject headings, but the best of them cut across several categories—speaking at once to whiteness and Americanism, to whiteness and class, and to whiteness and gender, for example. The brief headnotes to each selection identify the author and when needed, set up the context of an excerpt republished from a larger work. My introduction attempts to sketch the depth and dimensions of African-American studies of whiteness. Throughout I use the term "study" as in Black vernacular English, to describe both academic study and hard thought undertaken in much less formal contexts. The many selections in this volume make no claim to represent all African-American opinion about whites and whiteness. For example, the more reflexively anti-white tradition represented (at times) by the Nation of Islam, or by Leonard Jeffries's recent writings on whites as "ice people," is not substantially included. The aim is quite frankly to bring a usable tradition to light and to bear on further studies of what it has meant, and means, to be white in the United States.

—David R. Roediger
June 1997

INTRODUCTION

White people have not always been
"white," nor will they always be "white." It
is a political alliance. Things will change.
                                    AMOJA THREE RIVERS

Consider a slave on the auction block, awaiting sale. Imagine the slave being seen, indeed examined, by the potential bidders. Imagine what she felt. Think of her trembling and crying, breaking down, even fighting back. Such attempts to imagine looking in on the auction block and to empathize with those for sale have found a hard-won place in the mainstream of American culture. But little prepares us to see her as looking out, as studying the bidders. And yet, as recent and imaginative research has shown, slaves on the block often searched out every clue in sizing up the whites who would own them.[1] Did that scar represent a history of violence? What did that leer suggest? Was that accent familiar, or did it point to the possibility of being transported great distances, away from family and to the master's home? Did those clothes mean great wealth, declining fortunes, or poor whiteness? What could be learned of the buyers from other slaves? What strategies of self-presentation would discourage the attention of the bidder most feared, or encourage the potential buyer judged to be the best of terrible options?

When Langston Hughes published *The Ways of White Folks* some sixty years after the end of slavery, he featured the short story "Slave on the Block" near the book's outset. Set in early-twentieth-century New York City, not the antebellum South, and describing the experiences of a black servant rather than a slave, Hughes's story nonetheless claimed the angle of vision from the auction block as indispensable in describing how African Americans have learned about white ways.[2] In fact, the drama of the auction block highlights many of the major themes included in this volume regarding how African Americans have thought about and studied whiteness. The deep associations of whiteness with terror and with property were sharply posed at the point of sale. The auction block gave flesh to questions of sexual exploitation and of gender. Its stark realities laid bare the urgent imperative for slaves to penetrate the psychologies of whites and their necessity to make distinctions even among white slave buyers. All of these themes and more figure prominently in African-American thought concerning whiteness, and deserve our attention here.

But few Americans have ever considered the idea that African-Americans are extremely knowledgeable about whites and whiteness. In the mainstream of American culture, and certainly in intellectual circles, a rough and unproductive division of labor exists where the claiming of expert knowledge and commonsense wisdom on race are concerned. White writers have long been positioned as the leading and most dispassionate investigators of the lives, values, and abilities of people of color. White writing about whiteness is rarer, with discussions of what it means to be human standing in for considerations of how racial identity influences white lives. Writers of color, and most notably African-American writers, are cast as providing insight, often presumed to be highly subjective, of what it is like to be "a minority." Lost in this destructive shuffle is the fact that from folktales onward African Americans have been among the nation's keenest students of white consciousness and white behavior.

A story about each of the two greatest modern writers on whiteness in the United States, Toni Morrison and James Baldwin, allows us to see how African-American knowledge of whites is created and suppressed. In 1993, the journalist Bill Moyers asked Morrison when she would start writing about white people. Morrison wanted no part of Moyers's invitation to move into the white center of literary culture. She pledged to "stay out here at the margin and let the center come looking for me." Morrison had, however, already written considerably about whites, both in fictional work like "Recitatif" and in the brilliant 1990 volume *Playing in the Dark: Whiteness and the Literary Imagination*.[3] That challenging book was so little appreciated that Moyers could still ask when the writing on whites was to come. The fact that she had written the most important volume on whiteness published in this decade did not so much as establish Morrison's interest in the subject in the eyes of a relatively sophisticated observer of race in the United States like Moyers.

At nineteen, James Baldwin's visits to the Apollo Theatre, an art film house on 42nd Street in New York City, left him paralyzed by a terror born of looking into the faces of the white, gay male clientele there. The gay men he saw seemed "so far from being or resembling faggots." Indeed he thought that they "looked and sounded like vigilantes who banded together on weekends to beat faggots up." After much suffering, he found that it was often true that the men alternated between gay sexuality and homophobic violence. Baldwin situated his knowledge in the position from which he observed the men. He had "seen them in the men's room, sometimes on their knees, peering up into the stalls." But his racial position also mattered. "I might not have learned this had I been a white boy," he later wrote, regarding his knowledge of the coexistence of sex and violence, "but sometimes a white man will tell a black boy anything, everything, weeping briny tears. He knows that a black boy can never betray him, for no one will believe his testimony."[4] Baldwin's reminiscences complicate our tasks. They suggest that Moyers's dismissal of Morrison's work on whiteness might typify a larger pattern of the ways in which whites disbelieve and/or disregard how much African Americans know about them. Indeed, for Baldwin, the wholesale dismissal by whites of African-American expertise regarding whiteness was one critical condition under which such knowledge could be obtained.

At times African Americans have boldly claimed their expertise on whiteness. In the World War One era, James Weldon Johnson would assert as a "fact" that "colored people of this country know and understand the white people better than the white people know and understand them." A decade later, the African-American journalist and novelist George S. Schuyler held, "While the average Nordic knows nothing of how Negroes actually live and what they think, the Negroes know the Nordic intimately." The claims advanced by Johnson and Schuyler are serious and well-grounded, despite the fact that they would seem very unfamiliar and counterintuitive to most whites. Schuyler explained the insights of Black thinkers into "white lives" by observing that "blacks haven't been working with or for white folks all these years for nothing." W.E.B. Du Bois in *Darkwater* and bell hooks in *Black Looks* similarly emphasize the servants' ability to know the families for whom they work.[5] The contemporary mystery writer Barbara Neely captures this point wonderfully as her domestic worker/detective hero, Blanche White, solves murders by deploying her intimate knowledge of whites. Long experience with violence and sexual exploitation, Ida B. Wells-Barnett and Frederick Douglass argued, perfectly situated African-American Southerners to deflate the claims to chivalry, restraint, and civilization made by white males of that region. The drama and tragedy of passing as white, which is the subject of a large literature usually seen as portraying an exotic part of Black life, also turned on the close observation of white lives. Thus it should be no surprise that the legal theorist Cheryl Harris has recently used histories of passing by a family member to open discussions of the dynamics of white society.[6]

What bell hooks describes as the fantastic white ability to imagine "that black people cannot see them" constitutes a white illusion at once durable, powerful, and fragile. It exists alongside a profound fear of actually being seen by people of color. As Baldwin argued, ". . . a vast amount of the energy that goes into what we call the Negro problem is produced by the white man's desire not to be judged by those who are not white." From the beatings of house slaves who knew too much to the lynchings of African Americans thought to look too long, safety has often turned not just on being unseen, but also on being perceived as unseeing. Richard Wright's mother knew whereof she spoke when she responded fiercely and negatively to his apparently simple youthful question, "Can I go peep at the white folks?" The law under slavery went to considerable pains to keep slaves from testifying against, or even about, whites. After emancipation, keeping African Americans off juries became a central focus of racist state policy.[7] Discounting and suppressing the knowledge of whiteness held by people of color was not just a byproduct of white supremacy but an imperative of racial domination.

The exposure of the illusion that Blacks did not see and know whites was too troubling to be countenanced, even if indications of its implausibility came from white authors centrally placed within the canon of Western philosophy and literature. If Hegel's celebrated early-nineteenth-century reflections on "lordship and bondage" applied to slavery and racial oppression, white mastery was futile and the denial of African-American knowledge of whites was ridiculous. Hegel saw the slave as living always with the knowledge of the master's deadly power. Slaves therefore necessarily thought deeply about the dynam-

ics of lordship and bondage. The master could afford a lofty ignorance. As the slaves labored, stood in fear, and learned, they also
"worked on" escaping their chains. This probing analysis, philoso-
phers are anxious to tell us, represented Hegel's grappling with broad
issues of consciousness and mind, not with the slave systems of his
age. With this view, the implications of Hegel's work can neatly be
separated from Baldwin's insistence that "white men have for black
men a reality which is far from being reciprocal."[8]

Literary critics often manage to skirt the troubling implications of
the closest fictional approximation of Hegel's insights, Herman
Melville's classic novel of slave revolt, Benito Cereno. Critics have found
Benito Cereno to be fundamentally concerned with good and evil,
with civilization and savagery, with the confidence of the young
American nation—with, in short, everything but African-American
knowledge of whites. Not coincidentally, the writer who has done
the most to restore discussions of Black genius regarding whites to
discussions of the very plot of Benito Cereno (and to establish connections of Melville with Hegel) is the African-American historian of
slavery, Sterling Stuckey. "The slave perspective on the larger society,"
Stuckey has written in a passage suggesting one source of his insights
into Melville, "is seldom about the oppressed exclusively."[9]

Contemporary dismissals of African-American testimony regarding whiteness abound. The historian George Lipsitz recently called to
task a pair of political scientists who described changes in white racial
attitudes by using polling data from white respondents. How much
better it would be, Lipsitz argued, to concentrate equally on polling
data among people of color, who are in an excellent position to measure whether white attitudes have really changed.[10] However acute,
Lipsitz's point always provokes a smile when I repeat it. It is the same
kind of smile that the Chicago iconoclast Mike Royko knew he
would get when he described Spike Lee's Do the Right Thing as a classic cinematic study of Italian-American life.

I frequently copy for white students a report on a recent University of Michigan study which argues that, despite much talk about
self-segregation by students of color, such students are much more
likely than white students to socialize, date, and dine across the color

line.[11] The study typically provokes disbelief, disquiet, and then dismissal. Students of color must be more insular; everybody knows they
are. The deeper problem comes when I ask whether cross-racial experience by students of color makes it likely that they know more about
white students than white students know about them.

Mainstream scholarship provides little to challenge the students'
view regarding the implausibility of African-American expertise about
whites. In the hysteria over what gets called "political correctness,"
for example, much is sometimes made of the supposed animosity
directed at white scholars who write and teach about people of color.
But the converse—the almost utter failure to encourage or even notice studies of whiteness by scholars of color—draws no notice. A
significant literature in which whites are the main, or only, characters
in works of fiction by African-American authors has, for example,
engaged the talents of such great artists as Chester B. Himes, Paul
Laurence Dunbar, Wallace Thurman, Gordon Parks, Samuel R.
Delany, William Attaway, Charles Waddell Chesnutt, Willard Motley,
Ann Petry, James Baldwin, and Richard Wright. The serious "white
life novel" has left very little impact on American literary criticism.
Even its most spectacular successes, such as James Baldwin's *Giovanni's
Room* or Zora Neale Hurston's *Seraph on the Suwanee,* are little read.
Less artistically successful works, such as Richard Wright's pulpy and
revealing account of loss and violence in the white middle class in
Savage Holiday, vanish with hardly a trace.[12]

In my own field, that of history, the leading U.S. professional organization recently published a poll which asked members to list the
most important historians and books treating the American South.
Not a single respondent named W.E.B. Du Bois's *Black Reconstruction.* This omission, the rough equivalent of a group of theologians
neglecting the Bible in listing important books bearing on Christian tradition, came as part of a pattern. Among 111 responses naming historians of the South, only three identified African-American
historians. The early-twentieth-century apologist for slavery, U. B.
Phillips, by himself drew eight mentions. In part this reflects the
unstated and ridiculous assumption that Southern history somehow
means white Southern history. But even if this assumption were

somehow granted, we would confront the fact that historians ignoring Du Bois are ignoring a scholar whose accounts of the *white* South in *Black Reconstruction* remain unsurpassed. In any case, John Hope Franklin's *The Militant South,* a masterful study focusing squarely on whites, also failed to register more than token mention with the poll's respondents, just as it originally provoked puzzlement among white historians, who regarded its choice of topics, white violence, as a baffling one for a Black historian.[13]

Certainly a desire to strike back against racist stereotypes has served as a point of departure for many African-American studies of whiteness. Animated by what Ralph Ellison calls a desire to "change the joke [and] slip the yoke," such overturnings of racism took many forms. Thus from Frederick Douglass to the early-twentieth-century radical Cyril Briggs to the editors of *Ebony* in the 1960s, Black thinkers have answered pompous white pronouncements on the "Negro problem" by identifying the "white problem" at the center of American ills. If sentimental white Southerners waxed nostalgic with claims to write knowingly about "our black folks," the irascible George S. Schuyler turned the tables in a merciless 1927 essay entitled "Our White Folks." If lynch mobs justified themselves with lurid allegations of Black bestiality, and with homage to the manly and civilized self-control of even white mob members, Ida B. Wells-Barnett branded as savage, uncontrolled, cowardly, and sexually predatory those white males who led and joined crowds committing the public murders of Black men and sometimes women.[14]

At their simplest level, such reversals have focused on physical traits. The African-American abolitionist and lawyer, Dr. John S. Rock, spoke in 1861 of the contrast between the "fine, tough muscular system, the beautiful, rich color, the full broad features, and the gracefully frizzled hair of the Negro" and the "delicate physical organization, wan color, sharp features and long hair of the Caucasian." Rock surmised that "when the white man was created, nature was pretty well exhausted but, determined to keep up appearances, she pinched up his features and did the best she could under the circumstances." In an 1859 fantasy set in the year 4000, "Ethiop" wrote of African Americans remembering their defeated and disappeared oppressors as "milk white . . . like the chalk of foreign hills," with lank "un-comely" hair, sharp noses, and narrow faces. Six decades later, Du Bois would write, in a fanciful dialogue with a white supremacist, that as a "matter of taste" he, too, found "straight features" unattractive. "Needles and razors may be sharp," he reasoned, "but beautiful, never." This tradition continues, for example, in the recent satire of I. M. Blacque, self-published under the title *White Women Got Flat Butts*.[15]

More often, the "white problem" was seen as focusing on morality and history. When the historian Herbert Aptheker identified African-American superiority as a "neglected theme" in Black thought, his most convincing examples involved claims of the moral superiority of, as Du Bois put it, "the Lynched above the Lyncher . . . the Cruci-fied above Imperial Rome." In surveying the white, and particularly the Anglo-Saxon, past, African-American thinkers often returned charges of racial savagery more than in kind. When Marcus Garvey wrote "The Tragedy of White Injustice," he followed and made more extreme a significant line of thought emphasizing not only the bru-tality of slavery and racism, but of what Charles Chesnutt called the "Angry-Saxon" tradition more generally:

> Out of the cold of Europe these white men came /. . . eating their dead's flesh and sucking their blood / Relics of the Medi-terranean flood. . . .[16]

Such reversals often moved from simple returning of fire to rich irony, passionate practical concern, and a sharp questioning of white civilization. In 1964 Ralph Ellison described the folk verse "These white folk think / That they so fine, / But their dirty linen stinks / Just like mine" as a "sharp mused, clear-eyed observation of reality." In 1985, those lines (with slight variations) were for Ellison "not only childish but ultimately frustrating." More was required for Ellison, and more was often created. The African-American activist William J. Wilson, for example, changed the joke in 1860 when he observed that "for many centuries now [whites] have been on this continent; and for many years they have had entire rule and sway; yet they are

today no nearer to the problem—'Are they fit for self-government?'—
than they were at the beginning of their career." Absent guidance
from African Americans, the Brooklyn schoolteacher added, whites
would decline into "sure and certain barbarism." Wilson followed this
acid humor with a deadly earnest question—one which has perforce
engaged a part of African-American energy over the generations:
"What shall we do with the white people?"[17]

As they examined whiteness, many African-American thinkers
also came to see through the fictions of race as a scientific category,
although this did not always occur. From the nineteenth century's
replies to white racist "science," to the Nation of Islam and the
melanin-based theories of Frances Cress Welsing, a strain of biological race-thinking has had its appeals within African-American
thought. At times the attempt to counter essentialist, pseudoscientific,
white supremacist hierarchies by simply flipping them over stalled
once the flipping was done, because no fundamental critique of the
idea of race was generated. Much more impressive is the strength of a
tradition which did generate just such critiques. As Toni Morrison
argues:

> For three hundred years black Americans insisted that "race"
> was no usefully distinguishing factor in human relationships.
> During those same three centuries every academic discipline . . .
> insisted that "race" was the determining factor in human devel-
> opment.[18]

The African-American popular writer J. A. Rogers's early-
twentieth-century short story, "The Porter Debates the Senator,"
thoroughly debunks, through the wisdom of the porter, what Baldwin would later call the "lie of whiteness." Scoffing at notions of race
and racial purity and referring at times to all "race talk" as a "joke,"
Du Bois caught both the absurdity and gravity of racism in the
United States. His persona in *Dusk of Dawn* revealed the "quite easy"
rule-of-thumb for determining racial status in a very mixed population: "the black man is a person who must ride Jim Crow in Georgia." "The only whitey," Amiri Baraka recently added, "is system and

ideology." Malcolm X's phrasing on this score was still more striking. When writing from within the Nation of Islam, even before his conversion to changed attitudes about race in Mecca, Malcolm made a point of connecting whiteness with the exercise of power, not with biology. He looked forward, in *The End of White World Supremacy*, to the simultaneous demise of "colonialism," "white supremacy," and what he wonderfully named "white-ism." The end of white-ism, he hinted, in a provocative call for the abolition of whiteness, would end the "power" and therefore the "world" of white men.[19]

But African-American knowledge of whiteness amounts to much more than a denial of dominant assumptions regarding the reality of race and the superiority of whites. Based on artistry, study, and the intraracial exchange of ideas regarding struggle and survival, such knowledge did not simply react to what whites did and said. Broadly curious, and often strikingly compassionate, it necessarily considered the variety of white behavior. John Brown, the subject of a large body of African-American literary tributes, as well as a series of Jacob Lawrence paintings, was not George Wallace, and this is made clear by the way each of these men has been represented by African Americans. Whether surveying oppressors from the auction block, choosing employers, or searching for political allies, attention to nuances mattered greatly. Hughes qualified his puzzlement and disgust with the "ways of white folks" with "I mean some white folks."[20]

The issues of property, terror, and psychology represent areas in which African-American folklore, art, and academic study have pushed most persistently to unearth and answer fundamental questions regarding whiteness. Cheryl Harris's recent "Whiteness as Property," perhaps the most important historical treatment of whiteness since W.E.B. Du Bois's *Black Reconstruction,* offers a many-sided account of the ways in which the law and the practice of slave-trading, slaveholding, dispossession of American Indians, Jim Crow, and discrimination in wages and employment have trained whites to expect that their racial status will pay off. Harris shows that such expectations are not just the products of exploitation practiced long ago but also of recent history and contemporary oppression. Harris is right to place her striking essay within a tradition, noting the profound influences of Du Bois and of the African-American legal theorist Derrick Bell. She might have gone back to the folk tradition as well:

> *Nigger plants cotton,*
> *Nigger picks it out,*
> *White man pockets money,*
> *Nigger does without.*[21]

Indeed the earliest and most durable African-American folk traditions that sought to explain the differing values and fortunes of Blacks and whites center on the differing relations of Blacks and whites to a "box of work" stumbled upon by early men and women. Likewise anticipating important dimensions of Harris's analysis was Oliver Cromwell Cox, the great African-American sociologist of class and race. Other African-American leftists detailed the economic workings of what they called "white skin privilege"—the systematic favoritism which has allowed some white workers, as a character in Amiri Baraka's "The Motion of History" puts it, to get paid for "a dollar's worth of skin color" every hour of their working lives.[22]

Commentary on class divisions among whites is another important dimension of African-American thought. Slaves, who appreciated the hard fact that being held by poorer whites could mean more frequent sales and fewer opportunities for life in an African-American community in the quarters, were the initiators of this inquiry. Understanding, and at times internalizing, how the ruling race reckoned hierarchies of class and color, slaves skewered poorer whites for their poverty and sometimes for their sun-baked darkness. African-American speech spread the less-than-admiring terms for impoverished whites and often had a hand in their coinage or in their importation from African languages to the United States: *white trash, buckra, cracker, peckerwood,* and *redneck.* A keen interest in the white worker animates much African-American political writing. Authors continually judged, empirically and theoretically, the viability of alliances with white workers.[23] Labor historians, such as Sterling Spero and Abram Harris, sociologists, such as St. Clair Drake and Horace Cayton, and activist-intellectuals, such as Paul Robeson, Cyril Briggs, and Du Bois, reached different conclusions (and frequently changed their own minds) regarding the record and potential of such alliances.

"They tried to guarantee happiness to themselves," the poet Sterling A. Brown wrote of whites, work, and wealth in his classic, "Strong Men," "by shunting dirt and misery to you." Often, Black authors observed, there was to be no happiness. Elma Stuckey, whose work was inspired in large part by conversations with ex-slaves in her Memphis childhood, illustrates this theme in her poem "Enslaved," in which a "Red-necked cracker all alone" rages against an African American offering aid: "'Don't want your food, out of my sight! / I'm clinging to this—I'm white, I'm white!'"[24]

Du Bois, with a generosity not uncommon in African-American reflections on whiteness, confessed his "vast pity,—pity for [white working] people imprisoned and enthralled, hampered and made miserable" for the "phantasy" of white supremacy. He wrote of imperialism distorting and impoverishing the very ideals of the white worker, who wanted "not comfort for all men but power over other men," who "did not love humanity and hated 'niggers.'" In his *Black Reconstruction,* Du Bois provided the first history of the "white worker" and a still unequaled dissection of the attractions of the "public and psychological wages" of whiteness for laboring people of the dominant race. But those wages had a cost for whites as well as Blacks. He describes not only the glories of "the black laborer's Saturday off" but also the regimentation of white workers who too often accept that "daily toil is one of the Ten Commandments." "God made de world," as an African-American tale put it, "and de white folks made work."[25]

Equally compelling African-American studies treat whiteness as a species of terror. "White folks got my body," ran the refrain of the great Afro–South Carolinian folk poem "The Lynchers," in a moaning description of the survivors, not just the mobbed and murdered victims of lynch law. Paul Gilroy's recent *The Black Atlantic* uncompromisingly calls upon the tradition of connecting the terrors of the trade in Black bodies, the bloodiness of slave control, and the soul-killing violence of racial exploitation with the total experience of whiteness by people of color. bell hooks makes much the same points regarding the circumstances under which African Americans encounter and represent whiteness.[26]

Other Black thinkers have carried this insight still further. They contend that whiteness is also experienced through terror by whites, who find and reproduce unity by committing, and more often by witnessing, acts of violence. Slave tales and autobiographies, for example, at times insisted upon the centrality of stealing humans, breaking up families, "patrolling" plantations, and committing rape to the growth of a white identity. Those not active in the carnage, as Frederick Douglass emphasized in his discussions of planters' wives, were not only complicit in white terror, but also likely to fashion a tortured sense of white supremacy. When Zora Neale Hurston wrote that "Jim Crow laws have a purpose and that purpose is psychological," her point concerned the impact of systematic legal terror on the minds of whites as well as those of African Americans. "Seeing the daily humiliations of darker people," she wrote, "confirms the [white] child in its superiority." In a passage bound to be the envy of any postmodern theorist of race, Ralph Ellison likewise found white identity to be premised on and maintained through terror. Whiteness, for Ellison, was "a form of manifest destiny which designated Negroes as its territory and challenge." For Ellison the mob acted not only to brutalize its Black victims but also to "affirm white goals" and white unity. Both Ellison and Marion Vera Cuthbert created remarkable short stories describing a lynching from the viewpoint of a white onlooker devastated by the collective atrocities.[27]

The meticulous journalism on white terror by Wells-Barnett, Walter White, and others was never merely reporting. It documented, among much else, the mass experience of violence. We should consider that more than 3,000 lynchings of African Americans between 1890 and the Great Depression included many instances in which thousands and even upwards of 10,000 whites witnessed the horror. So planned as spectacles were some lynchings that excursion trains brought the huge crowds. Remains of the victims at times remained for days on public display. Crowds watched brawls over "souvenir" body parts. Folks songs memorialized the brutality. The sites of mob actions remained etched for decades in local memory, white as well as Black. It would seem beyond question that several million early twentieth century whites witnessed a lynching or touched its relics, and that tens of millions more were initiated into whiteness partly by hearing stories of racist terror from those closest to them.[28]

It is within the African-American tradition that the greatest awareness of such terror as a constituent part of white identity has been present. Indeed, even the daunting task of considering how whiteness as a system of property and whiteness as a system of terror have coexisted and shaped each other has received some attention in African-American thought. Slave autobiographies consistently emphasize both dynamics. Wells-Barnett, born just after slavery in Mississippi, cast white conservative political terror during Reconstruction, as well as waves of lynchings which followed, as responses to the fact that with emancipation "the vested interests of the white men in the Negro's body was lost." Walter White made "The Economic Foundations of Lynch Law" the centerpiece of *Rope and Faggot,* his classic study of racist terror. Wells-Barnett, White, and other African-American opponents of lynching also realized that economic success, not criminality, often exposed African Americans to mob violence. For Toni Morrison, the dangerous and dramatic white "playground of the imagination" which gave rise to a "uniquely American" white consciousness took root not just because it could "allay internal fears" but also because it could "rationalize external exploitation."[29]

Attempts to understand white terror and the psychologies of white people have productively focused on issues of gender and sexuality. Scrutiny of white manhood, so intimately and variously tied to the sexual exploitation of Black women, to the brutalization of Black men, and to white political mobilization and political violence, has, of course, been a staple of African-American writing from Harriet Jacobs to Jean Toomer to bell hooks. One of the most noteworthy characters in Richard Wright's *Eight Men* gains terrible knowledge of such white male sexuality as he attempts to pass as a Black female servant. But in many ways more remarkable, and more consistently revealing of the ways in which racism impacted on gender relations and domestic violence between white men and women, has been the significant discussion of the position of white women in African-American thought. Slave narratives often showed plantation mistresses pitiably attempting to live on a pedestal, to enforce oppression, and to ignore their husband's trips to the quarters. Often deeply compassionate, these narratives acknowledged both the harm done to slaveholding women and the harm which they in turn visited on slaves. After emancipation, Ida B. Wells-Barnett keenly observed that the "protection" white men offered from the alleged threat of Black rapists was hollow and destructive, that the "guardianship" of the "chivalrous white man" was the great misfortune of the Southern white woman. Walter White attempted to quantify the point. He counted the numbers of lynchings and the number of women listed in *Who's Who in America*. The more of the former in any given state, the less of the latter.[30]

Careful attempts to delineate what white and Black women did and did not share date to the words of Sojourner Truth, Frances E. W. Harper, and other nineteenth century women activists. They stretch to the works of Hortense Spillers, Angela Davis, Joy James, and the remarkable recent attempts of Cheryl Harris to consider the implications of white women typically reproducing free laborers, citizens, and even masters, while African-American women, at most times and places, reproduced the unfree. Studies which, from Wells-Barnett to Calvin Hernton to Trudier Harris to Lewis Gordon, explore the affinities between white women and Black men have been equally compelling. These affinities are traced to both a common humanity and to tangled connections between the oppression of both groups. By far the most provocative recent work in this area is Lewis Gordon's attempt to explore Black male and white female "effeminacy" in the worldview of white men. The white woman, according to Gordon, is not simply the "jewel of the antiblack racist" male, but also a "white blackness." Only she, as the United States reckons race, is capable of giving birth to white or Black babies. She is a "hole," Gordon argues, in a nation in which white heterosexual manliness is defined by a constant attempt to "close all . . . holes." She is as distrusted as she is glorified. Gordon's insistence on the denial of homoerotic desire as one central element in white maleness links his work to a substantial tradition of African-American gay and lesbian writing. At its best, from Baldwin to Audre Lorde, this tradition illuminates both race in the gay community and white heterosexuality as well.[31]

African-American thinkers have also fixed on the complex ways in which being American both has and has not implied being white. As Morrison argues, a crowning achievement of white domination in the United States has been that for most of the nation's history, "American" has silently signaled "white American." Adjectives were necessary only when nonwhite race or ethnicity within the white population had to be indicated. But at the same time, African-American intellectuals, such as Ralph Ellison and Albert Murray, have fully established that American culture is anything but white. South and North, the direct cultural influence of African Americans on whites loomed large. The "haunting" quality of Blackness further stemmed from the fact that white unity could only create itself against images of nonwhite others. In 1927, James Weldon Johnson wrote, "I am sure it would be safe to wager that no group of Southern white men could get together for sixty minutes without bringing up the race question. If the Northern white man happened to be in the group, the time could be safely cut to thirty minutes." Murray's characterization of U.S. culture as "incontestably mulatto" is, of course, too narrow to describe the many-sided hybridities which made America. And surely the incisive work on race and cultural borrowing by such scholars as Amiri Baraka and Nelson George requires us to attend to the deep inequalities of power which formed the context for both biological and cultural mixing across color lines. Greg Tate's homage to the brilliant white historian of African culture in the Americas, Robert Farris Thompson, sits hard by his disgust with young white males whose identification with Black culture consists of liking "to say *ho.*"[32] But such important complexities and qualifications aside, Ellison's (larger) point regarding African America's cultural impact on whites in the United States stands intact. In becoming both white and American, immigrants from Ireland and then from southern and east-ern Europe had to learn two lies—that they were white and that America was.

Until recently, the drama of such immigrants' history was supposed by almost all white scholars to be an encounter with Americanization and a contested acceptance of the requirements of assimilation. Such scholars missed the fact that immigrants often "became white" as well as they "became American." But exploration of the former drama is longstanding within the African-American tradition, at least since Chesnutt's "What Is a White Man" appeared in 1889. The simplest and perhaps most celebrated answer to how the whiteness of new immigrants can be historicized comes in the epilogue to Malcolm X's *Autobiography*. His collaborator on the book, Alex Haley, describes being in a U.S. airport with Malcolm and admiring an arriving family of European immigrants. They are, Malcolm predicts, about to learn their first word of English: *nigger*. Malcolm's one-liner is so precisely presaged and repeated in the works of Black artists from John Oliver Killens to Richard Pryor—Toni Morrison counts *nigger* as the second word in the immigrant's English vocabulary, with only "okay" coming before it—that it raises the possibility that each teller of the joke drew it from Black folk humor. Like the most enduring folklore, it distills a sharp point and operates on a number of levels. Pessimistic to the point of rancor, the joke nevertheless does not make immigrant racism a product of the essential "white" characteristics of the newcomers. The weight of U.S. racial division must be learned. The drama and tragedy arise from the knowledge that American realities were such brutal and effective teachers of that division, and that immigrants were such apt and ready learners of a word which, as Ralph Ellison wrote, "made them feel instantly American."[33]

Coexisting with the bitterness of Malcolm's joke is a much more lyrical tradition of Black commentary on the racial identity of new immigrants—a tradition equally premised on a deep sense of tragedy. In William Attaway's fine 1941 proletarian novel, *Blood on the Forge,* Melody and his half-brother, Chinatown, disagreed on the merits of the music made by the immigrants with whom they worked in Pittsburgh's steel mills. Chinatown heard in it but a "yowl," adding that "a

man can't understand one word they yowlin'." But Melody, who lived
to play the blues and who could "hear music in a snore," knew better.
He

> had heard some of these people from the Ukraine singing. He
> hadn't understood one word. Yet he didn't have to know the
> words to understand what they were wailing about. Words didn't
> count when the music had a tongue. The field hands of the
> sloping red-hill country in Kentucky sang that same tongue.

Attaway portrayed common oppression at every turn. Blacks and
Bohunks shared a wrenching from the land, lived in comparable
poverty, and died in the same industrial accidents. The same profit
motive and the same Irish-American petty bosses pitted African
Americans against hunkies. But the solidarities Melody heard in music
remained sadly absent from labor struggles and from everyday life.[34]

Hearing the wails of his (and Chinatown's) old Kentucky home in
Ukrainian music, Melody echoed Frederick Douglass's observations
of almost a century earlier. During his 1845–46 tour of Ireland,
Douglass heard the "wailing notes" of the music of the oppressed and
famished Irish people as close kin of the "wild notes" of the slaves'
sorrow songs. Douglass lingered over the wails of the Irish to emphasize the tragedy of Irish-American racism, seconding Irish nationalist
leader Daniel O'Connell's point that this was a "cruelty" not learned
in Ireland and was utterly inappropriate to the Irish experience. Morrison's description of her relationship with a new immigrant school-
mate in her Ohio hometown goes even further in illustrating the costs
of learning to be white in a racially driven society. In about second
grade, Morrison was paired in a "double-seat" with a newly arrived
boy who knew little or no English. She became his teacher and his
friend, until he learned the word *nigger* and the racial ground rules of
the United States. In short order, he tried *nigger* out on her and broke
the friendship. Striving to become white meant losing Morrison as an
English teacher.[35]

No thinker so fully brought together the many dimensions of
African-American studies of whiteness as James Baldwin. Attention

to power, to property, to work, to tragedy, to culture, to terror, to gender, to sexuality, to variety, to complexity, to contradiction, and to
change informed his deep and persistent inquiries into what it has
meant to be white. It is hard to imagine Baldwin resorting to language quite so cumbersome and clinical as the academically popular
phrase, the "social construction of whiteness." His subtle disarming
of biologically driven racial categories left room for individual deci-
sions and tragedies. Adopting and treasuring a white identity is, he
wrote, "absolutely a moral choice" since "there are no white people."
The choice was made by men and women themselves undergoing a
"vast amount of coercion" over generations. It was a choice based on
blood-soaked practices. "Slaughtering cattle, poisoning the wells, torching the houses, massacring Native Americans, raping Black women,"
were not, for Baldwin, mere symptoms of white racism but the terrors which forged white identity. Whiteness was a dramatic and an
American choice. At a time when immigration history missed the
drama of the European immigrant's learning of race relations in the
United States, Baldwin tellingly observed that Norwegians did not sit
around in Norway preening themselves about how wonderfully white
they were. Perhaps overdrawing a point, in that imperial expansion
and the slave trade made race resonate globally, Baldwin nonetheless
offered a useful provocation illuminating U.S. peculiarities. "No one,"
he wrote, "was white before he/she came to America."[36]

Baldwin insisted that whiteness was a desperate choice. It involved
not only a reckoning of whom to exclude from the private club of
full humanity but of what huge sections of the human experience to
exclude from one's sense of self or to only "visit surreptitiously after
dark." Such exclusions carried terrible consequences which reached
across the color line. "It's you who'll have the blues, not me, just wait
and see," he quoted Langston Hughes to his white readers. Baldwin's
concern with the "price of the ticket" for full admission to U.S. society animated many of his essays. That price, for European immigrants, "was to become white." No community, he emphasized, could
be built on this lie. But participation in the lie helped steal the vitality
from immigrant communities of the Irish, Italians, Jews, Poles, and
others.[37]

For Baldwin, whiteness involved more than the defense of white property and the defense of the history by which that property was obtained. It also involved the desperate belief that all the effort and carnage were worthwhile, a futile clinging to the hope that the pursuit of property really might be the pursuit of happiness. "White man," he warned, sounding much like American-Indian critics of whiteness, "you cannot endure the things you acquire." Choosing to opt "for safety instead of life," white-thinking Americans wound the circle of their experiences and dreams more and more tightly. What could not find a place in that constricted circle, "the white man's unadmitted—and apparently, to him, unspeakable—private fears and longings" were "projected onto the Negro." In a remarkable evocation of this policing of one's own humanity, and of its relation to the acceptance of inequality and alienating work, Baldwin likened the process of becoming white to remaining "trapped in [a] factory." Baldwin called white people out of the factory. "As long as you think you're white," he observed, tough-lovingly, "there's no hope for you."[38]

NOTES

1. See Walter Johnson's brilliant "Bargaining: Daily Life, Information and Opportunity in the New Orleans Slave Pens" from his forthcoming book. See also his "Masters and Slaves in the Market of Slavery and the New Orleans Trade, 1804–1864" (Ph.D. diss., Princeton University, 1995).

2. Langston Hughes, "Slave on the Block," in The Ways of White Folks (New York: Knopf, 1934), 19–31.

3. Robert Fikes, Jr., "Escaping the Literary Ghetto: African American Authors of White Life Novels, 1946–1994," Western Journal of Black Studies 19 (1995), 111; Toni Morrison, Playing in the Dark: Whiteness and the Literary Imagination (Cambridge, Mass., and London: Harvard University Press, 1992); Morrison, "Recitatif," in Confirmation: An Anthology of African American Women, Amiri and Amina Baraka, eds. (New York: Morrow, 1983), 243–61. For a brilliant appreciation of this aspect of Morrison's work, see Joy James, "Politicizing the Spirit: American Africanisms and African Ancestors in the Essays of Toni Morrison," Cultural Studies 9 (May 1995).

4. James Baldwin, "Here Be Dragons," in The Price of the Ticket: Collected Nonfiction, 1948–1985 (New York: St. Martin's Press, 1985), 682–83.

5. James Weldon Johnson, The Autobiography of an Ex-Colored Man (New York: Knopf, 1970, originally 1927); George S. Schuyler, "Our White Folks," The American Mercury (December 1927), 387; bell hooks, Black Looks: Race and Representation (Boston: South End Press, 1992), 165 and 168; W.E.B. Du Bois, Darkwater (New York: Harcourt, Brace and Howe, 1920), 111–13. The same point is forcefully made in Charles Payne's brilliant history of the Black freedom movement, I've Got the Light of Freedom (Berkeley and Los Angeles: University of California Press, 1995), 311.

6. See especially Barbara Neely, *Blanche on the Lam* (New York: St. Martin's Press, 1992), 39 and 115–16; Cheryl Harris, "Whiteness as Property," *Harvard Law Review* 106 (June 1993), 1710–13; on Wells, see Vron Ware, *Beyond the Pale: White Women, Racism and History* (New York: Verso, 1992), 167–224, and Martha Hodes, *Sex Across the Color Line,* forthcoming from Yale University Press.

7. hooks, *Black Looks,* 168 and 169; Baldwin, "The Fire Next Time," in *The Price of the Ticket,* 333; Richard Wright, *Black Boy* (New York: Harper and Brothers, 1945), 57.

8. G.W.F. Hegel, *The Phenomenology of Mind* (London: Allen and Unwin, 1910), I: 183ff; Paul Gilroy, *The Black Atlantic: Modernity and Double Consciousness* (Cambridge, Mass.: Harvard University Press, 1993), 49–51. Hegel's own views on the supposed backwardness of African people make the task of dismissing the historical rootedness of his insights much easier. See Hegel, *The Philosophy of History* (London: H. G. Bonn, 1894), 99. See also Baldwin, "The Fire Next Time," in *The Price of the Ticket,* 375.

9. Sterling Stuckey, "The Tambourine in Glory: African Culture and Melville's Art," forthcoming; Stuckey, "The Death of Benito Cereno: A Reading of Herman Melville on Slavery," in *Going Through the Storm: The Influence of African American Art in History* (New York and Oxford: Oxford University Press, 1994), 158–59 and 169. See also Carolyn Karcher, *Shadow Over the Promised Land: Slavery, Race and Violence in Melville's America* (Baton Rouge: Louisiana State University Press, 1980).

10. George Lipsitz, "'Swing Low Sweet Cadillac': White Supremacy, Antiblack Racism, and the New Historicism," *American Literary History* 7 (Winter 1995), 705–10.

11. The study is summarized in "Marginalia," *Chronicle of Higher Education* 9 (April 13, 1994), A-31.

12. Fikes, Jr., "Escaping the Literary Ghetto," 105–12. See also Gerald Early's afterword to the new edition of Wright's *Savage Holiday* (Jackson: University of Mississippi Press, 1994, originally 1954), 222–35.

13. Carl Abbott, "Tracing the Trends in U.S. Regional History" (American Historical Association), *Perspectives* 28 (February 1990), 8; Franklin discussed *The Militant South* and its reception in his presidential address to the Southern Historical Association, "Pursuing Southern History: A Strange Career" in Lexington in 1989. John Hope Franklin, *The Militant South, 1880–1861* (Cambridge, Mass.: Harvard University Press, 1956).

14. Schuyler, "Our White Folks," 385; Gail Bederman, *Manliness and Civilization: A Cultural History of Gender and Race in the United States, 1880–1917* (Chicago: University of Chicago Press, 1995), 60–76. Philip S. Foner, ed., *Life and Writings of Frederick Douglass,* 5 vols. (New York: International Publishers, 1950–1975), 4: 517; Editors of *Ebony, The WHITE Problem in America* (Chicago: Johnson Publications, 1966); for T. Thomas Fortune on "The Black Man's Burden," see Henry Louis Gates, Jr., *The Signifying Monkey: A Theory of African-American Literary Criticism* (New York and Oxford: Oxford University Press, 1988), 103. Waldo E. Martin, Jr., *The Mind of Frederick Douglass* (Chapel Hill and London: University of North Carolina Press, 1984), 112. Cyril Briggs, "Further Notes on [the] Negro Question in Southern Textile States," *The Communist* 8 (July 1929), 394. Lewis Gordon, *Bad Faith and Antiblack Racism* (Atlantic Highlands, N.J.: Humanities Press, 1995), 154, introduces another "white problem."

15. Du Bois and Rock as quoted in Herbert Aptheker, "Afro-American Superiority: A Neglected Theme in the Literature," *Phylon,* 31 (Winter 1970), 340; Mia

Bay's "The White Image in the Black Mind" (Ph.D. diss., Yale University, 1993), 166–73, with Ethiop quoted on 172. I. M. Blacque, *White Women Got Flat Butts* (Saint Paul, Minn.: by author, 1995).

16. Aptheker, "Afro-American Superiority," 336–43, quoting Du Bois on 340; Bay, "White Image," 177–203; Garvey, "The Tragedy of White Injustice," in Tony Martin, ed., *The Poetical Works of Marcus Garvey* (Dover, Mass.: Majority Press, 1983), 4; Charles Chesnutt, *The Marrow of Tradition* (New York: Penguin Books, 1993, originally 1901), 90. See also Stephen P. Knadler, "Untragic Mulatto: Charles Chesnutt and the Discourse on Whiteness," *American Literary History* 5 (Fall 1996), 426–48; William and Ellen Craft, *Running a Thousand Miles for Freedom* (New York: W. Tweedie, 1860); and David Roediger, "The Meaning of Africa for the American Slave," *Journal of Ethnic Studies* 4 (Winter 1977), 8–10.

17. Ethiop [Wilson], "What Shall We Do With White People?" *Anglo-African Magazine* (February 1860), 41–45. See also Bay, "White Image," 149–51. Ralph Ellison, *Going to the Territory* (New York: Random House, 1987), 99 and 166.

18. Morrison, "Unspeakable Things Unspoken: The Afro-American Presence in American Literature," *Michigan Quarterly Review* 28 (Winter 1989), 3; see also Eric Foner, "Review of Dinesh D'Souza's *End of Racism*," *Dissent* (Winter 1996), 107.

19. J. A. Rogers, "The Porter Debates the Senator," in *From Superman to Man* (St. Petersburg, Fla.: Helga M. Rogers, 1986, originally 1917); W.E.B. Du Bois, *Dusk of Dawn: An Essay Toward an Autobiography of a Race Concept* (New York: Harcourt, Brace and World, 1968), 137–41 and 153. Du Bois, *The Negro* (London and Oxford: Oxford University Press, 1970, originally 1915), 139; Amiri Baraka, *The LeRoi Jones / Amiri Baraka Reader,* ed. William J. Harris (New York: Morrow, 1991), xiii. Iman Benjamin Karim, ed., *The End of White World Supremacy: Four Speeches by Malcolm X* (New York: Merlin House, 1971), 130. For a 1919 use of "whiteocracy," see Richard R. Wright, Jr., as cited in Charles W. Mills, *The Racial Contract* (Ithaca and London: Cornell University Press, 1997), 131 and 161. Bernard W. Bell, Emily Grosholz and James B. Stewart, eds., *W.E.B. Du Bois on Race and Culture* (New York and London: Routledge, 1996), esp. the essays by Lucius Outlaw and Robert Gooding-Williams. James Baldwin, "On Being 'White' . . . and Other Lies," *Essence* (April 1984), 90–92. Lewis R. Gordon, *Fanon and the Crisis of European Man* (New York and London: Routledge, 1995), 12.

20. On Brown, see Benjamin Quarles, ed., *Blacks on John Brown* (Urbana: University of Illinois Press, 1972) and Paul Finkelman, ed., *His Soul Goes Marching On: Responses to John Brown and the Harpers Ferry Raid* (Charlottesville: University of Virginia Press, 1995); Hughes, *Ways of White Folks,* epigraph on dedication page.

21. Harris, "Whiteness as Property," 1709–91; the verses are from Philip Schatz, "Songs of the Negro Worker," *New Masses* 5 (May 1930), 7; see also Sterling Stuckey, "Through the Prism of Slavery: The Black Ethos in Slavery," in *Going Through the Storm,* 8–9. See also Helán E. Page and Brooke Thomas, "White Public Space and the Construction of White Privilege in U.S. Healthcare," *Medical Anthropology Quarterly* 8 (1994), 109–16.

22. Most directly, see Derrick Bell, "Property Rights in Whiteness—Their Legal Legacy, Their Economic Costs," *Villanova Law Review* 33 (1988); Cox, *Caste, Class, and Race: A Study in Social Dynamics* (Garden City, N.Y.: Doubleday, 1948); Ralph Bunche, *A World View of Race* (Washington, D.C.: The Associates on Negro Folk Education, 1936); Baraka, "Motion of History," in *The Motion of History and Other Plays* (New York: Morrow, 1976), 96. On folklore, race and work, see e.g., Zora Neale Hurston, *Mules and Men: Negro Folktales and Voodoo Practices in the South*

(New York: HarperCollins, 1990, originally 1935), 74–75. Harry Haywood, *Negro Liberation* (Chicago: Liberator Press, 1976, originally 1948).

23. The best single source on poor whites remains Ralph Ellison's wide-ranging essay "An Extravagance of Laughter," in *Going to the Territory*, 145–97; Eugene D. Genovese, "'Rather Be Nigger Than a Poor White Man': Slave Perceptions of Southern Yeomen and Poor Whites," in Hans L. Trefousse, ed., *Toward a New View of America: Essays in Honor of Arthur C. Cole* (New York: Burt Franklin, 1977), 79–96; and Richard Wright, *White Man, Listen* (Garden City, N.Y.: Doubleday, 1964, originally 1957), 101. Robert L. Chapman, ed., *New Dictionary of American Slang* (New York: Harper and Row, 1986); Clarence Major, ed., *Juba to Jive: A Dictionary of African-American Slang* (New York: Penguin Books, 1994).

24. Brown, "Strong Men," in *Southern Road* (Boston: Beacon Press, 1974, originally 1932), 52; Elma Stuckey, *The Collected Poems of Elma Stuckey* (Chicago: Precedent Publishers, 1987), 75.

25. Du Bois, *The World and Africa: An Inquiry Into the Part Which Africa Has Played in World History* (New York: International Publishers, 1972, originally 1946), 18–21; Julius Lester, ed., *The Seventh Son*, 2 vols. (New York: Random House, 1971), 2:508; Du Bois, *Black Reconstruction in America, 1860–1880* (New York: Atheneum, 1992, originally 1935), 17–31 and 700–701; Hurston, *Mules and Men*, 101.

26. Edward C. L. Adams, *Tales of the Congaree*, Robert G. O'Meally, ed. (Chapel Hill and London: University of North Carolina Press, 1987), 189–91; Gilroy, *The Black Atlantic*, 174–75; hooks, *White Looks*, 172.

27. Frederick Douglass, *Narrative of the Life of Frederick Douglass, An American Slave* (New York: Penguin Books, 1986, originally 1845), 77–80; Alice Walker, ed., *I Love Myself When I Am Laughing and Then Again When I Am Looking Mean and Impressive: A Zora Neale Hurston Reader* (Old Westbury, N.Y.: Feminist Press, 1979), 167–68; Sterling A. Brown, Arthur P. Davis, and Ulysses Lee, eds., *The Negro Caravan* (New York: Arno, 1970 originally 1941), 449; Ellison, *Going to the Territory*, 172 and 174. See also Daryl Cumber Dance, ed., *Shuckin' and Jivin': Folklore from Contemporary Black America* (Bloomington and London: Indiana University Press, 1978), 165–78; Ellison, "A Party Down at the Square," in John E. Callahan, ed., *Flying Home and Other Stories* (New York: Random House, 1996), 3–11, and Marion Vera Cuthbert, "Mob Madness," *The Crisis*, April 1936.

28. Ida B. Wells-Barnett, *On Lynchings: Southern Horrors, A Red Record and Mob Rule in New Orleans* (New York: Arno, 1969); Walter White, *Rope and Faggot* (New York: Knopf, 1929); Trudier Harris, *Exorcising Blackness: Historical and Literary Lynching and Burning Rites* (Bloomington: Indiana University Press, 1984).

29. Wells-Barnett, *A Red Record*, reprinted in *On Lynchings*, 7; White, *Rope and Faggot*, 82–113; C. L. R. James, "The Economics of Lynching," in Scott McLemee, ed., *C. L. R. James on the Negro Question* (Jackson: University of Mississippi Press, 1996), 34–36 (originally 1940); Morrison, "Unspeakable Things," 38.

30. Richard Wright, "Man of All Work," in *Eight Men* (New York, and Cleveland: World Publications, 1961), 117–62; White, *Rope and Faggot*, 158–61; Wells-Barnett, *A Red Record*, 12–13; Harriet Jacobs, *Incidents in the Life of a Slave Girl* (New York and Oxford: Oxford University Press, 1988, originally 1861), 49–57.

31. On Truth, and the complications involved in knowing her words, see Nell Irvin Painter, *Sojourner Truth: A Life, A Legend* (New York: Norton, 1996); Angela Y. Davis, *Women, Culture and Politics* (New York: Vintage, 1990); Joy James, *Transcending the Talented Tenth: Black Leaders and American Intellectuals* (New York and London: Routledge, 1977), 64–67; Calvin C. Hernton, *Sex and Racism in America* (New York:

Grove, 1965); Trudier Harris, *Exorcising Blackness;* Cheryl Harris, "Finding Sojourner's Truth: Race, Gender and the Institution of Slavery," forthcoming in *Cardozo Law Review;* Gordon, *Bad Faith and Antiblack Racism,* 124–29; Hortense J. Spillers: "Changing the Letter: The Yokes, the Jokes of Discourse, or, Mrs. Stowe, Mr. Reed," in Deborah E. McDowell and Arnold Rampersad, eds., *Slavery and the Literary Imagination* (Baltimore: Johns Hopkins University Press, 1989), 42–45; Morrison, *Playing in the Dark,* 15–28; Robin Wiegman, *American Anatomies: Theorizing Race and Gender* (Durham, N.C., and London: Duke University Press, 1995), 88–90. See also Randall Kenan's fine short story, "Tell Me, Tell Me," in *Let the Dead Bury Their Dead and Other Stories* (San Diego, New York, and London: Harcourt, Brace, 1992), 236–69. Baldwin, *Giovanni's Room* (New York: Dial Press, 1959) and "Here Be Dragons," in *The Price of the Ticket,* 667–78; Lorde, *Sister Outsider* (Freedom, Calif.: Crossing Press, 1984).

32. Morrison, *Playing in the Dark,* 47; Ellison, "What America Would Be Like Without Blacks," in *Going to the Territory,* 104–12; Johnson, *Autobiography of an Ex-Colored Man,* 76; Murray, *The Omni-Americans* (New York: Vintage, 1983), 22; Amiri Baraka [as LeRoi Jones], *Blues People* (New York: Morrow, 1963); Nelson George, *The Death of Rhythm & Blues* (New York: Pantheon, 1988), esp. 62–67; Greg Tate, *Flyboy in the Buttermilk: Essays on Contemporary America* (New York: Simon and Schuster, 1992), 178–84 and 99–107; Greg Tate, "The Sound and the Fury," *Vibe* 1 (September 1992), 15.

33. Chesnutt, "What Is a White Man?" *The Independent,* May 30, 1889; Malcolm X, with Alex Haley, *The Autobiography of Malcolm X* (New York: Ballantine, 1990, originally 1965), 399; Pryor, in John A. Williams and Dennis A. Williams, *If I Stop I'll Die: The Comedy and Tragedy of Richard Pryor* (New York: Thunder's Mouth Press, 1991), 94; Killens, in his foreword to William Attaway, *Blood on the Forge* (New York: Monthly Review Press, 1987, originally 1941), 9; Morrison in Derrick Bell, "Racial Libel as Ritual," *Village Voice,* November 21, 1995, 53 and in conversation in February 1996; Ellison, *Going to the Territory,* 111, counts *nigger* as "one of the first epithets that many European Americans learned when they got off the boat."

34. Attaway, *Blood on the Forge,* 130 and 120–23.

35. Attaway, *Blood on the Forge,* 130; Frederick Douglass, *My Bondage and My Freedom* (Chicago: Johnson Publications, 1970, originally 1855), 76; O'Connell, in George Potter, *To the Golden Door: The Story of the Irish in Ireland and America* (Boston: Little, Brown, 1960), 372; Morrison, in conversation, in February 1996.

36. James Baldwin, "On Being 'White' . . . and Other Lies," 90–92.

37. Baldwin, *The Price of the Ticket,* 375, and (including the Hughes quotation), 666; Baldwin, "The Fire Next Time," in *The Price of the Ticket,* 375; Baldwin, "On Being 'White' . . . and Other Lies," 90.

38. Baldwin, "White Man's Guilt," in *The Price of the Ticket,* 413–14; Baldwin in the 1985 film *The Price of the Ticket.*

PART I
CONFRONTING WHITENESS AND SEEING THROUGH RACE

White people cannot, in the generality,
be taken as models of how to live.

> —JAMES BALDWIN

They say we stink. But my ma says white
folks smell like dead folks.

> —RICHARD WRIGHT,
> CHARACTER IN *BLACK BOY*

The white race cannot tell when they
began to be known as such.

> —REV. HARVEY JOHNSON

The colored race is the best thermometer
of how things is going, because when
white folks feel good we know it, and
when white folks feel bad, we know it
too—even before they do—their appetites fall off.

> —FROM LANGSTON HUGHES AND
> ARNA BONTEMPS, EDS.,
> *THE BOOK OF NEGRO FOLKLORE*

"Caleb," I asked, "are white people people?"

"What are you talking about, Leo?"

"I mean—are white people—people? People like us?"

He looked down at me. His face was very strange and sad. It was a face I had never seen before. We climbed a few more stairs, very slowly. Then, "All I can tell you, Leo, is—well, they don't think they are."

—James Baldwin, dialogue from *Tell Me How Long the Train's Been Gone*

We would like to overhear St. Paul explain to this gentleman that truth with love is not truth with lies. It is precisely here that the white church is failing. . . . It dare not inveigh against the thief who is at the bottom of modern industrial organization. It dare not say of the Negro, "love your neighbor as yourself." Compelled to be dumb on these great matters of morality and decency it turns to Hell and Damnation and summons Billy Sunday to preach it.

—W.E.B. Du Bois

I got a funny feeling then; I began wondering when white people started getting white—or rather, when they started losing it.

—Chester B. Himes

DIALOGUE WITH A
WHITE FRIEND

W.E.B. Du Bois

The most eminent American intellectual of this century, W.E.B. Du Bois (1868–1963) philosophized, historicized, organized, and polemicized brilliantly during his long career. He wrote poems, pageants, editorials, novels, and classic works in sociology and history. Often a trenchant critic of "race talk," who saw the need to confront all assumptions of white supremacy, Du Bois also embraced a version of Black nationalism. Nowhere is his ability to see race as both a fanciful conceit and a consequential reality more apparent than in these pages from Dusk to Dawn *(1940), the second of his three major autobiographical works. Du Bois here creates a form of imagined dialogue now popularly and controversially used by scholars of race and the law.*

When, for example, the obsession of his race consciousness leaves him, my white friend, Roger Van Dieman (who, I hasten to add, is an abstraction and integration and never existed), is quite companionable; otherwise he is impossible. He has a way of putting an excessive amount of pity in his look and of stating as a general and incontrovertible fact that it is "horrible" to be an Exception. By this he means me. He is more than certain that I prove the rule. He is not a bright person, but of that famous average, standardized and astonished at anything that even seems original. His thesis is simple: the world is composed of Race superimposed on Race; classes superimposed on classes; beneath the whole thing is "Our Family" in capitals, and under that is God. God seems to be a cousin, or at least a blood relative, of the Van Diemans.

"Of course," he says, "you know Negroes are inferior."

I admit nothing of the sort, I maintain. In fact, having known with some considerable intimacy both male and female, the people of the British Isles, of Scandinavia, of Russia, of Germany, north and south, of the three ends of France and the two ends of Italy; specimens from the Balkans and black and white Spain; the three great races of Asia

and the melange of Africa, without mentioning America, I sit here
and maintain that black folk are much superior to white.

"You are either joking or mad," he says.

Both and neither. This race talk is, of course, a joke, and frequently it has driven me insane and probably will permanently in the
future; and yet, seriously and soberly, we black folk are the salvation of
mankind.

He regards me with puzzled astonishment and says confidentially:

"Do you know that sometimes I am half afraid that you really
believe this? At other times I see clearly the inferiority complex."

The former after lunch, I reply, and the latter before.

"Very well," he says, "let's lunch."

Where? I ask quizzically, we being at the time in the Roaring For-
ties.

"Why—oh, well—their refusal to serve you lunch at least does not
prove your superiority."

Nor yet theirs, I answer; but never mind, come with me to Second
Avenue, where Labor lives and food is bad.

We start again with the salad.

"Now, superiority consists of what?" he argues.

Life is, I remark (1) Beauty and health of body. (2) Mental clear-
ness and creative genius. (3) Spiritual goodness and receptivity. (4)
Social adaptability and constructiveness.

"Not bad," he answers. "Not bad at all. Now I contend that the
white race conspicuously excels in beauty, genius, and construction,
and is well abreast even in goodness."

And I maintain that the black race excels in beauty, goodness, and
adaptability, and is well abreast in genius.

"Sheer nonsense and pure balderdash. Compare the Venus of Milo
and the Apollo Belvedere with a Harlem or Beale Street couple."

I retort: in short, compare humanity at its worst with the Ideal,
and humanity suffers. But black folk in most attributes of physical
beauty, in line and height and curve, have the same norms as whites
and differ only in small details of color, hair and curve of countenance. Now can there be any question but that as colors, bronze,
mahogany, coffee and gold are far lovelier than pink, gray, and mar-

ble? Hair is a matter of taste. Some will have it drab and stringy and others in a gray, woven, unmoving mass. Most of us like it somewhere between, in tiny tendrils, smoking curls and sweeping curves. I have loved all these varieties in my day. I prefer the crinkly kind, almost wavy, in black, brown, and glistening gold. In faces, I hate straight features; needles and razors may be sharp—but beautiful, never.

"All that is personal opinion, I prefer the colors of heaven and day: sunlight hair and sky-blue eyes; straight noses and thin lips, and that incomparable air of haughty aloofness and aristocracy."

And I, on the contrary, am the child of twilight and night, and choose intricately curly hair, black eyes, full and luscious features; and that air of humility and wonder which streams from moonlight. Add to this voices that caress instead of rasp, glances that appeal rather than repel, and a sinuous litheness of movement to replace Anglo-Saxon stalking—there you have my ideal. Of course, you can bury any human body in dirt and misery and make it horrible. I have seen the East End of London.

"Beauty seems to be simply opinion, if you put it that way."

To be sure. But whose opinion?

"Bother beauty. Here we shall never agree. But, after all, I doubt if it makes much difference. The real point is Brains: clear thinking, pure reason, mathematical precision and creative genius. Now, without blague, stand and acknowledge that here the white race is supreme."

Quite the contrary. I know no attribute in which the white race has more conspicuously failed. This is white and European civilization; and as a system of culture it is idiotic, addle-brained, unreasoning, topsy-turvy, without precision; and its genius chiefly runs to marvelous contrivances for enslaving the many, and enriching the few, and murdering both. I see absolutely no proof that the average ability of the white man's brain to think clearly is any greater than that of the yellow man or of the black man. If we take even that doubtful but widely heralded test, the frequency of individual creative genius (when a real racial test should be the frequency of ordinary common sense)—if we take the Genius as the savior of mankind, it is only possible for the white race to prove its own incontestable superiority by appointing both judge and jury and summoning its own witnesses.

I freely admit that, according to white writers, white teachers, white historians, and white molders of public opinion, nothing ever happened in the world of any importance that could not or should not be labeled "white." How silly. I place black iron-welding and village democracy, and yellow printing and state building, side by side with white representative government and the steam engine, and unhesitatingly give the palm to the first. I hand the first vast conception of the solar system to the Africanized Egyptians, the creation of Art to the Chinese, the highest conception of Religion to the Asiatic Semites, and then let Europe rave over the Factory system.

"But is not well-being more widely diffused among white folk than among yellow and black, and general intelligence more common?"

True, and why? Ask the geography of Europe, the African Slave Trade and the industrial technique of the nineteenth-century white man. Turn the thing around, and let a single tradition of culture suddenly have thrust into its hands the power to bleed the world of its brawn and wealth, and the willingness to do this, and you will have exactly what we have today, under another name and color.

"Precisely. Then, at least, the white race is more advanced and no more blameworthy than others because, as I insist, its native intelligence is greater. It is germ plasm, seed, that I am talking about. Do you believe in heredity?"

Not blindly; but I should be mildly surprised to see a dog born of a cat.

"Exactly; or a genius born of a fool."

No, no; on the contrary, I rather expect fools of geniuses and geniuses of fools. And while I stoutly maintain that cattiness and dogginess are as far apart as the East from the West, on the other hand, I just as strongly believe that the human ass and the superman have much in common and can often, if not always, spawn each other.

"Is it possible that you have never heard of the Jukes, or of the plain results of hereditary degeneration and the possibilities of careful breeding?"

It is not possible; they have been served up to me ad infinitum. But they are nothing. I know greater wonders: Lincoln from Nancy

Hanks, Dumas from a black beast of burden, Kant from a saddler, and Jesus Christ from a manger.

"All of which, instead of disproving, is exact and definite proof of the persistence of good blood."

Precisely, and of the catholicity of its tastes; the method of proof is this: when anything good occurs, it is proof of good blood; when anything bad occurs, it is proof of bad blood. Very well. Now good and bad, native endowment and native deficiency, do not follow racial lines. There is good stock in all races and the outcropping of bad individuals, too; and there has been absolutely no proof that the white race has any larger share of the gifted strains of human heritage than the black race or the yellow race. To be sure, good seed proves itself in the flower and the fruit, but the failure of seed to sprout is no proof that it is not good. It may be proof simply of the absence of manure—or its excessive presence.

Granted, that when time began, there was hidden in a Seed that tiny speck that spelled the world's salvation, do you think today it would manifest itself crudely and baldly in a dash of skin color and a crinkle of hair? Is the subtle mystery of life and consciousness and of ability portrayed in any such slapdash and obvious marks of difference?

"Go out upon the street; choose ten white men and ten colored men. Which can carry on and preserve American civilizations?"

The whites.

"Well, then."

You evidently consider that a compliment. Let it pass. Go out upon the street and choose ten men and ten women. Which could best run a Ford car? The men, of course; but hold. Fly out into the sky and look down upon ten children of Podunk and ten children of Chicago. Which would know most about elevated railroads, baseball, zoology, and movies?

"The point is visible, but beyond that, outside of mere experience and education, and harking back to native gift and intelligence, on your honor, which has most, white folk or black folk?"

There you have me deep in the shadows, beyond the benign guidance of words. Just what is gift and intelligence, especially of the native sort? And when we compare the gift of one human soul with that of another, are we not seeking to measure incommensurable things; trying to lump things like sunlight and music and love? And if a certain shadowy Over-soul can really compare the incomparable with some transcendental yardstick, may we not here emerge into a super-equality of man? At least this I can quite believe.

"But it is a pious belief, not more."

Not more; but a pious belief outweighs an impious unbelief.

Admitting that the problem of native human endowment is obscure, there is no corresponding obscurity in spiritual values. Goodness and unselfishness; simplicity and honor; tolerance, susceptibility to beauty in form, color, and music; courage to look truth in the face; courage to live and suffer in patience and humility, in forgiveness and in hope; eagerness to turn, not simply the other cheek, but the face and the bowed back; capacity to love. In all these mighty things, the greatest things in the world, where do black folk and white folk stand?

Why, man of mine, you would not have the courage to live one hour as a black man in America, or as a Negro in the whole wide world. Ah, yes, I know what you whisper to such accusation. You say dryly that if we had good sense we would not live either; and the fact that we do submit to life as it is and yet laugh and dance and dream, is but another proof that we are idiots.

This is the truly marvelous way in which you prove your superiority by admitting that our love of life can only be intelligently explained on the hypothesis of inferiority. What finer tribute is possible to our courage?

What great works of Art have we made? Very few. The Pyramids, Luxor, the Bronzes of Benin, the Spears of the Bongo, "When Malinda Sings" and the Sorrow Song she is always singing. Oh, yes, and the love of her dancing.

But art is not simply works of art; it is the spirit that knows Beauty, that has music in its soul and the color of sunsets in its headkerchiefs; that can dance on a flaming world and make the world dance, too. Such is the soul of the Negro.

Why, do you know the two finest things in the industry of the West, finer than factory, shop or ship? One is the black laborer's Saturday off. Neither the whip of the driver, nor the starvation wage, nor the disgust of the Yankee, nor the call of the cotton crop, has yet convinced the common black variety of plantation laborer that one day in the week is enough for rest and play. He wants two days. And, from California to Texas, from Florida to Trinidad, he takes two days while the planter screams and curses. They have beaten the English slavey, the French and German peasants, and the North Italian contadini into twelve-hour, six-day slaves. They crushed the Chinese and Indian coolie into a twenty-four-hour beast of burden; they have even made the American, free, white and twenty-one, believe that daily toil is one of the Ten Commandments. But not the Negro. From Monday to Friday the field hand is a slave; then for forty-eight golden hours he is free, and through these same forty-eight hours he may yet free the dumb, driven cattle of the world.

Then the second thing, laughter. This race has the greatest of the gifts of God, laughter. It dances and sings; it is humble; it longs to learn; it loves men; it loves women. It is frankly, baldly, deliciously human in an artificial and hypocritical land. If you will hear men laugh, go to Guinea, "Black Bottom," "Niggertown," Harlem. If you want to feel humor too exquisite and subtle for translation, sit invisibly among a gang of Negro workers. The white world has its gibes and cruel caricatures; it has its loud guffaws; but to the black world alone belongs the delicious chuckle.

"But the State; the modern industrial State. Wealth of work, wealth of commerce, factory and mine, skyscrapers; New York, Chicago, Johannesburg, London and Buenos Aires!"

This is the best expression of the civilization in which the white race finds itself today. This is what the white world means by culture.

"Does it not excel the black and yellow race here?"

It does. But the excellence here raises no envy; only regrets. If this vast Frankenstein monster really served its makers; if it were their minister and not their master, god and king; if their machines gave us rest and leisure, instead of the drab uniformity of uninteresting drudgery; if their factories gave us gracious community of thought and feeling; beauty enshrined, free and joyous; if their work veiled them with tender sympathy at human distress and wide tolerance and understanding—then, all hail, White Imperial Industry! But it does not. It is a Beast! Its creators even do not understand it, cannot curb or guide it. They themselves are but hideous, groping hired Hands, doing their bit to oil the raging devastating machinery which kills men to make cloth, prostitutes women to rear buildings and eats little children.

Is this superiority? It is madness. We are the supermen who sit idly by and laugh and look at civilization. We, who frankly want the bodies of our mates and conjure no blush to our bronze cheeks when we own it. We, who exalt the Lynched above the Lyncher, and the Worker above the Owner, and the Crucified above Imperial Rome.

"But why have you black and yellow men done nothing better or even as good in the history of the world?"

We have, often.

"I never heard of it."

Lions have no historians.

"It is idiotic even to discuss it. Look around and see the pageantry of the world. It belongs to white men; it is the expression of white power; it is the product of white brains. Who can have the effrontery to stand for a moment and compare with this white triumph, yellow and brown anarchy and black savagery?"

You are obsessed by the swiftness of the gliding of the sled at the bottom of the hill. You say: what tremendous power must have caused its speed, and how wonderful is Speed. You think of the rider as the originator and inventor of that vast power. You admire his poise and *sang-froid,* his utter self-absorption. You say: surely here is the son of God and he shall reign forever and forever.

You are wrong, quite wrong. Away back on the level stretches of the mountain tops in the forests, amid drifts and driftwood, this sled was slowly and painfully pushed on its little hesitating start. It took power, but the power of sweating, courageous men, not of demigods. As the sled slowly started and gained momentum, it was the Law of Being that gave it speed, and the grace of God that steered its lone, scared passengers. Those passengers, white, black, red and yellow, de-serve credit for their balance and pluck. But many times it was sheer luck that made the road not land the white man in the gutter, as it had others so many times before, and as it may him yet. He has gone far-ther than others because of others whose very falling made hard ways iced and smooth for him to traverse. His triumph is a triumph not of himself alone, but of humankind, from the pusher in the primeval forests to the last flier through the winds of the twentieth century.

REPRESENTATIONS OF WHITENESS IN THE BLACK IMAGINATION

bell hooks

Born in Kentucky as Gloria Jean Watkins, bell hooks (1952–) is among the most prolific and influential contemporary feminist and antiracist cultural critics. Her essays on advertising, literature, film, sexuality, pedagogy, nationalism, popular culture, hiphop, freedom, and more are collected in such volumes as Yearning *(1990),* Outlaw Culture *(1994),* Ain't I a Woman *(1981), and* Talking Back *(1989). The essay which follows appeared in* Black Looks *(1992), perhaps hooks's most sustained inquiry into how race is seen and reproduced.*

Although there has never been any official body of black people in the United States who have gathered as anthropologists and/or ethnographers to study whiteness, black folks have, from slavery on, shared in conversations with one another "special" knowledge of whiteness gleaned from close scrutiny of white people. Deemed special because it was not a way of knowing that has been recorded fully in written material, its purpose was to help black folks cope and survive in a white supremacist society. For years, black domestic servants, working in white homes, acting as informants, brought knowledge back to segregated communities—details, facts, observations, and psychoanalytic readings of the white Other.

Sharing the fascination with difference that white people have collectively expressed openly (and at times vulgarly) as they have traveled around the world in pursuit of the Other and Otherness, black people, especially those living during the historical period of racial apartheid and legal segregation, have similarly maintained steadfast and ongoing curiosity about the "ghosts," "the barbarians," these strange apparitions they were forced to serve. In the chapter on "Wildness" in *Shamanism, Colonialism, and The Wild Man,* Michael Taussig urges a stretching of our imagination and understanding of the Other to include inscriptions "on the edge of official history."

Naming his critical project, identifying the passion he brings to the quest to know more deeply *you who are not ourselves,* Taussig explains:

> I am trying to reproduce a mode of perception—a way of see-
> ing through a way of talking—figuring the world through dia-
> logue that comes alive with sudden transformative force in the
> crannies of everyday life's pauses and juxtapositions, as in the
> kitchens of the Putumayo or in the streets around the church in
> the Niña Maria. It is always a way of representing the world in
> the roundabout "speech" of the collage of things . . . It is a
> mode of perception that catches on the debris of history . . .

I, too, am in search of the debris of history. I am wiping the dust off past conversations to remember some of what was shared in the old days when black folks had little intimate contact with whites, when we were much more open about the way we connected white-ness with the mysterious, the strange, and the terrible. Of course, everything has changed. Now many black people live in the "bush of ghosts" and do not know themselves separate from whiteness. They do not know this thing we call "difference." Systems of domination, imperialism, colonialism, and racism actively coerce black folks to internalize negative perceptions of blackness, to be self-hating. Many of us succumb to this. Yet, blacks who imitate whites (adopting their values, speech, habits of being, etc.) continue to regard whiteness with suspicion, fear, and even hatred. This contradictory longing to possess the reality of the Other, even though that reality is one that wounds and negates, is expressive of the desire to understand the mystery, to know intimately through imitation, as though such knowing worn like an amulet, a mask, will ward away the evil, the terror.

Searching the critical work of post-colonial critics, I found much writing that bespeaks the continued fascination with the way white minds, particularly the colonial imperialist traveler, perceive black-ness, and very little expressed interest in representations of whiteness in the black imagination. Black cultural and social critics allude to such representations in their writing, yet only a few have dared to make explicit those perceptions of whiteness that they think will discomfort or antagonize readers. James Baldwin's collection of essays, *Notes of A Native Son,* explores these issues with a clarity and frankness that is no longer fashionable in a world where evocations of pluralism and diversity act to obscure differences arbitrarily imposed and maintained by white racist domination. Addressing the way in which whiteness exists without knowledge of blackness even as it collectively asserts control, Baldwin links issues of recognition to the practice of imperialist racial domination. Writing about being the first black person to visit a Swiss village with only white inhabitants in his essay "Stranger in the Village," Baldwin notes his response to the village's yearly ritual of painting individuals black who were then positioned as slaves and bought so that the villagers could celebrate their concern with converting the souls of the "natives":

> I thought of white men arriving for the first time in an African village, strangers there, as I am a stranger here, and tried to imagine the astounded populace touching their hair and marveling at the color of their skin. But there is a great difference between being the first white man to be seen by Africans and being the first black man to be seen by whites. The white man takes the astonishment as tribute, for he arrives to conquer and to convert the natives, whose inferiority in relation to himself is not even to be questioned, whereas I, without a thought of conquest, find myself among a people whose culture controls me, has even, in a sense, created me, people who have cost me more in anguish and rage than they will ever know, who yet do not even know of my existence. The astonishment with which I might have greeted them, should they have stumbled into my African village a few hundred years ago, might have rejoiced their hearts. But the astonishment with which they greet me today can only poison mine.

My thinking about representations of whiteness in the black imagination has been stimulated by classroom discussions about the way in which the absence of recognition is a strategy that facilitates making a group the Other. In these classrooms there have been heated debates among students when white students respond with disbelief, shock, and rage, as they listen to black students talk about whiteness, when they are compelled to hear observations, stereotypes, etc., that are offered as "data" gleaned from close scrutiny and study. Usually, white students respond with naive amazement that black people critically assess white people from a standpoint where "whiteness" is the privileged signifier. Their amazement that black people watch white people with a critical "ethnographic" gaze, is itself an expression of racism. Often their rage erupts because they believe that all ways of looking that highlight difference subvert the liberal belief in a universal subjectivity (we are all just people) that they think will make racism disappear. They have a deep emotional investment in the myth of "sameness," even as their actions reflect the primacy of whiteness as a sign informing who they are and how they think. Many of them are shocked that black people think critically about whiteness because racist thinking perpetuates the fantasy that the Other who is subjugated, who is subhuman, lacks the ability to comprehend, to understand, to see the working of the powerful. Even though the majority of these students politically consider themselves liberals and anti-racist, they too unwittingly invest in the sense of whiteness as mystery.

In white supremacist society, white people can "safely" imagine that they are invisible to black people since the power they have historically asserted, and even now collectively assert over black people, accorded them the right to control the black gaze. As fantastic as it may seem, racist white people find it easy to imagine that black people cannot see them if within their desire they do not want to be seen by the dark Other. One mark of oppression was that black folks were compelled to assume the mantle of invisibility, to erase all traces of their subjectivity during slavery and the long years of racial apartheid, so that they could be better, less threatening servants. An effective strategy of white supremacist terror and dehumanization during slavery centered around white control of the black gaze. Black slaves, and later manumitted servants, could be brutally punished for looking, for appearing to observe the whites they were serving, as only a subject can observe, or see. To be fully an object then was to lack the

capacity to see or recognize reality. These looking relations were rein-
forced as whites cultivated the practice of denying the subjectivity of
blacks (the better to dehumanize and oppress), of relegating them to
the realm of the invisible. Growing up in a Kentucky household
where black servants lived in the same dwelling with the white family
who employed them, newspaper heiress Sallie Bingham recalls, in her
autobiography *Passion and Prejudice,* "Blacks, I realized, were simply
invisible to most white people, except as a pair of hands offering a
drink on a silver tray." Reduced to the machinery of bodily physical
labor, black people learned to appear before whites as though they
were zombies, cultivating the habit of casting the gaze downward so
as not to appear uppity. To look directly was an assertion of subjectivity, equality. Safety resided in the pretense of invisibility.

Even though legal racial apartheid no longer is a norm in the
United States, the habits that uphold and maintain institutionalized white supremacy linger. Since most white people do not have to
"see" black people (constantly appearing on billboards, television,
movies, in magazines, etc.) and they do not need to be ever on guard
nor to observe black people to be safe, they can live as though black
people are invisible, and they can imagine that they are also invisible
to blacks. Some white people may even imagine there is no representation of whiteness in the black imagination, especially one that is
based on concrete observation or mythic conjecture. They think they
are seen by black folks only as they want to appear. Ideologically,
the rhetoric of white supremacy supplies a fantasy of whiteness.
Described in Richard Dyer's essay "White," this fantasy makes whiteness synonymous with goodness:

> Power in contemporary society habitually passes itself off as
> embodied in the normal as opposed to the superior. This is
> common to all forms of power, but it works in a peculiarly
> seductive way with whiteness, because of the way it seems
> rooted, in common-sense thought, in things other than ethnic
> difference . . . Thus it is said (even in liberal textbooks) that
> there are inevitable associations of white with light and there-
> fore safety, and black with dark and therefore danger, and that

this explains racism (whereas one might well argue about the safety of the cover of darkness, and the danger of exposure to the light); again, and with more justice, people point to the Jewish and Christian use of white and black to symbolize good and evil, as carried still in such expressions as "a black mark," "white magic," "to blacken the character" and so on. Socialized to believe the fantasy, that whiteness represents goodness and all that is benign and non-threatening, many white people assume this is the way black people conceptualize whiteness. They do not imagine that the way whiteness makes its presence felt in black life, most often as terrorizing imposition, a power that wounds, hurts, tortures, is a reality that disrupts the fantasy of whiteness as representing goodness.

Collectively black people remain rather silent about representations of whiteness in the black imagination. As in the old days of racial segregation where black folks learned to "wear the mask," many of us pretend to be comfortable in the face of whiteness only to turn our backs and give expression to intense levels of discomfort. Especially talked about is the representation of whiteness as terrorizing. Without evoking a simplistic essentialist "us and them" dichotomy that suggests black folks merely invert stereotypical racist interpretations so that black becomes synonymous with goodness and white with evil, I want to focus on that representation of whiteness that is not formed in reaction to stereotypes but emerges as a response to the traumatic pain and anguish that remains a consequence of white racist domination, a psychic state that informs and shapes the way black folks "see" whiteness. Stereotypes black folks maintain about white folks are not the only representations of whiteness in the black imagination. They emerge primarily as responses to white stereotypes of blackness. Lorraine Hansberry argues that black stereotypes of whites emerge as a trickle-down process of white stereotypes of blackness, where there is the projection onto an Other all that we deny about ourselves. In Young, Gifted, and Black, she identifies particular stereotypes about white people that are commonly cited in black communities and urges us not to "celebrate this madness in any direction":

It is not "known" in the ghetto that white people, as an entity, are "dirty" (especially white women—who never seem to do their own cleaning); inherently "cruel" (the cold, fierce roots of Europe; who else could put all those people into ovens *scientifically*); "smart" (you really have to hand it to the m.f.'s), and anything *but* cold and passionless (because look who has had to live with little else than their passions in the guise of love and hatred all these centuries)? And so on.

Stereotypes, however inaccurate, are one form of representation. Like fictions, they are created to serve as substitutions, standing in for what is real. They are there not to tell it like it is but to invite and encourage pretense. They are a fantasy, a projection onto the Other that makes them less threatening. Stereotypes abound when there is distance. They are an invention, a pretense that one knows when the steps that would make real knowing possible cannot be taken or are not allowed.

Looking past stereotypes to consider various representations of whiteness in the black imagination, I appeal to memory, to my earliest recollections of ways these issues were raised in black life. Returning to memories of growing up in the social circumstances created by racial apartheid, to all black spaces on the edges of town, I reinhabit a location where black folks associated whiteness with the terrible, the terrifying, the terrorizing. White people were regarded as terrorists, especially those who dared to enter that segregated space of blackness. As a child, I did not know any white people. They were strangers, rarely seen in our neighborhoods. The "official" white men who came across the tracks were there to sell products, Bibles and insurance. They terrorized by economic exploitation. What did I see in the gazes of those white men who crossed our thresholds that made me afraid, that made black children unable to speak? Did they understand at all how strange their whiteness appeared in our living rooms, how threatening? Did they journey across the tracks with the same "adventurous" spirit that other white men carried to Africa, Asia, to those mysterious places they would one day call the "third world"?

Did they come to our houses to meet the Other face-to-face and enact the colonizer role, dominating us on our own turf?

Their presence terrified me. Whatever their mission, they looked too much like the unofficial white men who came to enact rituals of terror and torture. As a child, I did not know how to tell them apart, how to ask the "real white people to please stand up." The terror that I felt is one black people have shared. Whites learn about it second-hand. Confessing in *Soul Sister* that she too began to feel this terror after changing her skin to appear "black" and going to live in the south, Grace Halsell described her altered sense of whiteness:

> Caught in this climate of hate, I am totally terror-stricken, and I search my mind to know why I am fearful of my own people. Yet they no longer seem my people, but rather the "enemy" arrayed in large numbers against me in some hostile terri-tory . . . My wild heartbeat is a secondhand kind of terror. I know that I cannot possibly experience what *they,* the black people, experience . . .

Black folks raised in the North do not escape this sense of terror. In her autobiography, *Every Good-bye Ain't Gone,* Itabari Njeri begins the narrative of her northern childhood with a memory of southern roots. Traveling south as an adult to investigate the murder of her grandfather by white youth who were drag racing and ran him down in the streets, Njeri recalls that for many years "the distant and acci-dental violence that took my grandfather's life could not compete with the psychological terror that had begun to engulf my own." Ultimately, she begins to link that terror with the history of black people in the United States, seeing it as an imprint carried from the past to the present:

> As I grew older, my grandfather assumed mythic proportions in my imagination. Even in absence, he filled my room like music and watched over me when I was fearful. His fantasized pres-ence diverted thoughts of my father's drunken rages. With age,

my fantasizing ceased, the image of my grandfather faded. What lingered was the memory of his caress, the pain of something missing in my life, wrenched away by reckless white youths. I had a growing sense—the beginning of an inevitable comprehension—that this society deals blacks a disproportionate share of pain and denial.

Njeri's journey takes her through the pain and terror of the past, only the memories do not fade. They linger as does the pain and bitterness: "Against a backdrop of personal loss, against the evidence of history that fills me with a knowledge of the hateful behavior of whites toward blacks, I see the people of Bainbridge. And I cannot trust them. I cannot absolve them." If it is possible to conquer terror through ritual reenactment, that is what Njeri does. She goes back to the scene of the crime, dares to face the enemy. It is this confrontation that forces the terror of history to loosen its grip.

To name that whiteness in the black imagination is often a representation of terror. One must face written histories that erase and deny, that reinvent the past to make the present vision of racial harmony and pluralism more plausible. To bear the burden of memory one must willingly journey to places long uninhabited, searching the debris of history for traces of the unforgettable, all knowledge of which has been suppressed. Njeri laments that "nobody really knows us." She writes, "So institutionalized is the ignorance of our history, our culture, our everyday existence that, often, we do not even know ourselves." Theorizing black experience, we seek to uncover, restore, as well as to deconstruct, so that new paths, different journeys, are possible. Indeed, Edward Said, in "Traveling Theory," argues that theory can "threaten reification, as well as the entire bourgeois system on which reification depends, with destruction." The call to theorize black experience is constantly challenged and subverted by conservative voices reluctant to move from fixed locations. Said reminds us:

Theory . . . is won as the result of a process that begins when consciousness first experiences its own terrible ossification in the general reification of all things under capitalism; then when consciousness generalizes (or classes) itself as something opposed to other objects, and feels itself as contradiction to (or crisis within) objectification, there emerges a consciousness of change in the *status quo;* finally, moving toward freedom and fulfillment, consciousness looks ahead to complete self-realization, which is of course the revolutionary process stretching forward in time, perceivable now only as theory or projection.

Traveling, moving into the past, Njeri pieces together fragments. Who does she see staring into the face of a southern white man who was said to be the murderer? Does the terror in his face mirror the look of the unsuspecting black man whose death history does not name or record? Baldwin wrote that "people are trapped in history and history is trapped in them." There is then only the fantasy of escape, or the promise that what is lost will be found, rediscovered, and returned. For black folks, reconstructing an archaeology of memory makes return possible, the journey to a place we can never call home even as we reinhabit it to make sense of present locations. Such journeying cannot be fully encompassed by conventional notions of travel.

Spinning off from Said's essay, James Clifford, in "Notes on Travel and Theory," celebrates the idea of journeying, asserting:

> This sense of worldly, "mapped" movement is also why it may be worth holding on to the term "travel," despite its connotations of middle class "literary" or recreational journeying, spatial practices long associated with male experiences and virtues. "Travel" suggests, at least, profane activity, following public routes and beaten tracks. How do different populations, classes and genders travel? What kinds of knowledges, stories, and theories do they produce? A crucial research agenda opens up.

Reading this piece and listening to Clifford talk about theory and travel, I appreciated his efforts to expand the travel/theoretical frontier so that it might be more inclusive, even as I considered that to answer the questions he poses is to propose a deconstruction of the conventional sense of travel, and put alongside it, or in its place, a theory of the journey that would expose the extent to which holding on to the concept of "travel" as we know it is also a way to hold on to imperialism.

For some individuals, clinging to the conventional sense of travel allows them to remain fascinated with imperialism, to write about it, seductively evoking what Renato Rosaldo aptly calls, in *Culture and Truth,* "imperialist nostalgia." Significantly, he reminds readers that "even politically progressive North American audiences have enjoyed the elegance of manners governing relations of dominance and subordination between the 'races.'" Theories of travel produced outside conventional borders might want the Journey to become the rubric within which travel, as a starting point for discourse, is associated with different headings—rites of passage, immigration, enforced migration, relocation, enslavement, and homelessness. Travel is not a word that can be easily evoked to talk about the Middle Passage, the Trail of Tears, the landing of Chinese immigrants, the forced relocation of Japanese-Americans, or the plight of the homeless. Theorizing diverse journeying is crucial to our understanding of any politics of location. As Clifford asserts at the end of his essay:

> Theory is always written from some "where," and that "where" is less a place than itineraries: different, concrete histories of dwelling, immigration, exile, migration. These include the migration of third world intellectuals into the metropolitan universities, to pass through or to remain, changed by their travel but marked by places of origin, by peculiar allegiances and alienations.

Listening to Clifford "playfully" evoke a sense of travel, I felt such an evocation would always make it difficult for there to be recognition of an experience of travel that is not about play but is an encounter with terrorism. And it is crucial that we recognize that the hegemony of one experience of travel can make it impossible to articulate another experience or for it to be heard. From certain standpoints, to travel is to encounter the terrorizing force of white supremacy. To tell my "travel" stories, I must name the movement from racially segregated southern community, from rural black Baptist origin, to prestigious white university settings. I must be able to speak about what it is like to be leaving Italy after I have given a talk on racism and feminism, hosted by the parliament, only to stand for hours while I am interrogated by white officials who do not have to respond when I enquire as to why the questions they ask me are different from those asked the white people in line before me. Thinking only that I must endure this public questioning, the stares of those around me, because my skin is black, I am startled when I am asked if I speak Arabic, when I am told that women like me receive presents from men without knowing what those presents are. Reminded of another time when I was stripped searched by French officials, who were stopping black people to make sure we were not illegal immigrants and/or terrorists, I think that one fantasy of whiteness is that the threatening Other is always a terrorist. This projection enables many white people to imagine there is no representation of whiteness as terror, as terrorizing. Yet it is this representation of whiteness in the black imagination, first learned in the narrow confines of poor black rural community that is sustained by my travels to many different locations.

To travel, I must always move through fear, confront terror. It helps to be able to link this individual experience to the collective journeying of black people, to the Middle Passage, to the mass migration of southern black folks to northern cities in the early part of the 20th century. Michel Foucault posits memory as a site of resistance. As Jonathan Arac puts it in his introduction to *Postmodernism and Politics,* the process of remembering can be a practice which "transforms history from a judgement on the past in the name of a present truth to a 'counter-memory' that combats our current modes of truth and justice, helping us to understand and change the present by placing it in a new relation to the past." It is useful, when theorizing black experience, to examine the way the concept of "terror" is linked to representations of whiteness.

In the absence of the reality of whiteness, I learned as a child that to be "safe," it was important to recognize the power of whiteness, even to fear it, and to avoid encounter. There was nothing terrifying about the sharing of this knowledge as survival strategy, the terror was made real only when I journeyed from the black side of town to a predominantly white area near my grandmother's house. I had to pass through this area to reach her place. Describing these journeys "across town" in the essay "Homeplace: A Site of Resistance," I remembered:

> It was a movement away from the segregated blackness of our community into a poor white neighborhood. I remember the fear, being scared to walk to Baba's, our grandmother's house, because we would have to pass that terrifying whiteness—those white faces on the porches staring us down with hate. Even when empty or vacant those porches seemed to say *danger,* you do not belong here, you are not safe.

Oh! that feeling of safety, of arrival, of homecoming when we finally reached the edges of her yard, when we could see the soot black face of our grandfather, Daddy Gus, sitting in his chair on the porch, smell his cigar, and rest on his lap. Such a contrast, that feeling of arrival, of homecoming—this sweetness and the bitterness of that journey, that constant reminder of white power and control. Even though it was a long time ago that I made this journey, associations of whiteness with terror and the terrorizing remain. Even though I live and move in spaces where I am surrounded by whiteness, there is no comfort that makes the terrorism disappear. All black people in the United States, irrespective of their class status or politics, live with the possibility that they will be terrorized by whiteness.

This terror is most vividly described by black authors in fiction writing, particularly the recent novel by Toni Morrison, *Beloved.* Baby Suggs, the black prophet, who is most vocal about representations of whiteness, dies because she suffers an absence of color. Surrounded by a lack, an empty space, taken over by whiteness, she remembers: "Those white things have taken all I had or dreamed and broke my heartstrings too. There is no bad luck in the world but white folks." If the mask of whiteness, the pretense, represents it as always benign, benevolent, then what this representation obscures is the representation of danger, the sense of threat. During the period of racial apartheid, still known by many folks as Jim Crow, it was more difficult for black people to internalize this pretense, hard for us not to know that the shapes under white sheets had a mission to threaten, to terrorize. That representation of whiteness, and its association with innocence, which engulfed and murdered Emmett Till was a sign; it was meant to torture with the reminder of possible future terror. In Morrison's *Beloved,* the memory of terror is so deeply inscribed on the body of Sethe and in her consciousness, and the association of terror with whiteness is so intense that she kills her young so that they will never know the terror. Explaining her actions to Paul D., she tells him that it is her job "to keep them away from what I know is terrible." Of course Sethe's attempt to end the historical anguish of black people only reproduces it in a different form. She conquers the terror through perverse reenactment, through resistance, using violence as a means of fleeing from a history that is a burden too great to bear.

It is the telling of our history that enables political self-recovery. In contemporary society, white and black people alike believe that racism no longer exists. This erasure, however mythic, diffuses the representation of whiteness as terror in the black imagination. It allows for assimilation and forgetfulness. The eagerness with which contemporary society does away with racism, replacing this recognition with evocations of pluralism and diversity that further mask reality, is a response to the terror. It has also become a way to perpetuate the terror by providing a cover, a hiding place. Black people still feel the terror, still associate it with whiteness, but are rarely able to articulate the varied ways we are terrorized because it is easy to silence by accusations of reverse racism or by suggesting that black folks who talk about the ways we are terrorized by whites are merely evoking victimization to demand special treatment.

I was reminded of the way in which the discourse of race is increasingly divorced from any recognition of the politics of racism when I attended a recent conference on Cultural Studies. Attending the conference because I was confident that I would be in the company of like-minded, "aware," progressive intellectuals, I was disturbed when the usual arrangements of white supremacist hierarchy were mirrored both in terms of who was speaking, of how bodies were arranged on the stage, of who was in the audience. All of this revealed the underlying assumptions of what voices were deemed worthy to speak and be heard. As the conference progressed, I began to feel afraid. If these progressive people, most of whom were white, could so blindly reproduce a version of the *status quo* and not "see" it, the thought of how racial politics would be played out "outside" this arena was horrifying. That feeling of terror that I had known so intimately in my childhood surfaced. Without even considering whether the audience was able to shift from the prevailing standpoint and hear another perspective, I talked openly about that sense of terror. Later, I heard stories of white women joking about how ludicrous it was for me (in their eyes I suppose I represent the "bad" tough black woman) to say I feel terrorized. Their inability to conceive that my terror, like that of Sethe's, is a response to the legacy of white domination and the contemporary expressions of white supremacy is an indication of how little this culture really understands the profound psychological impact of white racist domination.

At this same conference, I bonded with a progressive black woman and her companion, a white man. Like me, they were troubled by the extent to which folks chose to ignore the way white supremacy was informing the structure of the conference. Talking with the black woman, I asked her: "What do you do, when you are tired of confronting white racism, tired of the day-to-day incidental acts of racial terrorism? I mean, how do you deal with coming home to a white person?" Laughing she said, "Oh, you mean when I am suffering from White People Fatigue Syndrome? He gets that more than I do." After we finish our laughter, we talk about the way white people who shift locations, as her companion has done, begin to see the world differently. Understanding how racism works, he can see the way in which whiteness acts to terrorize without seeing himself as bad, or all white people as bad, and all black people as good. Repudiating us-and-them dichotomies does not mean that we should never speak of the ways observing the world from the standpoint of "whiteness" may indeed distort perception, impede understanding of the way racism works both in the larger world as well as in the world of our intimate interactions.

In *The Post-Colonial Critic,* Gayatri Spivak calls for a shift in locations, clarifying the radical possibilities that surface when positionality is problematized. She explains that "what we are asking for is that the hegemonic discourses, and the holders of hegemonic discourse, should dehegemonize their position and themselves learn how to occupy the subject position of the other." Generally, this process of repositioning has the power to deconstruct practices of racism and make possible the disassociation of whiteness with terror in the black imagination. As critical intervention it allows for the recognition that progressive white people who are anti-racist might be able to understand the way in which their cultural practice reinscribes white supremacy without promoting paralyzing guilt or denial. Without the capacity to inspire terror, whiteness no longer signifies the right to dominate. It truly becomes a benevolent absence. Baldwin ends his essay "Stranger in the Village" with the declaration: "This world is white no longer, and it will never be white again." Critically examining the association of whiteness as terror in the black imagination, deconstructing it, we both name racism's impact and help to break its hold. We decolonize our minds and our imaginations.

WHITES AS HEATHENS
AND CHRISTIANS
David Walker

David Walker (1785–1830), a Boston dealer in used clothing and self-described "restless disturber of the peace," addressed his fellow "coloured citizens of the world" in three editions of his self-published Appeal *in 1829 and 1830. Born to a slave father and a free mother in North Carolina, Walker had traveled widely in the South and reflected deeply on the revolutionary tradition in the United States. Looking to a god who would intervene on "behalf of the oppressed," and advocating physical resistance to tyranny,* David Walker's Appeal *was suppressed vigorously in the South. A landmark document of pan-African revolt in the United States, it featured an extensive and bitter critique of white civilization.*

The whites have always been an unjust, jealous, unmerciful, avaricious and blood-thirsty set of beings, always seeking after power and authority.—We view them all over the confederacy of Greece, where they were first known to be any thing, (in consequence of education) we see them there, cutting each other's throats—trying to subject each other to wretchedness and misery—to effect which, they used all kinds of deceitful, unfair, and unmerciful means. We view them next in Rome, where the spirit of tyranny and deceit raged still higher. We view them in Gaul, Spain, and in Britain.—In fine, we view them all over Europe, together with what were scattered about in Asia and Africa, as heathens, and we see them acting more like devils than accountable men. But some may ask, did not the blacks of Africa, and the mulattoes of Asia, go on in the same way as did the whites of Europe. I answer, no—they never were half so avaricious, deceitful and unmerciful as the whites, according to their knowledge.

But we will leave the whites or Europeans as heathens, and take a view of them as Christians, in which capacity we see them as cruel, if not more so than ever. In fact, take them as a body, they are ten times more cruel, avaricious and unmerciful than ever they were; for while they were heathens, they were bad enough it is true, but it is positively a fact that they were not quite so audacious as to go and take vessel loads of men, women and children, and in cold blood, and through devilishness, throw them into the sea, and murder them in all kind of ways. While they were heathens, they were too ignorant for such barbarity. But being Christians, enlightened and sensible, they are completely prepared for such hellish cruelties.

Now suppose God were to give them more sense, what would they do? If it were possible, would they not *dethrone* Jehovah and seat themselves upon his throne? I therefore, in the name and fear of the Lord God of Heaven and of earth, divested of prejudice either on the side of my colour or that of the whites, advance my suspicion of them, whether they are *as good by nature* as we are or not. Their actions, since they were known as a people, have been the reverse, I do indeed suspect them, but this, as I before observed, is shut up with the Lord, we cannot exactly tell, it will be proved in succeeding generations.—The whites have had the essence of the gospel as it was preached by my master and his apostles—the Ethiopians have not, who are to have it in its meridian splendor—the Lord will give it to them to their satisfaction. I hope and pray my God, that they will make good use of it, that it may be well with them.

ON RACE AND CHANGE
William Wells Brown

Born in a slave family in Kentucky, William Wells Brown (1814?–1884) escaped to the North from St. Louis in 1834. An active abolitionist on both sides of the Atlantic, Brown published the pioneering African-American novel Clotel *in 1853. A medical doctor, Brown also wrote sweeping works of history, including* The Rising Son; or, The Antecedents and Achievements of the Colored Race *(1874). It is from that volume that the following striking passage on race, history, and environment is drawn.*

We all acknowledge the Anglo-Saxon to be the highest type of civilization. But from whence sprang this refined, proud, haughty, and intellectual race? Go back a few centuries, and we find their ancestors described in the graphic touches of Caesar and Tacitus. See them in the gloomy forests of Germany, sacrificing to their grim and gory idols; drinking the warm blood of their prisoners, quaffing libations from human skulls; infesting the shores of the Baltic for plunder and robbery; bringing home the reeking scalps of enemies as an offering to their king.

Macaulay says:—"When the Britons first became known to the Tyrian mariners, they were little superior to the Sandwich Islanders."

Hume says:—"The Britons were a rude and barbarous people, divided into numerous clans, dressed in the skins of wild beasts: druidism was their religion, and they were very superstitious." Caesar writing home, said of the Britons,—"They are the most degraded people I ever conquered." Cicero advised his friend Atticus not to purchase slaves from Briton, "because," said he, "they cannot be taught music, and are the ugliest people I ever saw."

An illustration of the influence of circumstances upon the physical appearance of man may be found still nearer our own time. In the Irish rebellion in 1641, and 1689, great multitudes of the native Irish were driven from Armagh and the South down into the mountainous tract extending from the Barony of Flews eastward to the sea; on the other side of the kingdom the same race were expelled into Litrin, Sligo, and Mayo. Here they have been almost ever since, exposed to the worst effects of hunger and ignorance, the two great brutalizers of the human race.

The descendants of these exiles are now distinguished physically, from their kindred in Meath, and other districts, where they are not in a state of personal debasement. These people are remarkable for open, projecting mouths, prominent teeth, and exposed gums; their advancing cheek-bones and depressed noses carry barbarism on their very front.

In Sligo and northern Mayo, the consequences of two centuries of degradation and hardship exhibit themselves in the whole physical condition of the people, affecting not only the features, but the frame, and giving such an example of human degradation as to make it revolting.

They are only five feet two inches, upon an average, bow-legged, bandy-shanked, abortively-featured; the apparitions of Irish ugliness and Irish want.

WHAT SHALL WE DO
WITH THE WHITE PEOPLE?

"Ethiop" (William J. Wilson)

Signing himself as "Ethiop," the Brooklyn schoolteacher William J. Wilson (1818–?) wrote many articles for Frederick Douglass' Paper *and for the* Anglo-African Magazine *in the two decades before the Civil War. In one extended fantasy he imagined a future in which African Americans looked back during the year 4000, recalling their former oppressors, now extinct, as "milk white" beings, who were "terrible to look upon, yea even fearful." In the remarkable 1860* Anglo-African Magazine *article reprinted below, Wilson's concerns are largely with past and present, though he raises large questions concerning the future.*

This is a grave question, and gravely will we attempt to consider it. But before entering upon the discussion, a brief outline of the rise and career of this people in this country may be necessary.

For many centuries now have they been on this continent; and for many years have they had entire rule and sway; yet they are to-day no nearer the solution of the problem, *"are they fit for self-government"*— than they were at the commencement of their career. Discontent and disaffection have marked every footstep, and the word *"failure"* is to-day written on every door-post.

They came over to this country in the first instance in small numbers, and forthwith began upon a course of wrong doing. The Aborigines were the first victims of their cupidity. They took advantage of them in every conceivable manner. They robbed them of their lands, plundered their wigwams, burned their villages, and murdered their wives and children. This may seem over-drawn; for in some instances small purchases of lands were made; but this was merely for the sake of foothold—a kind of entering-wedge; when once gained, the work of ravage and devastation would commence. Thus, step by step they advanced, until now they have almost the entire possession of the continent.

One would naturally conclude, that with such a condition of

things, this people would be content, that a condition seemingly so favorable, would ensure some sort of quietude, some substantial peace. Not so this people. Restless, grasping, unsatiated, they are ever on the lookout for not what is, or ought to be theirs, but for what they can get. Like a band of sailors (call them by what name you please), who, after having appropriated all the rich treasures of a merchantman, make the captain, crew and passengers walk the plank, so these white people insist not merely in having country and government and everything else therein, but that rightful owners shall vacate and tread the plank in the bargain. Twice they have quarreled with, stripped off, and fought the mother who gave them origin and nursed them till they were grown; and once have they most unmercifully beaten their weaker and more pacific neighbor; and then despoiled him of a large portion of his lands, and are now tormented with longings after the balance.

If we go back to an earlier page in their history, we find them stealing and appropriating what? Why, men, women and children from abroad and consigning them to a perpetual bondage; them and their children, and their children's children forever. This infamous business they continued unmolested for over a century; but for some reasons, certainly not from any convictions of wrong they abandoned the practice; only however, as it has subsequently appeared to fasten the chains tighter and to press harder the hereditary victims they so cruelly hold in bondage. It is but just to add, that the internal slave trade, is, to-day, more actively carried on than was ever the foreign trade by this people, and, too, with great pecuniary advantages, which, with them, is sufficient for a full justification of the business.

Let us turn our attention to another page of their history. Prior to their broil with the English people in Europe, they framed a form of government, which to all human appearance promised well. It seemed to contain all the elements of success. Its foundation had the look of solidity and its frame work, that of strength and durability. "*We hold these truths to be self-evident, that all men are created free and equal; and endowed with certain and inalienable rights; among which are life, liberty, and the pursuits of happiness.*"

This grand, this lofty, this truthful language constituted its four corner stones; and the civilized world naturally enough looked for a noble and lasting superstructure to be built thereon. The great masses of the old world sighed and hoped for it: and the *Crowns* trembled and feared because of it. Both clearly expected the rearing high up in its topmost lattice a beacon light that would lead to a new era among the governments of the world; but both have been disappointed.

Disaffection and discontent came almost simultaneously with the bud and the blossom, and ere the first summer fruits, confusion and division had entire sway. From thence forth have they gone on, amidst the jar and confusion of tongues, until we stand, to-day, a most perfect Babel; out-rivalling in every respect that ancient one so summarily disposed of by the Great Disposer himself.

Scarce three-fourths of a century has passed away since the basis of the government was laid, and we find the foremost of their leaders earnestly and laboriously engaged in pulling out the foundation stones thereof and anathematizing them as "glittering generalities"; gross blunders, untempered mortar, &c., &c. Dissolution and overthrow are the war-whoop of the entire *corps* of their leaders; not one of whom, but would, were it in his power, pull down the pillars of the Republic over his own head: Such is the unbridled sway the vilest of passions have over them.

If, in our scrutiny, we pass down to the present, we shall find increased discontent and disruption. Looking at this people in the light of their present existing institutions, what do we behold? Strife, confusion and disaffection. If we peruse their journals, which constitute the true index of the general mind, without exception we find nothing but grumblings, murmurings and moanings over the sad state things are in; coupled with a war of words, gross language and shameful vituperation.—These make up the sum of all you find therein. If we go into the Halls of Legislation, which are the exponents of the will of this people, we shall discover that fearful quarrels, brutal fights, cowardly assassinations, bludgeons, knives and pistols, are the chief arguments used, the weighty bills passed, the grave laws made; the burthen of the legislation accomplished; True, there are other arguments offered, other bills passed, and other codes enacted; but these play but a secondary part, and fall as dead weights at the feet of the people. In these little or no interest is taken. They afford the people no satisfaction: they bring them no content, no happiness.

If we ascend to the Judicial Chamber, we shall find there operations in process, producing the same unsatisfactory results to this people. We shall find there instead of laws, wicked codes; for justice we find injustice; for truth, falsehood; for right, wrong; and these perversions insisted on and enforced to the very letter. They reverse there the very principle of law, so that in doubtful cases, or where the interpretation may favour right or wrong, justice or injustice, humanity or inhumanity; they give wrong, injustice and inhumanity the benefit of the doubt. And moreover, that these worst of codes, may be enforced and recognized as law, and this perversion of principles swelled and digested the worst and most unprincipled of men—*men without scruple* and without conscience, are selected to do their work; and faithfully do they execute their task. "The people," say they, "must be made to conquer their prejudices and accept these proceedings."

If we go to the pulpits we behold the same unsatisfactory state of things. We find these places filled with men who, to do them credit, we firmly believe, try to preach the gospel of Christ but fail in the attempt. The fault is not so much theirs as the system under which they have been reared. A system under which, instead of proclaiming the everlasting gospel of Christ, they are compelled to look after their bread, or places of preferment. Instead of uttering the truths that Christ's system teaches and applying them to the hearts and consciences of men, and bringing them to bear upon their daily life and practice, we find them wholly absorbed in cutting and trimming theological garments to suit their various patrons. Though, notwithstanding all this, manifestations of dissatisfaction may be traced through all their clerical performances. How can it be otherwise. They feel that something is wrong, that a screw is somewhere loose in the general machinery of society. Standing by, they dare not bind what they find loosed, and they dare not loosen what they find bound.

They stand a powerless, self-condemned body, and call up all our pity, and we can scarcely mingle with it any tincture of bitterness. The congregations who gather round these pulpits make God's word of none effect. No love, no humility, such as Christ taught, is there. They build costly and gorgeous temples, and worshiping instead the Great God therein they turn them into engines, for generating prejudice and bitter hate against the oppressed, the outcast, and the lowly, thus making God's word a contempt, and their own conduct a wonder to angels.

If we look into their social state, we shall discover but strife, bitterness, and distraction. Not those honest and frank differences of opinion that beget and strengthen sound opinion, but low petty captiousness and cowardly vindictiveness, everywhere pervade. On looking over the country as a whole, we see section divided against section, and clan pitted against clan, and each cheered on by fierce leaders and noisy demagogues on the one side; while compromises and harmony and quiet are sued for on the other by men who are denounced as fogies and fossils by the general voice of the whole people. If we take locality after locality, we shall find the same state of turmoil and confusion. Hand raised against hand, and frown meeting frown. Everywhere is the exclamation sounding "Am I my brother's keeper!!" Everywhere is written the sentence "What have I to do with thee!" It would seem as if this people anew had builded a tower of Babel, and that a confusion of ideas infinitely more disintegrating than a confusion of tongues had begun the work of separation and isolation,—their first step in the downward path of barbarism, just as truly as "*E Pluribus Unum*" was their first step to progress and civilization.

Go with us over the plains of Kansas, and witness there the recent death struggle between sections of this people for the supremacy of wrong over right. Go stand by the grave mounds made there by that fierce struggle; or returning go through the guilded palaces and gorgeous streets, and then through the low sickening hovels of the metropolis of the country; or go with us even to cold philosophical New England, even industrious intellectual Massachusetts, and wander about the factories there; and above all, go with us to the regions of the sunny South, where, without shadow of law, they torture men to their death, outraged women gather up their own little children as calves for the slaughter, and sell them to the highest bidder. Witness all this, and tell us if these things of this people are not true?

The manifold blessings, physical and intellectual, with which God and nature have crowned them in granting them a country so manifestly fitted for the development of a people—a people especially of their peculiar bent and endowments; stand out in wonderful contrast with their conduct, their course, their abuse of the great privileges so kindly bestowed upon them. Climate the finest in the world, soil the most fertile, topographical facilities the best conceivable; resources greater than that of any other part of the globe, and facilities for their development beyond that of any other country extant; with just enough difficulties—(no more)—to develop in addition, their genius in overcoming the same. These all have been theirs. Everything that nature could bestow and art devise has been placed at their hands, and yet the blight of discord disruption and disunion, has, like a Simoon settled down upon this people.

What then shall we Anglo-Africans do with these white people? *"What shall we do with them?"* It may seem strange, that a people so crushed and trodden upon; so insignificant as the Anglo-Africans, should even ask the question "what shall we do with the whites?" Indeed, the question may seem presumptuous, quizzical ridiculous; but the truth is, that these white people themselves, through their Press and Legislative Halls, in their pulpits, and on their Rostrums, so constantly talk of nothing but us black people, and have apparently got so far beyond every thing else, that it would seem that their very instincts regard us as in a measure able to settle and make quiet their restlessness, and hence they have actually forced upon us the question which is, the title of this article. It has indeed become a serious question with us: What shall we do with the white people?

We have, perhaps, been too modest, else we would have raised the question before; and might, it may be, ere this, have found its proper solution. Let us endeavor to compensate for past neglect by an earnest endeavor to settle this important question. But before proceeding to the answer we find another and equally vital question forcing itself in our way, which demanding a moment's attention, viz: What is the cause of all this discontent, this unquiet state, this distress? This answer we think may be found in this, viz: *a long continued, extensive, and almost complete system of wrong-doing.* Like a man who commences the life of a pick-pocket and changes not his way, becomes not only an adept in the profession, but a hardened offender, and reaps the bitter fruits in the end thereof, so also this people. They commenced with the plunder of the Indian, theft of the African, followed by the grossest wrongs upon the Africo-American, and broils with their neighbors without, and stripes among themselves within, the fruits of which are thorough disaffection and agitation.

But another and equally important question forces itself upon us, viz: whither are this people tending? If permitted in their course; if no restraining hand arrest them, who does not foresee that the goal at which they will ultimately arrive will be sure and certain barbarism. Already do we hear it proclaimed through their *presses* that if other hands than their own are not compelled to labour for them, want and starvation will stalk abroad through the land; blood will flow through the streets like water from the fountain, and repine follow in its train. That where now they have thrift and plenty, dirth will abound, the thorn and the thistle and the deadly brier will spring up and grow, and the more deadly serpent will hiss and nestle therein, that the harvest will be passed and ended, the summer over and gone, and the voice of the turtle be no more heard in the land.

And, indeed, this picture which is not ours but theirs, seems to be not an exaggeration, no fancy sketch, but a reality; for already do we find them grappling each other by the throat for opinion sake—opinions, the result of honest convictions of right and truth. In a large portion of the country already no man among them can express honest truth, without risk of life while everywhere will the hiss of contempt follow him, and the finger of scorn point toward him if he venture upon it. Honesty and truth, unless they be of a certain character, are at discount among this people, and like Rachel for her children go weeping through the land; while dishonesty and falsehood, if of a certain character, stalk boldly forth with the laugh and the joy of demons, and exclaiming, "we have triumphed! we have triumphed!!"

And verily they have triumphed; and in that triumph and what else we have instanced, who does not see that this people are on the direct road to barbarism.

What then shall we Anglo-Africans do with them? How save them and the country from their sure and impending fate? What agencies shall we put forth to arrest so direful a calamity? These are indeed serious questions, and reviewed in the light of earnestness demand, if possible, immediate solution.

This people must be saved; quiet and harmony must be restored. Plans for the removal of these white people as all such schemes are—such for example as these people have themselves laid for the removal of others out of their midst—would be wrong in conception, and prove abortive in attempt; nor ought it be desirable on our part were it even possible to forcibly remove them. It is their right to stay, only they have no right to jeopard the interest or the peace of the country if permitted to remain. God, in his all wise purpose, has reserved this fair land for other, and higher and nobler purposes than a theatre for the exhibition of prejudices, bitter hates, fierce strifes, dissentions, oppressions, frauds. On the contrary, it was so to speak, reserved for centuries, like a sealed book, and then thrown open just when needed by the *Great Author himself* that men of every tongue, and clime and hue, should gather thereon, and perfect their development.

So long as we have entertained the belief that this people would ultimately approach toward this point, we have silently bowed without remonstrance or even murmur. We have labored long and faithfully with little or no remuneration, we have been patient, under every trial, and enduring under every burthen placed upon us or self-imposed, that these people might redeem themselves, that they might retrieve their past errors and return to a sense of right. Pressed and circumscribed by them, we have been disposed to make the best of our way; narrow as the space we have as yet been enabled to acquire for our labours, we have been content. But the white people, on the other hand, are not content. We find even under depressing circumstances room enough for us in this country, they the white people and they alone, find its boundaries too circumscribed for their greedy grasp. Possessing acres by the millions, yet they would elbow us and all others off of what we possess, to give them room for what they cannot occupy. We want this country, say they, for ourselves, and ourselves alone. What right have they but that of might, to put forth such a cool assumption? Who are these people that they come forth in the light of the Nineteenth century, and, too, after creating the agitation and confusion which now effervesce the entire nation and demand the whole country for themselves and their posterity.

Seriously do we hope, that if the peace of the country is to be so continuously disturbed that they would withdraw. We have arrived at a period when they could easily be spared. We have ceded to these people energy and force of character, and we may add one other characteristic, viz: a roving, *unsettled, restless* disposition. They are in inclination if not habit, marauders.

It may be, unless we shall find some other effective means of adjusting existing difficulties, that from this point we may have some hope for their Exodus.

We give them also high credit for their material progress. Who knows, but that some day, when, after they shall have fulfilled their mission, carried arts and sciences to their highest point, they will make way for a milder and more genial race, or become so blended in it, as to lose their own peculiar and objectionable characteristics? In any case, in view of the existing state of things around us, let our constant thought be, *what for the best good of all shall we do with the White people?*

THE COLOR OF HEAVEN

Mia Bay

The historian Mia Bay (1961–), a professor at Rutgers University, completed the most systematic study of African-American thought concerning whites in her 1994 Yale University doctoral dissertation, "The White Image in the Black Mind." In the only piece written originally for inclusion in this collection, Bay draws from her forthcoming book on African-American views of whites, concentrating specifically on antebellum Southern views of a race-blind God and of the moral superiority of slaves to their enslavers.

The fate of races in the hereafter was a subject of intense concern in the antebellum South. "Jordan's stream is wide and deep," African Americans sang during slavery, "Jesus stand on t'oder side . . . I wonder if my maussa deh." Their song focused on a question that prompted endless speculations among slave-owners as well. Who would get to heaven? The slaves and their masters shared a Protestant religious faith which promised them that death would bring an end to the earthly distinctions that divided the living. Their Bible told them that all souls would meet as equals in heaven, but masters and slaves alike found that prospect hard to imagine. Both wondered how the races would be divided after death. Ex-slave testimony illustrates that the slaves and their masters came to very different conclusions when they considered this subject.

Evangelical slaveholders feared that death would bring an end to all racial distinctions, and worse, be the moment when they were judged for the inequities they had perpetuated. Less pious Southern whites, however, often assumed that heaven would be theirs alone. "Nigger obey your master and mistress," a Texas slave woman was told, "'cause what you get from dem here in dis world is all you ever goin' git, 'cause you jes' like the hogs and the other animals, when you dies you ain't no more." Other slave-owners imagined a white heaven while offering their slaves a less dispiriting fate. They promised them that if they behaved themselves they could hope to go to "negro heaven"—or "kitchen heaven" as it was sometimes called.

Despite the appealing prospect of an all-white heaven, evidently not all masters and mistresses were willing to give up their slaves when they crossed the great divide. "De white folks dat owned slaves," one ex-slave reported, "thought that when dey got to heaven de colored folks would be dar to wait on them." One slave mistress worried that heaven would not be heaven without the services of her slave maid. "I would give anything if I could have Maria in heaven with me to do little things for me."

African-American slaves also imagined a commingling of the races in the hereafter. But it was a prospect which troubled many of them. "I was setting up here thinkin' the other night 'bout talk of them white folks going to heaven," one freedman said. "Lord God, they'd turn heaven wrong side out and have the angels working to make something they could take away from them." Long after slavery, many ex-slaves abhorred the prospect of meeting their former owners in the hereafter. "I'se done ready declared to see God when I'se die," declared the elderly Ben Simpson. "But boss, I hopes my old master is not up there to torment this old negro again."

Such hopes were sustained by the religious worship of slaves who prayed that "God don' think different of the blacks and whites." A shared belief that these prayers were heard was, perhaps, what gave so many slaves confidence that their white owners ultimately would have to account for their sins. Like their white Southern counterparts, black Southerners often foresaw a "negro heaven," but they believed the preponderance of black people in heaven would be achieved by the judgments of a just God rather than by segregation. White Southerners, one freedwoman observed, "can't expect to beat up us people and jump on a bed and close their eyes and go to heaven." Confident that their own race would be well represented in heaven, the question that the slaves debated was how many whites would find a place there.

"No white people went to heaven," wrote a correspondent to a black newspaper in 1897, recalling the slaves' religious beliefs. "Many believe the same until this day." Texas freedwoman Millie Manuel put it another way, declaring "the Good Shepard will give the best white man a heaben that is hotter than the worstest nigger's hell." Such opinions were common enough to convince Emily Burke, a Northern white woman who visited Georgia in the 1840s, that "I never saw a negro a Universalist. They all believe in the future retribution for their masters in the hands of a just God."

Surprisingly few slaves, however, insisted that all whites had to be barred from heaven. Even fugitive slave Charles Ball, who maintained that the slaves abhorred the idea of an afterlife of living in "a state of perfect affection with equity, and boundless affection, with white people," did not portray the slave's heaven as a segregated place. "As a matter of special favor," Ball explained, the slaves would by special intercession open the Pearly Gates very occasionally to masters and mistresses who had been particularly kind, although even these favored white souls would "by no means be of equal rank with those who shall be raised from the depths of misery, in the world."

The vision of heaven that Ball describes came out of an African-American slave culture sustained by what W.E.B. Du Bois described as an enduring "faith in the ultimate justice of things." Heaven, in the minds of the slaves, was not the racially divided place their masters envisioned. At the same time, while not ruling out the possibility of salvation for deserving whites, the slaves did not expect to meet many white people in heaven. "They was good whites I heard tell of," said Mary Reynolds, whose slave experience was harrowing, adding "they is plenty mo' of them in hell, too."

"Oh, heaven, heaven," sang the African-American slaves as they worked, "Everybody talking 'bout heaven ain't going there." For Reynolds and other slaves the prospect of heaven was made all the more alluring by the anticipation of how the unsuspecting whites would fare under a just God. "Hebben?" replied Mary Bracey, when asked about the afterlife. "De tree of life in Hebben, an' honey an' milk for eat. Dey be no houses, dere be no rain an' cold dere. Dey be no black an' white; we be all alike den, an' play de harp. De fine white folks ob Charleston gonna be surprise, w'en dey miss an' go down dere, where de black an' white burn alike."

KLANSMAN'S PRAYER

Charles Johnson

The deeply philosophical, brilliantly comic novelist Charles Johnson (1948–), whose Middle Passage *received the National Book Award in 1990, learned cartooning by mail-order instruction in the 1960s. His cartoons, many of them prepared for the student newspaper at Southern Illinois University, were collected in* Black Humor *(1970).*

Give me the strength to eliminate the inferior people ruining my nation.

Sho 'nuff, boss!

OUR WHITE FOLKS

George S. Schuyler

*The combative novelist, essayist, and journalist George S. Schuyler
(1895–1977) moved from socialism to the far-right during a lengthy career
of provocations. A descendant of Revolutionary War fighters and himself a
lieutenant in the army during the World War One years, Schuyler mocked
ideas of both racial traits and white superiority in a variety of writings in the
1920s and 1930s. His celebrated essay "The Negro-Art Hokum" (1926)
lampooned the idea of "fundamental, eternal and inescapable" racial differences, including, and especially, the exotic and "natural" creativity which he
argued that literary critics imputed to African Americans. Schuyler's* Slaves
Today *(1931), a novel describing modern slavery in Liberia, and* Black
No More *(1931), a wild science fiction satire in which a Black doctor per-
fects a process to blanch skins, continued his refusal to take seriously appeals
to transhistorical racial characteristics. In "Our White Folks," a 1927 essay
for H. L. Mencken's* The American Mercury, *Schuyler concentrated his
fire on white pretensions to an understanding of race, turning the tables
playfully and earnestly.*

Numerous and ponderous tomes have been written about Negroes
by white folks. With a pontifical air they rush into print on the slightest provocation to tell the world all about the blackamoor. These
writings range all the way from alarmist gabble about the Black Menace or the tragedy of the dark brethren suffocating in the midst of
white civilization to sloppy sentimentalities by the lunatic fringe of
Liberals and the mooney scions of Southern slaveholders who de-
plore the passing of Uncle Tom and Aunt Beckie, who knew how
to "act properly" and did not offend them by being self-respecting
or intelligent. This fervent scribbling has been going on for a dozen
decades or more, until today the libraries and attics of the country are
crammed with more books and papers on the Negro than on any
other American group. With so much evidence of what the Nordic
thinks of his black brother, no one need remain ignorant on the subject. And if one doesn't read one may learn his attitude and opinion

by observing the various Jim-crow laws and other such exhibits throughout this glorious land.

We Ethiops, one gathers from this mass of evidence, are a childish, shiftless, immoral, primitive, incurably religious, genially incompetent, incredibly odoriferous, inherently musical, chronically excitable, mentally inferior people with pronounced homicidal tendencies. We are incapable of self-government or self-restraint, and irresponsible except when led by white folks. We possess a penchant for assaulting white females and an inordinate appetite for chicken, gin and watermelon. While it is finally and reluctantly admitted that we belong to the human race, we are accorded only the lowest position in the species, a notch or two above the great apes. We make good domestics but hopeless executives. Even at this late date, all coons look alike to the great majority of Nordic Americans, and even the highest type of Negro is under no consideration to be accorded a higher position than the lowest type of white. In short, from examining the bulk of the evidence, the impartial investigator must conclude that the Negro has almost a monopoly of all the more discreditable characteristics of mankind. But at the same time one is effusively informed that he is deeply loved and thoroughly understood, especially by his pork-skinned friends of southern derivation.

As a result of this attitude of his pale neighbors, the lowly moke has about ten times as many obstacles to hurdle in the race of life as the average peckerwood. It is difficult enough to survive and prosper in this world under the best of conditions, but when one must face such an attitude on the part of those who largely control the means of existence, the struggle is great indeed. Naturally there is deep resentment and bitterness among the more intelligent Negroes, and there always has been. Nothing else could be expected from a people who confront a continuous barrage of insult and calumny and discrimination from the cradle to the grave. There are Negroes, of course, who publicly claim to love the white folks, but privately the great majority of them sing another tune. Even the most liberal blacks are always suspicious, and have to be on the alert not to do or say anything that will offend the superior race. Such an atmosphere is not conducive to great affection, except perhaps on the part of halfwits.

Is it generally known that large numbers of Negroes, though they openly whooped it up for Uncle Sam, would have shed no tears in 1917–18 if the armies of the Kaiser had by some miracle suddenly swooped down upon such fair cities as Memphis, Tenn., Waycross, Ga., or Meridian, Miss. The Negro upper class, in press and pulpit, roared and sweated to keep the dinges in line by telling them how much the white folks would do to improve their status after the war if they would only be loyal, but the more enlightened Ethiops were frankly skeptical, a skepticism justified later on. On several occasions during that struggle for democracy I sounded out individual Sambos here and there, and was somewhat surprised to find many of them holding the view that it made no difference to them who won the war, since the Germans could hardly treat them any worse than the Nordics of the U. S. A., and might treat them a lot better. Any number of intelligent Negroes expressed the opinion under the breath that a good beating would be an excellent thing for the soul of America. Even some of the actual black soldiers were observed on occasion to indulge in cynical smirks and sarcastic exclamations during the reading of tracts from Mr. Creel's propaganda mill.

II

Of course the attitude of the Negro toward the Nordics varies with the locality he lives in, the conditions under which he lives, and the class to which he belongs. Traveling in the South, it is difficult to get the truth about race relations in a given community unless one is very painstaking. This is due to the fact that among both whites and blacks down there, there is a great deal of local patriotism, no matter how bad conditions may actually be. The whites will claim that their niggers are the best in the world and that those in all of the surrounding towns are gorillas, while the Ethiops will speak highly of their own white folks, but heap maledictions upon the heads of the crackers further down the line. It is always wise to let them talk themselves out of breath in praise of their particular community, and then inquire discreetly about the schools, the courts, the franchise, economic opportunities, civic improvements, health conditions, and so forth. As the Negroes discuss such things one begins to get an indication of their real feelings, which are seldom flattering to their townsfolk of paler hue.

Curiously enough, the majority of Nordics seem to believe that all Negroes look upon them as some sort of demigods—as paragons of intelligence, efficiency, refinement and morality. No doubt they have arrived at this curious conclusion by observing how the blackamoors ape their appearance with skin whiteners and hair straighteners, and how they are given to disparaging the efforts and attainments of other Negroes. They have probably heard such Negroisms as "A nigger ain't nuthin," "What more can you expect from a nigger?" and "Why don't you be like white folks?"

The Negro, it is true, is cynical and skeptical about his own, and often his castigations of his brethren are more devastating than any administered by the white folks. In this respect, he resembles his Jewish brother. But the crow is equally critical of his red-necked comrades. Only infrequently do the white folks perceive that this indirect flattery is a sort of combination of protective coloration, group discipline, and feeling of annoyance and futility. It does not in the majority of cases mean that the individual Negro they see in front of them thinks that they are his superiors—except in power.

If the Southern white, as is his wont, can with any justification trumpet to the world that he knows the Negro, the Aframerican can with equal or greater truth claim to have the inside information on the cracker. Knowing him so intimately, the black brother has no illusions about either his intelligence, his industry, his efficiency, his honor, or his morals. The blacks haven't been working with and for the white folks all these decades and centuries for nothing. While the average Nordic knows nothing of how Negroes actually live and what they actually think, the Negroes know the Nordics intimately. Practically every member of the Negro aristocracy of physicians, dentists, lawyers, undertakers and insurance men has worked at one time or another for white folks as a domestic, and observed with cynical detachment their orgies, obsessions and imbecilities, while contact with the white proletariat has acquainted him thoroughly with their gross stupidity and often very evident inferiority.

Toward the white working classes, indeed, there is a great suspicion and ill-feeling among the Negroes of the United States, much to the discomfiture of labor organizers and radicals. The superior posture of the poor whites is based on nothing but the fortuitous circumstance that created them lighter in color. The Negro puts this down to mere ignorance and a fear of competition for jobs. He believes that the white workers would have nothing to lose by ditching their color prejudice and aligning themselves with him. Ever since the so-called Civil War, he has been attempting to make the white proletariat see the light, but the mudsill Caucasians are obdurate. They think far more of an empty color superiority than they do of labor solidarity. Even the Jewish working-people, of whom solidarity might be expected, are far from being free of color prejudice.

Quite naturally, the Negroes feel far more kindly toward the whites of wealth and influence. From them they have obtained quite a few favors and largesses, but they do not lose sight of the fact that in the face of a group crisis, such as a lynching or a race riot, they cannot depend upon these upper class Nordics, who invariably desert when the mob heaves into sight, if indeed they do not join it. Directing and controlling the social and economic life of the country, they have allowed to go almost unquestioned all sorts of legislation inimical to the Negro's advancement. Toward individual Negroes they may be kindly and helpful, but except in the case of those who support Negro colleges and schools, they do not seem to care a rap about how the mass of blacks gets along. They allow gross inequalities in the appropriation of school funds; they allow Negro residential sections to go without adequate health inspection; they allow the compulsory school laws to remain unenforced in so far as the blacks are concerned; they make little or no protest against peonage and the horrors of Southern prisons and chain-gangs; they allow petty officials to make a mockery of the judicial system where Negroes are involved; and they refuse to see to it that the Negro is given the means to protect himself, if possible, through the franchise.

These upper class white folks contend that the workings of democracy prevent them from forcing the poor whites to toe the mark, but the Negroes observe that when it is desired to put over anything else that is deemed important, some way is always found. It seems to the thinking black man that, even granting that the white ruling class is incapable of assisting the masses of his people, they could at least openly enlist themselves on the side of honesty, fairness and square dealing, and thereby set an example to the others. But in the main they prefer to remain silent, and so leave the Negro to the mercies of the white rabble. Is it any wonder that he views them with distrust?

The attitude of the Northern white folks, in particular, puzzles and incenses him. Very often he feels that they are more dangerous to him than the Southerners. Here are folks who yawp continuously about liberty, justice, equality and democracy, and whoop with indignation every time a Senegambian is incinerated below the Potomac or the Belgians burn another village in the Congo, but toward the Negro in their midst they are quite as cruel as the Southern crackers. They are wont to shout, in their liberal moments, that the Negro is as good as they are—as if that were a compliment!—and to swear by all the gods that they want to give him a square deal and a chance in the world, but when he approaches them for a job they offer him a mop and pail or a bellhop's uniform, no matter what his education and training may be. And except in isolated instances they see that he remains permanently in the lowly position they have given him.

The majority of them are almost as prejudiced as their Southern brethren, as any Negro knows who has ever attempted to enter a public place or to attend their social gatherings. Unlike the crackers, they only grudgingly give him a chance to earn a living, even as a menial. The restriction of European immigration has helped the Negro in the North considerably in the field of industry, but in the marts of commerce there seems to be an impression that he is incapable of functioning in the field of general business. At present, in the city of New York, which is considered a heaven for Negroes, and the tolerance and liberality of which are widely advertised throughout the nation, it is harder for a capable young Negro to get a decent job in a business house than it is for a comely Negro girl to escape being approached by white men in a Southern town.

To the intelligent Aframerican, an individual who has color prejudice seems manifestly to belong in the same intellectual class as the Holy Rollers and the Ku Kluxers. To judge an individual solely on the basis of his skin color and hair texture is so obviously nonsensical that he cannot help classing the bulk of Nordics with the inmates of an insane asylum. He views with mingled amusement and resentment the stupid reactions of white folks to a black skin. It excites his bitter mirth to observe how his entrance into almost any public place is sufficient to spoil the evening of the majority of the proud Caucasians present, no matter how intelligent they may claim to be. Nor is this insanity restricted alone to Anglo-Saxons, for Jews, Irish, Greeks, Poles, Russians, Italians, and Germans, even those who know little of the American language and less of the national customs, grow quite as apoplectic at the sight of a sable countenance.

III

Because the whites bellow so much about their efficiency and thrift, the Negro marvels that they go to the expense of a dual school system, Jim-crow railroad coaches and waiting-rooms, separate cemeteries, and segregated parks, libraries and street cars, with the obvious economic waste entailed, when the two peoples are so intimately associated all day, not to mention at night. Indeed, an examination of family trees will reveal that a large number of the whites and blacks are really related, especially in the land of cotton, where most of the hue and cry is raised about Anglo-Saxon purity. The South, the Negro does not fail to note, has actually retarded its own progress by maintaining this hypocritical double standard. And now it is threatening the standards of living in the New England mill towns and Northern coal fields by offering cheaper labor and lower taxes,—an offer that it can make only because of the ready acceptance of low living standards by the Southern white mob out of fear that Negroes will take its poorly paid jobs. Thus the results of the stupid system are felt in sections where hardly any Negroes live at all.

Almost every thoughtful Negro believes that the scrapping of the color caste system would not hinder but rather help the country. In their zeal to keep the black brother away from the pie counter, the whites are depriving the nation of thousands of individuals of extra-ordinary ability. The rigid training and discipline that the Negro has received since his arrival on these sacred shores has left him with a lower percentage of weaklings and incompetents than is shown by any other group. He has always had to be on the alert, ever the diplo-mat and skillful tactician, facing more trying situations in a week than the average white citizen faces in a year. This experience has certainly fitted him for a more important position than he now holds in the Republic. He is still imbued with the pioneering spirit that the bulk of the whites have had ironed out of them. He has energy and origi-nality, the very qualities being sought today in business and govern-ment. Yet narrow bigotry and prejudice bar his way.

When the Southern white man asks the liberal Caucasian, "Do you want your daughter to marry a nigger?", he is probably hitting the nail on the head, for that is the crux of the entire color problem. Fear of economic and political competition is a factor, but above it is the bogey of sex competition. Equality in one field will unquestion-ably lead to equality in the other. And yet there is no law compelling blacks and whites to intermarry, and if the natural aversion that the scientists shout of really exists there need be no fears on that score. The Anglo-Saxons will retain their polyglot purity if they wish to do so—and if they actually find the Ethiops as repellant as the authorities on the subject allege.

But there is considerable doubt in the mind of the Negro as to whether this aversion actually exists, and whether the Anglo-Saxons actually *think* it exists. He tries to reconcile the theory that it does with the fact that nearly thirty States have laws prohibiting intermar-riage between the so-called races, and with the additional fact that half of the Negroes in America obviously possess more or less Cau-casian blood, thus being neither black nor white. The dark brother is convulsed with mirth over the famous one-drop theory, that distinctive American contribution to the science of anthropology which lists as Negroes all people having the remotest Negro ancestry, despite the fact that they may be, and often are, indistinguishable from the purest Nordic. He whoops with glee over the recent incident in Virginia, where the workings of the new Racial Integrity Law caused fifty white children to be barred from the white schools and ordered to attend Negro schools on the ground that they were Negroes, although no one knew it except the official genealogists, whereas all the while, in the States of Texas and Oklahoma, dark brown Mexicans and Indians were listed as white, and their children attended white schools. Knowing how much racial intermixture has been going on in this country since the Seventeenth Century, he is eager to see racial integrity laws passed in all of the States, as has been done in Georgia and Virginia, so that the genealogists may get busy on a national scale and thus increase the "Negro" population to at least four times its present number.

The Negro listens with a patient tolerance born of much knowledge and observation to the gabble of white gentlemen concerning the inferior morality of black women. These chivalrous folk, in some sections, do not hesitate to discuss these illicit amours within hearing of their Negro servitors, who boil within as they listen to the racy conversation of the advocates of racial separatism. The whites, of course, never hear the Negro's side of the story. Indeed, it is doubtful whether they realize that he *has* a side. For many and obvious reasons, he keeps his very interesting information to himself and grins along his way. He knows that no one group in this country monopolizes sex morality. Some day a black American Balzac is going to gather material for another volume of Droll Stories that will be quite as interesting and entertaining as the original.

The attitude of the whites toward the Negro's participation in politics seems very absurd to the contemplative dinge. He is a part of American life and he knows very well what is going on in politics. If his sooty brethren are not yet ready to be trusted with the ballot, neither for that matter are the ruck of peckerwoods. He has heard the yells and moans of the ex-Confederates about the alleged horrors of the Reconstruction period, when Negro legislators (who never controlled a single Southern State) are said to have indulged in graft on a great scale and squandered the public funds, but after careful investigation he has failed to learn of a single State or community in the whole country in which precisely the same thing is not true of white politicians. If Negroes sell their votes for a quart of corn liquor and two dollars, they are, he observes, by no means alone. Surely, he concludes, no Legislature composed of Negroes could pass more imbecile legislation than is the annual product of every legislative body in the land, not by any means excluding Congress. He concludes that he is barred from the ballot in the South only in order to keep capable Negroes from competing with broken-down Nordic lawyers for political sinecures. The excuse that his inability to use the ballot intelligently is the cause of his disfranchisement is highly amusing to him after a glance at the national scene.

The amazing ignorance of whites—even Southern whites—about Negroes is a constant source of amusement to all Aframericans. White men who claim to be intelligent and reasonable beings persist in registering surprise whenever they hear of or meet a Negro who has written a novel, a history, or a poem, or who can work a problem in calculus. Because of this naïveté, many mediocre Negroes are praised to the high heavens as geniuses of the first flight, and grow sleek and fat. Such fellows are frequently seized upon by gullible whites and labeled as leaders of the Negro race, without the Negroes being consulted on the matter. It seems incredible to most white folks that within the Negro group are social circles quite as cultured and refined as those existing among whites. I recall with amusement the story circulating the rounds of Aframerica concerning a wealthy white woman in a Southern city who asked her Negro maid if it was true that there were Negro homes in New York City such as those described by Carl Van Vechten in "Nigger Heaven," and who was quite astonished and incredulous when the girl informed her that not only were there such homes in New York but also in that town as well.

IV

Those Negroes who have entrée to white intellectual circles do not return to their own society with regret, but rather with relief, for they rightly observe that the bulk of the white intellectuals have more form than content; that they have a great deal of information but are not so long on common sense; and that they lack that sense of humor and gentle cynicism which one expects to find in the really civilized person, and which are the chief characteristics of even the most lowly and miserable Aframerican.

These so-called sophisticated whites leap from one fad to another, from mah jong to "Ask Me Another," with great facility, and are usually ready to embrace any cause that comes along thirsting for supporters. They are obsessed by sex and discuss it interminably, with long dissertations on their moods and reactions, complexes and sublimations. Life to them seems to be one perpetual psychoanalytical clinic. This appears to the Negro observer as a sure sign of sexual debility. The lusty, virile fellow, such as is the average shine, is too busy really living to moon overly much about the processes of life. It is difficult to imagine a group of intelligent Negroes sprawling around a drawing-room, consuming cigarettes and synthetic gin while discussing their complexes and inhibitions.

The Negroes have observed, too, that they know how to have a good time, despite all their troubles and difficulties, while the majority of white people certainly do not. Indeed, the frantic efforts of the crackers to amuse themselves is a never-ending source of amusement to the blacks. The Nordics take all amusements so seriously! They cannot swim without attempting to cross the English Channel or the Gulf of Mexico; they cannot dance without organizing a marathon to see which couple can dance the longest. They must have their Charleston contests, golf contests, coffee-drinking contests, frankfurter-eating contests. In short, they always go to extremes. The Negroes, on the other hand, have learned how to enjoy themselves without too much self-consciousness and exhibitionism.

The efforts of the Nordics to be carefree are grotesque; the so-called emancipated whites being the worst of the lot. No group of

Negroes anywhere could be louder or rowdier than they are in their efforts to impress the neighborhood with the fact that they are having a good time. Look, for example, at their antics in Greenwich Village. It is not without reason that those white folks who want to enjoy themselves while in New York hustle for Harlem. The less emancipated ones go to the cabarets, where they can sit and watch Negroes dance and caper; the more sensible go to a Negro dance-hall, where they can participate in the fun. It is not uncommon to hear them say that the only time they thoroughly enjoy themselves is when they journey to the so-called Black Belt, where joy is not shackled or saddled.

This is probably the reason why, to the white brethren, the blacks are supposed to be happy-go-lucky children, with never a serious thought in their polls. But the Negro, recalling how the white folks swarm to hear such mountebanks as Billy Sunday, Krishnamurti, Conan Doyle, Imperial Wizard Evans and William Hale Thompson, and eagerly swallow all of the hokum flowing through the Republic, concludes that the Sambos have no monopoly on intellectual infantilism.

The Negro is a sort of black Gulliver chained by white Lilliputians, a prisoner in a jail of color prejudice, a babe in a forest of bigotry, but withal a fellow philosophical and cynical enough to laugh at himself and his predicament. He has developed more than any other group, even more than the Jews, the capacity to see things as they are rather than as he would have them. He is a close student of the contradictory pretensions and practices of the ofay gentry, and it is this that makes him really intelligent in a republic of morons. It is only during the last few years that the cracker *intelligentsia* have begun to sniff suspiciously at the old Anglo-Saxon slogans and concepts of justice, democracy, chivalry, honor, fair play, and so forth. The Negro has always been skeptical about them, knowing that they were conditioned by skin color, social position and economic wealth.

He is sick and tired of the holier-than-thou attitude of the white folks. On what, he inquires, do they base the contention that they are superior? He puts the history of the blacks down through the ages alongside that of the whites and is not ashamed of the comparison.

He knows that there is as much evidence that black men founded human civilization as there is that white men did, and he doubts whether the occidental society of today is superior to the monarcho-communist society developed in Africa. He knows that neither intellectually nor physically is he inferior to the Caucasians. The fact is that in America conditions have made the average Negro more alert, more resourceful, more intelligent, and hence more interesting than the average Nordic. Certainly if the best measure of intelligence is ability to survive in a changing or hostile environment, and if one considers that the Negro is not only surviving but improving all the time in health, wealth, and culture, one must agree that he possesses a high degree of intelligence. In their efforts to fight off the ravages of color prejudice, the blacks have welded themselves into a homogeneity and developed a morale whose potentialities are not yet fully appreciated.

V

They laugh to themselves when they hear white folks refer to them as ugly and black. Thanks to the whites who are always talking about racial purity, the Negroes possess within their group the most handsome people in the United States, with the greatest variety of color, hair and features. Here is the real melting-pot, and a glorious sight it is to see. Ugly people there are, certainly, but the percentage of beautiful folk is unquestionably larger than among the ofay brethren. One has but to venture abroad in a crowd of whites and then go immediately to a fashionable Negro thoroughfare to be impressed with this fact. Black? Well, yes, but how beautiful! How well it blends with almost every color! How smooth the skin; how soft and rounded the features! But there are browns, chocolates, yellows and pinks as well. Here in Aframerica one finds such an array of beauty that it even attracts Anglo-Saxons, despite their alleged color aversion.

The dark brother looks upon himself as an American, an integral part of this civilization. To him it is not a white civilization, but a white and black civilization. He rightly feels that it is partially his, because for three hundred years he toiled to make it possible. He wants no more than an equal break with everybody else, but he feels that he has much greater contributions to make to our national life than he has so far been allowed to make. There is hope among the more enlightened Negroes that the similar group among the Nordics can be educated to see the social value and necessity of removing the barriers that now hamper the black citizen. The country can lose nothing and may gain much by a step. Strange as it may seem, many Negroes look to the enlightened Southern whites as the force that will help bring about the change. While these ofays do not understand the blacks as well as they think, they do at least know them fairly well, and there is, propaganda to the contrary, some good feeling between the two groups. This emerging group of southern whites is gradually becoming strong enough to make its voice heard and respected, and in the years to come it will have more and more influence.

The Aframerican, being more tolerant than the Caucasian, is ready to admit that all white people are not the same, and it is not unusual to read or hear a warning from a Negro orator or editor against condemning all crackers as prejudiced asses, although agreeing that such a description fits the majority of them. The Ethiop is given to pointing out individual pinks who are exceptionally honorable, tolerant and unprejudiced. In this respect, I venture to say, he rises several notches higher than the generality of ofays, to whom, even in this day and time, all coons look alike.

DEBATING THE SENATOR
J. A. Rogers

Jamaican-born Joel Augustus Rogers (1883–1966) played a major role in the popularization of African and African-American history. A writer of fiction and a journalist as well as an historian, Rogers also produced the fine cartoon series Your History. *Although he is best known for such histories as* The World's Greatest Men of African Descent *(1931) and topical studies like* Sex and Race *(1941), Rogers's first major book was the novel* From Superman to Man *(1917). In that work, excerpted here, Rogers's protagonist, a Pullman porter, combines common sense and science to deflate every argument for racism, and indeed for the very idea of separate races, offered by his passenger, a senator from Oklahoma.*

While the senator was still laughing, the train began to slow down, and Dixon, asking to be excused, slid to the other end of the seat to look out, thus leaving the book he had placed behind him, exposed. The senator saw the book, and his laughter soon changed to curiosity.

The volume stood end up on the seat and he could discern from its size and binding that it might contain serious thought. Did it? He had somehow felt that this Negro was above the ordinary and the sight of the book confirmed the feeling.

A certain forced quality in the timbre of Dixon's laughter, as also the merry twinkle in his eye, had made him feel at times just a bit uncomfortable. His curiosity getting the better of him, he reached over to take the volume, but at the same instant Dixon's slipping back to his former seat caused him to hesitate. Yet he determined to find out. He demanded flippantly, pointing to the book,—"Reading the Bible, George?"

"No, sir."

"What then?"

"Oh, only a scientific work," said the other, carelessly, not wishing to broach the subject of racial differences that the title of the book suggested.

Dixon's evident desire to evade a direct answer sharpened his curiosity. He suggested off-handedly, but with ill-concealed eagerness: "Pretty deep stuff, eh? Who's the author?"

Dixon saw the persistent curiosity in his eye. Knowing too well the type of the man before him, he did not wish to give him the book, but unable to find further pretext for withholding it, he took it from the seat, turned it right side up, and handed it over. The senator took it with feigned indifference. Moistening his forefinger, he turned over the leaves, then settled down to read the marked passages. Now and then he would mutter: "Nonsense! Ridiculous!" Suddenly in a burst of impatience he turned to the frontispiece, and exclaimed in open disgust: "Just as I thought. Written by a Frenchman." Then, before he could recollect to whom he was talking—so full was he of what he regarded as the absurdity of Finot's view—he demanded—"Do you believe all this rot about the equality of the races?"

Dixon's policy was to avoid any topic that was likely to produce a difference of opinion with a passenger, provided it did not entail any sacrifice of his self-respect. He regarded his questioner as one to be humored, rather than vexed. He remembered a remark, made by this legislator that afternoon:

"The Jew, the Frenchman, the Dago and the Spaniards are all 'niggers' to a greater or less extent. The only white people are the Anglo-Saxon, Teutons and Scandinavians." This, Dixon surmised, accounted for the remark he had made about Finot's adopted nationality, and it amused him.

Dixon pondered the question. Then there occurred to him a way by which he could retain his own opinion and yet be in apparent accord with the passenger. He responded:

"No, sir, I do not believe in the equality of the races. As you say, it is impossible."

The senator looked up as if he had not been expecting a response; but, seemingly pleased with Dixon's acquiescence, he continued as he turned the leaves: "Writers of this type don't know what they are talking about. They write from mere theory. If they had to live among 'niggers,' they would sing an entirely different tune."

Dixon felt that he oughtn't to let this remark go unchallenged. He protested courteously: "Yet, sir, M. Finot had proved his argument admirably. I am sure if you were to read this book you would agree with him, too."

The senator looked up.

"Didn't you just say you didn't agree with this book?" he questioned sharply.

"I fear you misunderstood me, sir."

"Didn't you say you did not believe in the equality of the races?"

"Yes, sir."

"Then why?"

"Because as you said, sir, it is impossible."

"Why? Why?"

"Because there is but one race—the human race."

The senator did not respond. Though angry at the manner in which Dixon had received and responded to his question, he stopped to ponder the situation in which his unwitting question had placed him. As he had confessed, he did not like educated Negroes, and had no intention of engaging in a controversy with one. His respect and his aversion for this porter increased with a bound. Now he was weighing which was the better of the two possible courses—silence and response. If he said nothing, this Negro might think he had silenced him, while to respond would be to engage in an argument, thus treating the Negro as an equal. After weighing the matter for some time he decided that silence was the less compatible with his racial dignity, and with much condescension, his stiff voice and haughty manner a marked contrast to his jollity of a few minutes past, he demanded:

"You say there is only one race. What do you call yourself?"

"An American citizen," responded the other, composedly.

"Perhaps you have never heard of the word, 'nigger'?"

"Couldn't help it, sir," said Dixon, evenly.

"Then, do you believe the 'nigger' is the equal of the Anglo-Saxon race?" he demanded with ill-concealed anger.

"I have read many books on anthropology, sir, but I have not seen mention of either a 'nigger' race or an Anglo-Saxon one."

"Very well, do you believe your race—the black race—is equal to the Caucasian?"

Dixon stopped to weigh the wisdom of his answering. What good would it do to talk with a man seemingly so rooted in his prejudices? Then a simile came to him. On a visit to the Bureau of Standards at Washington, D. C., he had seen the effect of the pressure of a single finger upon a supported bar of steel three inches thick. The light strain had caused the steel to yield one-twenty-thousandth part of an inch, as the delicate apparatus, the interferometer, had registered. Since every action, he went on to reason, produces an effect, and truth, with the impulse of the Cosmos behind it, is irresistible, surely if he advanced his views in a kindly spirit, he must modify the error in this man. But still he hesitated. Suddenly he recalled that here was a legislator, one, who, above all others, ought to know the truth. This decided him. He would answer to the point, but would restrict any conversation that might ensue to the topic of the human race as a whole. Above all he would steer clear of the color question in the United States. He said with soft courtesy:

"I have found, sir, that any division of humanity according to physique, can have but a merely nominal value, as differences in physiques are caused by climatic conditions and are subject to a re-change by them. As you know, both Science and the Bible are agreed that all so-called races came from a single source. Pigmented humanity becomes lighter in the temperate zone, while unpigmented humanity becomes brown in the tropics. One summer's exposure at a bathing beach is enough to make a life-saver darker than many Indians. The true skin of all human beings is of the same color: all men are white under the first layer.

"Then it is possible by the blending of human varieties to produce innumerable other varieties, each one capable of reproducing and continuing itself.

"Again, anthropologists have never been able to classify human varieties. Huxley, as you know, named 2, Blumenbach 5, Burke 63, while others, desiring greater accuracy, have named hundreds. Since these classifications are so vague and changeable, it is evident, is it not, sir, that any division of humanity, whether by color of skin, hair or facial contour, to be other than purely nominal, must be one of mentality? And to classify humanity by intellect, would be, as you know, an impossible task. Nature, so far as we know, made only the individual. This idea has been ably expressed by Lamarck, who, in speaking of the human race says,—'Classifications are artificial, for nature has created neither classes, nor orders, nor families, nor kinds, nor permanent species, but only individuals.'"

The senator handed back the book to Dixon, huffily. "But, you have not answered my question," he insisted, "I asked, do you believe the black race will ever attain the intellectual standard of the Caucasian?"

"Intellect, whether of civilized or uncivilized humanity, as you know, sir, is elastic in quality. That is, primitive man when transplanted to civilization not only becomes civilized, but sometimes excels some of those whose ancestors have had centuries of culture, and the child of civilized men when isolated among primitives becomes one himself. We would find that the differences between a people who had acquired say three or four generations of beneficent culture, and another who had been long civilized would be about the same as that between the individuals in the long civilized group. That is, the usual human differences would exist. To be accurate we would have to appraise each individual separately. Any comparison between the groups would be inexact."

"But," reiterated the other, sarcastically, "you have not answered my question. Do you believe the black man will ever attain the high intellectual standard of the Caucasian? Yes or no."

"For the most authoritative answer," responded Dixon in the calm manner of the disciplined thinker, "we must look to modern science. If you don't mind, sir, I will give you some quotations from scientists of acknowledged authority, all of your own race."

Dixon drew out his notebook.

"Bah," said the other savagely, "opinions! Mere opinions! I asked you what you think and you are telling me what someone else says. What I want to know is, what do YOU think."

"Each of us," replied Dixon, evenly, "however learned, however independent, is compelled to seek the opinion of someone else on some particular subject at some time. There is the doctor and the other professionals, for instance. Now in seeking advice one usually places the most reliance on those one considers experts, is it not? This afternoon I overheard you quoting from one of Lincoln's debates with Douglas in order to prove your views."

Silence.

Dixon opened his notebook, found the desired passage, and said:

"In 1911 most of the leading sociologists and anthropologists of the world met in a Universal Races Congress in London. The opinion of that congress was that all the so-called races of men are essentially equal. Gustav Spiller, its organizer and secretary, voiced the findings of that entire body of experts when, after a careful weighing of the question of superiority and inferiority, he said (here Dixon read from the notebook):

" 'We are then under the necessity of concluding that an impartial investigator would be inclined to look upon the various important peoples of the world as, to all intents and purposes, essentially equal in intellect, enterprise, morality and physique.' "

Dixon found another passage and said: "Finot, whose findings ought to be regarded as more valuable than the expressions of those who base their arguments on sentiment or on Hebrew mythology, says,—'All peoples may attain this distant frontier which the brains of the whites have reached.' He also says:

"'The conclusion, therefore, forces itself upon us, that there are no inferior and superior races, but only races and peoples living outside or within the influence of culture.

"'The appearance of civilization and its evolution among certain white peoples and within a certain geographical latitude is only the effect of circumstances.'

"Zamenhof, the inventor of Esperanto, in his paper before the Universal Races Congress, says:

"'Give the Africans without any mingling of rancor or oppression, a high and humane civilization, and you will find their mental level will not differ from ours. Abolish the whole of our civilization and our minds will sink to the level of an African cannibal. It is not a difference of mentality in the race, but a difference of instruction.'"

Dixon closed his note-book and said, "The so-called savage varieties of mankind are the equal of the civilized varieties in this:—there is latent within them the same possibilities of development. Then the more developed peoples have the germ of decay more or less actively at work within them."

The senator had been awaiting his turn with impatience. Now drawing up his overcoat over his pajama-clad knees, and raising his voice in indignation, he flung at Dixon, apparently forgetting all previous qualms of lowered racial pride, "That's all nonsense. It is not true of the Negro, for while the white, red and yellow races have, or have had, civilizations of their own, the black has had none. All he has even accomplished has been when driven by the whites. Indigenous to a continent of the greatest natural resources, he has all these ages produced absolutely nothing. Geographical position has had absolutely nothing to do with it, or we would not have had Aztec civilization. Tell me, has the Negro race ever produced a Julius Caesar, a Shakespeare, a Montezuma, a Buddha, a Confucius? The Negro and all the Negroid races are inherently inferior. It is idiocy to say the Negro is the equal of the Caucasian. God Almighty made black to serve white. He placed an everlasting curse on all the sons of Ham and the black man shall forever serve the white." His face flushed with excitement.

Dixon was apparently unmoved. He responded with courtesy, his well-modulated voice and even tones in sharp contrast to the bluster and hysteria of the other. "The belief that the history of the Negro began with his slavery in the New World, while popular, is highly erroneous. The black man, like the Aztec, was civilized when the dominant branches of the Caucasian variety were savages. You will remember sir, that Herodotus, the Father of History, an eye-witness, distinctly mentions the black skins, and woolly hair of the Egyptians of his day. In Book II, Chapter 104, of his history he says:

"'I believe the Colchians are a colony of Egyptians, because like them they have black skin and woolly hair.'

"Aristotle in his 'Physiognomy,' Chapter VI, distinctly mentions the Ethiopians as having woolly hair and the Egyptians as being black-skinned. Count M. C. de Volney, author of 'The Ruins of Empire,' says:

"'The ancient Egyptians were real Negroes of the same species as the other present natives of Africa.'

"A glance at the Sphinx or at any of the ancient Egyptian statues in the British Museum will confirm these statements. When I saw the statue of Amenemphet III, I was immediately struck by the facial resemblance to Jack Johnson. I have seen Negroes here and in Africa, who bore a striking resemblance to Seti the Great. The latter was worshipped as the god, Amen, on whose name good white Christians still call. By the light of modern research it does appear as if white-skinned humanity got its civilization from the black-skinned variety, and even its origin. Volney says:

"'To the race of Negroes . . . the object of our extreme contempt . . . we owe our arts, sciences and even the very use of speech!'

"And with reference to the production of great men by the Negro . . ."

The senator had been fidgeting in his chair. He interrupted testily, "But what about the Negro's low, debased position in the scale of civilization? Look at the millions of Negroes in Africa little better than gorillas! They are still selling their own flesh and blood, eating human flesh and carrying on their horrible voodoo! All of the white race is civilized and all the other races, to some extent. Consider the traditions of the white man and all it means! Look at the vast incomprehensible achievements of the white man,—the railroads, the busy cities, the magnificent edifices, the wireless telegraph, the radio, the ships of the air,—yes, consider all the marvels of science! What has the white man not done? He has weighed the atom and the star with perfect accuracy. He has probed the uttermost recesses of infinity and fathomed the darkest mysteries of the ocean; he has challenged the lightning for speed and equalled it; he has competed with the eagle in the air, and outstripped him; he has rivalled the fish in his native element. In fact, there is not one single opposing force in Nature that he has not bent to his adamant will. He has excelled even the excellence of Nature. Consider, too, the philosophies, the religions, the ennobling works of art and of literature. Has the Negro anything to compare? Has he anything at all to boast of? Nothing! And yet in the face of all of these overwhelming facts, things patent to even the most ignorant, you tell me the Negro is the equal of the breed of supermen—wondermen—I represent? Really this childlike credulity of yours reaches the acme of absurdity. More than ever do I perceive a Negro is incapable of reasoning."

He caught for breath as he lolled back in the chair, and a smile of supreme satisfaction lit his features.

Dixon, who had been listening patiently, was seemingly unaffected. He responded composedly:—"The white man's civilization is only a continuation of that which was passed on to him by the Negro, who has simply retrogressed. 'Civilizations,' as Spiller has pointed out, 'are meteoric, bursting out of obscurity only to plunge back again.' Macedonia, for example! In our own day we have seen the decline of Aztec and Inca civilizations. Of the early history of man we know nothing definite. Prior even to paleolithic man there might have been civilizations excelling our own. In the heart of Africa, explorers may yet unearth marks of some extinct Negro civilization in a manner similar to the case of Assyria forgotten for two thousand years, and finally discovered by accident under forty feet of earth. For instance, the Chicago Evening Post of Oct. 11, 1916, speaking editorially of the discoveries made at Nepata by Dr. Reisner of Harvard, says—"To his amazement he found even greater treasures of the Ethiopian past. Fragment after fragment was unearthed until at least he had reconstructed effigies of no less than eleven monarchs of the forgotten Negro empire." Since then the tombs of fourteen other kings and fifty-five queens have been unearthed by the Reisner expedition. Among them is that of King Tirkaqua, mentioned in the book of Isaiah. An account of this appeared in the New York Times, November 27, 1921. Again, great Negro civilizations like that of Timbuctoo flourished even in the Middle Ages. Then there have been such purely Negro civilizations as that of Uganda and Songhay, which were of high rank. Boas says in his 'Mind of Primitive Man' (here Dixon took out his notebook): 'A survey of African tribes exhibits to our view cultural achievements of no mean order. All the different kinds of activities that we consider desirable in the citizens of our country may be found in aboriginal Africa.'"

The senator did not reply. His eyes, narrowed to slits, were peering at Dixon piercingly. The latter, returning his gaze, continued undaunted, "Spiller also says—'The status of a race at any particular moment of time offers no index to its capacities.' How true has this been of Britons, Picts and Scots, and Huns. Nineteen hundred years ago England was inhabited by savages, who stained themselves with woad, offered human sacrifices and even practiced cannibalism. Nor is culture a guarantee against decay or Greece would not have decayed. You may be sure the Roman had the same contempt for the savages of the North, who finally conquered him and almost obliterated his civilization, as have the self-styled superior peoples of today for the less developed ones. But these undeveloped peoples should not be despised. Nature, it certainly appears, does not intend to have the whole world civilized at the same time. Even as a thrifty housewife retains a balance in the bank to meet emergencies, so Nature retains these undeveloped varieties as a reserve fund to pay the toll which civilization always exacts. Finot says that many biologists regard the Caucasian as having arrived at the limit of his evolution, and that he can go no higher without danger to his overdeveloped brain. Underdeveloped peoples, like undeveloped resources, sir, are simply Nature's bank account."

The senator readjusted his slippers and went over to the water cooler for a drink. He did not like to argue in this vein. Dixon's quiet assurance and well-bred air, too, surprised him, and made him unconsciously admit to himself that here was a Negro different from his concept of that race, and not much different from himself after all. Yet his racial pride would not permit him to be outwitted by one he regarded as an inferior in spite of that 'inferior's' apparent intelligence. He would try the tactics best known to him,—the same that he had more than once used successfully with Negroes. He would outface his opponent, awe him, as it were, by his racial prestige. With this determination he returned to his seat and calmly seated himself. After a few leisurely puffs of a freshly-lighted cigarette he turned to Dixon, who had not moved, and in pretty much the same tone that a bullying lawyer would use to a timid witness, shaking an extended forefinger and glaring from under his knitted eyebrows, he demanded:—

"Do you mean to tell me that you really believe the Negro is the equal of the white man? That YOU think you are as good as a white man? Come on now, none of your theories."

Dixon appeared far from being intimidated. Indeed, he was secretly amused. Carefully repressing his mirth, he asked with sprightly ingenuousness:—

"In what particular, sir?"

The senator, it appears, had not foreseen an analysis of his question, for he stammered:

"Oh, you know very well what I mean. I mean—well—well—do you feel you are the equal of a white man?"

"Your question has answered itself, sir."

"In what way?"

"Well, sir, if I could tell how a white man feels, which I would have to do to make the comparison, then it would mean that I, a Negro, have the same feelings as a white man."

No response. Silence, except for the rumbling of the train. After a short pause, Dixon continued,—"Since, as your question implies, I must use the good in me as a standard by which to measure the good in a white man, I believe that any white man, who, like myself, is endeavoring to do the right thing, is as good a man as I. And more, sir," he added in a tone of gentle remonstrance, "your question has been most uncomplimentary to yourself, for, in asking me whether I consider myself as good as a white man, you are assuming that all white men, irrespective of reputation, are alike."

The senator appeared more confused than ever. His face flushed and his eyes moved shiftily. But he was determined not to be beaten. Rallying to the charge, he began in an irritable and domineering tone: "You said you were born in Alabama?"

"Yes, sir."

"Your father was a slave, wasn't he?"

"My grandmother, sir," corrected Dixon frankly.

"Well, what I want to get at is this:—do you, the descendant of a slave, consider yourself the social equal of a white man, who has always been free, and who owned your people as chattels?" And he finished austerely: "Come on now, no more beating around the bush."

Dixon decided to accept his meaning. In a tone that implied a perfect mutual understanding, he began:—"Of course, sir, this is a matter that deeply concerns our country and humanity, and so I feel that we two can speak on it calmly and without any ill feeling." Then in a polite and convincing tone, he explained,—"Reared, as I was, in a part of the South where a white skin is deified and a black one vilified, candidly, in my childhood, I did believe that there was something about the white man that made him superior to me. But, fortunately for me, I have travelled and read considerably. I once worked for one Mr. Simpson, a lecturer. While with him I visited the principal countries of the world. In one English town, where I lived six months, I didn't see a dark face. Living thus exclusively among whites, I observed that, except for differences due entirely to environment, my people were essentially the same as the whites. Indeed, what struck me most in my travels was the universality of human nature. European-reared Negroes possessed, so far as I could discern, the same temperament and manner, class for class, as the whites. Then my position on these cars has given me a rare opportunity for continued observations. I have met white persons in all kinds of relationships, and if there is any inherent difference between Negro and Caucasian, I have failed to find it after more than thirty years of rather careful observation. It is needless to say, sir, that my ideas of superiority based on lack of pigment or texture of hair evaporated long ago."

This reply nettled the senator still more. He demanded with increased irritation, "But what about slavery? The Negro has been a slave since the dawn of history. Consult any dictionary of synonyms, and you will see the term 'Negro' is synonymous with 'slave.' A black skin has ever been a livery of servitude. Isn't this world-old slavery a sign of the Negro's hopeless inferiority? My father had hundreds of slaves!"

Dixon noticed the senator's increased agitation and determined to be calmer than ever. He replied with a blandness that exasperated the other still more:—"Strange as it may sound, sir, the Caucasian has never been really free. The vast majority of its members are today, industrially, the serfs, and mentally, the slaves of the few. But, if we accept the term literally, all or nearly all branches of the white variety of mankind have been slaves that could be bought or sold. Britons were slaves to the Romans. Cicero, writing to his friend, Atticus, said,—"The stupidest and ugliest slaves come from Britain.' Later they were slaves of the Normans. Palgrave, an English historian, says of the Anglo-Saxon period:

> "'The Theowe (Anglo-Saxon slave) was entirely the property of his master, body as well as labor; like the Negro, he was part of the live stock, ranking in use and value with the beasts of the plough.'

"Villenage persisted in England until the sixteenth century. Certain classes of Anglo-Saxon slaves were not even permitted to buy their freedom, since it was contended that their all was the property of their masters. Serfdom was not abolished in Prussia until 1807, and in Austria until 1848. Even here in America white persons were slaves. There were Irish slaves in New England."

"Irish slaves in New England?" echoed the other in scornful surprise.

"Yes, sir, Irish men and women were slaves in New England, being sold like black slaves and treated not a whit better. Many of the most socially prominent in America have slave ancestors. Lincoln's ancestors were white slaves. According to Professor Cigrand, Grover Cleveland's great-grandfather, Richard Falley, was an Irish slave in Connecticut. There were also white slaves in Virginia. Black and white slaves used to work together in the fields in Barbadoes. Indeed, it would be quite possible to find white persons living in this country who were born in actual slavery, such having come from Russia, where slavery was abolished the same year our Emancipation Proclamation was signed . . . Ah, and that reminds me. The word, slave, has a white origin."

"A white origin!"

"Yes, sir, it comes from 'Slav,' a very white-skinned people who were reduced to slavery by the Germans. . . ."

PART II

WHITENESS AS PROPERTY: THE WORKINGS OF RACE

Sterling Brown tells the story of the two men standing on the corner. One was a white man, the other wasn't. The first said, "I've got nothing but trouble. My house just burned down and I had no insurance. My wife just ran away with my best friend in my automobile and there are still ten payments due on it. My doctor just told me that I have to go to the hospital and have a serious operation. I sure have tough luck." The second just looked at him and said, "What you kickin' 'bout? Yuh white, ain't yuh?"
—From Langston Hughes and
Arna Bontemps, eds.,
The Book of Negro Folklore

The white people owed the colored race a big debt, and if they paid it all back, they wouldn't have anything left for seed.
—Sojourner Truth,
as summarized by
George Brown Yerrinton

At the entrance to the dock the guard said, "Put out that cigarette, boy, What's the matter you colored boys can't never obey no rules?"

I tossed it over on the wooden craneway, still burning. He muttered something as he went over to step on it.

The white folks had sure brought their white to work with them that morning.

—CHESTER B. HIMES,
DIALOGUE FROM
IF HE HOLLERS LET HIM GO

"Don't never worry about work," says Jim Presley. "There's more work in the world than there is anything else. God made de world and de white folks made work."

—ZORA NEALE HURSTON

"I wake up and there's no smell of bacon frying . . . Why?" "Because that white motherfucker got it in his house!"

—AFRICAN-AMERICAN JOKE

White in America has always signified who is entitled to privilege. In this sense, the phrase "white privilege" is a redundancy [since] Whiteness has always signified worthiness, inclusion and acceptance.

—JOHN A. POWELL

It must be remembered that the white group of laborers, while they received a low wage, were compensated in part by a sort of public and psychological wage. They were given public deference and titles of courtesy because they were white.

—W.E.B. DU BOIS

they felt the long-standing priority of their superior status to blacks had been unjustly repealed. This year, we celebrate the thirty-fourth anniversary of the Court's rejection of the "separate but equal" doctrine of *Plessy v. Ferguson,* but in the late twentieth century, the passwords for gaining judicial recognition of the still viable property right in being white include "higher entrance scores," "seniority," and "neighborhood schools." There is as well, the use of impossible to hurdle intent barriers, to deny blacks remedies for racial injustices where the relief sought would either undermine white expectations and advantages gained during years of overt discrimination, or where such relief would expose the deeply imbedded racism in a major institution, such as the criminal justice system.

The continuing resistance to affirmative action plans, set-asides, and other meaningful relief for discrimination-caused harm, is based in substantial part on the perception that black gains threaten the main component of status for many whites: the sense that as whites, they are entitled to priority and preference over blacks. The law has mostly encouraged and upheld what Mr. Plessy argued in *Plessy v. Ferguson* was a property right in whiteness, and those at the top of the society have been benefitted because the masses of whites are too occupied in keeping blacks down to note the large gap between their shaky status and that of whites on top.

Blacks continue to serve the role of buffers between those most advantaged in the society, and those whites seemingly content to live the lives of the rich and famous through the pages of the tabloids and television dramas, like Dallas, Falcon Crest and Dynasty. Caught in the vortex of this national conspiracy that is perhaps more effective because it apparently functions without master plans or even conscious thought, the wonder is, not that so many blacks manifest self-destructive or non-functional behavior patterns, but that there are so many who continue to strive and sometimes succeed, despite all.

The cost to black people of racial discrimination is high, but beyond the bitterness that blacks understandably feel, there is the reality that most whites too, are, as Jesse Jackson puts it, victims of economic injustice. Indeed, allocating the costs is not a worthwhile use of energy when the need now is so clearly a cure.

There are today—even in the midst of outbreaks of anti-black hostility on our campuses and elsewhere—some indications that an increasing number of working class whites are learning what blacks have long known: that the rhetoric of freedom so freely voiced in this country is no substitute for the economic justice that has been so long denied.

True, it may be that the structure of capitalism, supported as was the Framers' intention by the constitution, will never give sufficiently to provide real economic justice for all. But in the beginning, that constitution deemed those who were black as the fit subject of property. The miracle of that document—too little noted during its bicentennial—is that those same blacks and their allies have in their quest for racial justice brought to the Constitution much of its current protection of individual rights.

The challenge is to move the document's protection into the sacrosanct area of economic right this time to insure that opportunity in this sphere is available to all. Progress in this critical area will require continued civil rights efforts, but may depend to a large extent on whites coming to recognize that their property right in being white has been purchased for too much and has netted them only the opportunity, as C. Vann Woodward put it, "to hoard sufficient racism in their bosoms to feel superior to blacks while working at a black's wages."

In this regard, I hope you realize that we are witnessing a historic event as Rev. Jesse Jackson attempts to convince whites of the truth that blacks have long known: that the rhetoric of liberty so freely offered is no substitute for the economic justice that has been so long denied.

True, it may be that the structure of capitalism, supported as was the Framers' intention by the Constitution, will never give sufficiently to provide real economic justice for all. There is more than ample reason to question with Tilden J. LeMelle:

Whether a society in which racism has been internalized and institutionalized to the point of being an essential and inherently functioning component of that society—a culture from whose inception racial discrimination has been a regulative force for maintaining stability and growth and for maximizing other cultural values—whether such a society *of itself* can even legislate (let alone enforce) public policy to combat racial discrimination is most doubtful.

"A racist culture," LeMelle fears, "can move to eradicate or make racism ineffective only when racism itself becomes a serious threat to the culture and its bearers." In this regard, the current presidential campaign is both a hope and a discouragement. It is a hope because a surprisingly substantial group of whites—including working class whites—have evidenced an ability to overcome the fatal attraction of the ethereal property right in whiteness, and are recognizing the need to rally with blacks—and a black candidate—for economic protection against exploiters who are mainly white.

The discouragement is that so many leaders of the party supposedly committed to social welfare and economic justice for the working classes are so willing to stop at all costs a candidate with the proven potential to unite blacks and whites across the race-as-property color-line. It is said that a black man—and particularly this black man—cannot be elected.

This prediction, voiced by experts, and trumpeted by the media, is accepted as gospel by the powers in the party whose strongly supported candidate in 1984 lost in 49 states. The Democratic party powers are so convinced that American intolerance will bar the election of a black that they are ready to embrace and deem electable America's first ethnic President whose wife is a Jew, and whose economic miracle in Massachusetts will prove—under close scrutiny—to be more the result of good fortune than good government.

I hope you do not miss the paradox of a people who have been the historic victims of American racism, and their candidates, who evidence more faith in the ability of white people to overcome their racism than do the leaders of the party that blacks have supported unstintingly for more than half a century. I do not hope to change the minds of those who oppose Jesse Jackson. He, like the other candidates, has weaknesses as well as strengths. I do urge that you place in context my message regarding the need, by whites as well as blacks, for decolonization of racial-mindsets.

The cost of racial discrimination is levied against us all. Blacks feel the burden and strive to remove it. Too many whites have felt that it was in their interest to resist those freedom efforts. Those pulls, despite the counter-indicators provided by history, logic and simple common sense, remain strong. But the efforts to achieve racial justice have already performed a miracle of transforming the Constitution— a document primarily intended to protect property rights—into a vehicle that provides a measure of protection for those whose rights are not bolstered by wealth, power, and property.

PART III

THE WHITE WORLD AND WHITER AMERICA

It would be interesting to make a comparison between so-called white civilization and the civilizations of darker races in the light of absolute fulfillment of human happiness.

—James Weldon Johnson

There will be white mythologies, invented Orients, invented Africas, invented Americas, with a correspondingly fabricated population, countries that never were, inhabited by people who never were—Calibans and Tontos, Man Fridays and Sambos—but who attain a virtual reality through their existence in traveler's tales, folk myth, popular and highbrow fiction, colonial reports, scholarly theory, Hollywood cinema, living in the white imagination and determinedly imposed on their alarmed real-life counterparts.

—Charles W. Mills

White men put on black masks and became another self, one which was loose of limbs, innocent of obligation to anything outside the self, indifferent to success . . . and thus a creature totally devoid of tension and deep anxiety. The verisimilitude of this *persona* to actual Negroes, who were around to be seen, was at best incidental. For the white man who put on the black mask modeled himself after a subjective black man—a black man of lust and passion and natural freedom (license) which white men carried within themselves and harbored with both fascination and dread.

—NATHAN HUGGINS,
ON NINETEENTH CENTURY
BLACKFACE MINSTRELSY

The discovery of personal whiteness among the world's peoples is a very modern thing. . . .

—W.E.B. DU BOIS

Us slaves watched white folks' parties where the guests danced a minuet and then paraded in a grand march, with the ladies and gentlemen going different ways and meeting again, arm in arm, and marching down the center together. Then we'd do it, too, but we used to mock 'em, every step. Sometimes the white folks noticed, but they seemed to like it; I guess they thought we couldn't dance any better.

—QUOTED IN MARSHALL
AND JEAN STEARNS'S
JAZZ DANCE

If the cakewalk is a Negro dance caricaturing certain white customs, what is that dance when, say, a white theatre company attempts to satirize it as a Negro dance?

—LeRoi Jones [Amiri Baraka]

When I went to New York, the white people were not the same white people. . . . They were too dark. I tried to make them become Black. They didn't like that at all. I would try to ask them: Who are you and where are you from? They say: Well, what do you mean? And I say: Well you don't look white. And they say: Well, we're white. But you don't look white-white. If you all had let me run it, we would all be colored.

—Bernice Johnson Reagon

They go back in history to erase us, imperialism must be Elvis Presley to our Big Mama Thornton's Dis'd and Covered (they call it *Discovered!*)

—Amiri Baraka

America for Americans! This is the white man's country! The Chinese must go, shrieks the exclusionist. Exclude the Italians! Colonize the blacks in Mexico or deport them to Africa. Lynch, suppress, drive out, kill out! America for Americans!

Who are Americans? comes rolling back from ten million throats. Who are to do the packing and delivering of goods? Who are the homefolks and who are the strangers? Who are the absolute and original tenants in fee-simple?

—Anna Julia Cooper

. . . Negroes in America have the same life as the Jew in Poland. Ridiculed, segregated. We were hung and burned for just being alive.

—WALTER MOSLEY, CHARACTER IN
A RED DEATH, DESCRIBING
A JEWISH RADICAL

But for the Old Settlers and those wishing to be mistaken for such, assimilation via careful Anglo-conformism was the narrow gate to the *real America* and to being *real* Americans.

—C. ERIC LINCOLN

What is the Black Man's Burden,
Ye hypocrites and vile,
Ye whited sepulchres
From th' Amazon to the Nile?
What is the Black Man's Burden,
Ye Gentile parasites,
Who crush and rob your brother
Of his manhood and his rights?

—T. THOMAS FORTUNE

FROM *PLAYING IN THE DARK*

Toni Morrison

Born in Ohio during the Great Depression, Nobel Laureate Toni Morrison (1931–) graduated from Howard University and then attended Cornell University, where she received her master's degree in English in 1955 (writing a thesis on William Faulkner and Virginia Woolf). Her earliest novel, The Bluest Eye *(1970), was the first of several luminous works of fiction, including* Song of Solomon *(1977) and* Beloved *(1987). In addition to her fiction, Morrison has received acclaim for her works of literary and cultural criticism.* Playing in the Dark *(1992), her collection of critical essays from which the selection below is excerpted, argues that an Africanist presence has been instrumental in the development of American literature.*

Eventually individualism fuses with the prototype of Americans as solitary, alienated, and malcontent. What, one wants to ask, are Americans alienated from? What are Americans always so insistently innocent of? Different from? As for absolute power, over whom is this power held, from whom withheld, to whom distributed?

Answers to these questions lie in the potent and ego-reinforcing presence of an Africanist population. This population is convenient in every way, not the least of which is self-definition. This new white male can now persuade himself that savagery is "out there." The lashes ordered (500 applied five times is 2500) are not one's own savagery; repeated and dangerous breaks for freedom are "puzzling" confirmations of black irrationality; the combination of Dean Swift's beatitudes and a life of regularized violence is civilized; and if the sensibilities are dulled enough, the rawness remains external.

These contradictions slash their way through the pages of American literature. How could it be otherwise? As Dominick LaCapra reminds us, "Classic novels are not only worked over . . . by common contextual forces (such as ideologies) but also rework and at least partially work through those forces in critical and at times potentially transformative fashion."

As for the culture, the imaginative and historical terrain upon which early American writers journeyed is in large measure shaped by the presence of the racial other. Statements to the contrary, insisting on the meaninglessness of race to the American identity, are themselves full of meaning. The world does not become raceless or will not become unracialized by assertion. The act of enforcing racelessness in literary discourse is itself a racial act. Pouring rhetorical acid on the fingers of a black hand may indeed destroy the prints, but not the hand. Besides, what happens in that violent, self-serving act of erasure to the hands, the fingers, the fingerprints of the one who does the pouring? Do they remain acid-free? The literature itself suggests otherwise.

Explicit or implicit, the Africanist presence informs in compelling and inescapable ways the texture of American literature. It is a dark and abiding presence, there for the literary imagination as both a visible and an invisible mediating force. Even, and especially, when American texts are not "about" Africanist presences or characters or narrative or idiom, the shadow hovers in implication, in sign, in line of demarcation. It is no accident and no mistake that immigrant populations (and much immigrant literature) understood their "Americanness" as an opposition to the resident black population. Race, in fact, now functions as a metaphor so necessary to the construction of Americanness that it rivals the old pseudo-scientific and class-informed racisms whose dynamics we are more used to deciphering.

As a metaphor for transacting the whole process of Americanization, while burying its particular racial ingredients, this Africanist presence may be something the United States cannot do without. Deep within the word "American" is its association with race. To identify someone as a South African is to say very little; we need the adjective "white" or "black" or "colored" to make our meaning clear. In this country it is quite the reverse. American means white, and Africanist people struggle to make the term applicable to themselves with ethnicity and hyphen after hyphen after hyphen. Americans did not have a profligate, predatory nobility from which to wrest an identity of national virtue while continuing to covet aristocratic license and luxury. The American nation negotiated both its disdain and its envy in the same way Dunbar did: through a self-reflexive contemplation of fabricated, mythological Africanism. For the settlers and for American writers generally, this Africanist other became the means of thinking about body, mind, chaos, kindness, and love; provided the occasion for exercises in the absence of restraint, the presence of restraint, the contemplation of freedom and of aggression; permitted opportunities for the exploration of ethics and morality, for meeting the obligations of the social contract, for bearing the cross of religion and following out the ramifications of power.

Reading and charting the emergence of an Africanist persona in the development of a national literature is both a fascinating project and an urgent one, if the history and criticism of our literature is to become accurate. Emerson's plea for intellectual independence was like the offer of an empty plate that writers could fill with nourishment from an indigenous menu. The language no doubt had to be English, but the content of that language, its subject, was to be deliberately, insistently un-English and anti-European, insofar as it rhetorically repudiated an adoration of the Old World and defined the past as corrupt and indefensible. In the scholarship on the formation of an American character and the production of a national literature, a number of items have been catalogued. A major item to be added to the list must be an Africanist presence—decidedly not American, decidedly other.

The need to establish difference stemmed not only from the Old World but from a difference in the New. What was distinctive in the New was, first of all, its claim to freedom and, second, the presence of the unfree within the heart of the democratic experiment—the critical absence of democracy, its echo, shadow, and silent force in the political and intellectual activity of some not-Americans. The distinguishing features of the not-Americans were their slave status, their social status—and their color.

It is conceivable that the first would have self-destructed in a variety of ways had it not been for the last. These slaves, unlike many others in the world's history, were visible to a fault. And they had inherited, among other things, a long history on the meaning of color. It was not simply that this slave population had a distinctive color; it was that this color "meant" something. That meaning had been named and deployed by scholars from at least the moment, in the eighteenth century, when other and sometimes the same scholars started to investigate both the natural history and the inalienable rights of man—that is to say, human freedom.

One supposes that if Africans all had three eyes or one ear, the significance of that difference from the smaller but conquering European invaders would also have been found to have meaning. In any case, the subjective nature of ascribing value and meaning to color cannot be questioned this late in the twentieth century. The point for this discussion is the alliance between visually rendered ideas and linguistic utterances. And this leads into the social and political nature of received knowledge as it is revealed in American literature.

Knowledge, however mundane and utilitarian, plays about in linguistic images and forms cultural practice. Responding to culture—clarifying, explicating, valorizing, translating, transforming, criticizing—is what artists everywhere do, especially writers involved in the founding of a new nation. Whatever their personal and formally political responses to the inherent contradiction of a free republic deeply committed to slavery, nineteenth-century writers were mindful of the presence of black people. More important, they addressed, in more or less passionate ways, their views on that difficult presence.

The alertness to a slave population did not confine itself to the personal encounters that writers may have had. Slave narratives were a nineteenth-century publication boom. The press, the political campaigns, and the policy of various parties and elected officials were rife with the discourse of slavery and freedom. It would have been an *isolato* indeed who was unaware of the most explosive issue in the nation. How could one speak of profit, economy, labor, progress, suffragism, Christianity, the frontier, the formation of new states, the acquisition of new lands, education, transportation (freight and passengers), neighborhoods, the military—of almost anything a country concerns itself with—without having as a referent, at the heart of the discourse, at the heart of definition, the presence of Africans and their descendants?

It was not possible. And it did not happen. What did happen frequently was an effort to talk about these matters with a vocabulary designed to disguise the subject. It did not always succeed, and in the work of many writers disguise was never intended. But the consequence was a master narrative that spoke *for* Africans and their descendants, or *of* them. The legislator's narrative could not coexist with a response from the Africanist persona. Whatever popularity the slave narratives had—and they influenced abolitionists and converted antiabolitionists—the slave's own narrative, while freeing the narrator in many ways, did not destroy the master narrative. The master narrative could make any number of adjustments to keep itself intact.

Silence from and about the subject was the order of the day. Some of the silences were broken, and some were maintained by authors who lived with and within the policing narrative. What I am interested in are the strategies for maintaining the silence and the strategies for breaking it. How did the founding writers of young America engage, imagine, employ, and create an Africanist presence and persona? In what ways do these strategies explicate a vital part of American literature?

WHAT AMERICA WOULD BE LIKE WITHOUT BLACKS

Ralph Ellison

Although his literary reputation has rested principally on his towering Invisible Man *(1952) and riveting short stories, Ralph Ellison (1914–1994) was also among the top literary and social critics in the late twentieth century United States. Able to show why cultural debates matter in everyday life, and vice-versa, Ellison wrote criticism for a broad audience. An Oklahoman who credited that state's frontier spirit for much of his creativity, Ellison left Tuskegee University and Alabama-style segregation for New York City, after his junior year. He reflected on the work of Twain, Faulkner, and Hemingway in passionate essays published alongside discussions of jazz musicians and bluesmen. "What America Would Be Like Without Blacks," first published in* Time *in 1970, typifies Ellison's insistence that American culture is not white.*

The fantasy of an America free of blacks is at least as old as the dream of creating a truly democratic society. While we are aware that there is something inescapably tragic about the cost of achieving our democratic ideals, we keep such tragic awareness segregated to the rear of our minds. We allow it to come to the fore only during moments of great national crisis.

On the other hand, there is something so embarrassingly absurd about the notion of purging the nation of blacks that it seems hardly a product of thought at all. It is more like a primitive reflex, a throwback to the dim past of tribal experience, which we rationalize and try to make respectable by dressing it up in the gaudy and highly questionable trappings of what we call the "concept of race." Yet, despite its absurdity, the fantasy of a blackless America continues to turn up. It is a fantasy born not merely of racism but of petulance, of exasperation, of moral fatigue. It is like a boil bursting forth from impurities in the bloodstream of democracy.

In its benign manifestations, it can be outrageously comic—as in the picaresque adventures of Percival Brownlee who appears in

William Faulkner's story "The Bear." Exasperating to his white masters because his aspirations and talents are for preaching and conducting choirs rather than for farming, Brownlee is "freed" after much resistance and ends up as the prosperous proprietor of a New Orleans brothel. In Faulkner's hands, the uncomprehending drive of Brownlee's owners to "get shut" of him is comically instructive. Indeed, the story resonates certain abiding, tragic themes of American history with which it is interwoven, and which are causing great turbulence in the social atmosphere today. I refer to the exasperation and bemusement of the white American with the black, the black American's ceaseless (and swiftly accelerating) struggle to escape the misconceptions of whites, and the continual confusing of the black American's racial background with his individual culture. Most of all, I refer to the recurring fantasy of solving one basic problem of American democracy by "getting shut" of the blacks through various wishful schemes that would banish them from the nation's bloodstream, from its social structure, and from its conscience and historical consciousness.

This fantastic vision of a lily-white America appeared as early as 1713, with the suggestion of a white "native American," thought to be from New Jersey, that all the Negroes be given their freedom and returned to Africa. In 1777, Thomas Jefferson, while serving in the Virginia legislature, began drafting a plan for the gradual emancipation and exportation of the slaves. Nor were Negroes themselves immune to the fantasy. In 1815, Paul Cuffe, a wealthy merchant, shipbuilder, and landowner from the New Bedford area, shipped and settled at his own expense thirty-eight of his fellow Negroes in Africa. It was perhaps his example that led in the following year to the creation of the American Colonization Society, which was to establish in 1821 the colony of Liberia. Great amounts of cash and a perplexing mixture of motives went into the venture. The slave owners and many Border-state politicians wanted to use it as a scheme to rid the country not of slaves but of the militant free Negroes who were agitating against the "peculiar institution." The abolitionists, until they took a lead from free Negro leaders and began attacking the scheme, also participated as a means of righting a great historical injustice. Many blacks went along with it simply because they were sick of the black and white American mess and hoped to prosper in the quiet peace of the old ancestral home.

Such conflicting motives doomed the Colonization Society to failure, but what amazes one even more than the notion that anyone could have believed in its success is the fact that it was attempted during a period when the blacks, slave and free, made up eighteen percent of the total population. When we consider how long blacks had been in the New World and had been transforming it and being Americanized by it, the scheme appears not only fantastic, but the product of a free-floating irrationality. Indeed, a national pathology.

Nevertheless, some of the noblest of Americans were bemused. Not only Jefferson but later Abraham Lincoln was to give the scheme credence. According to historian John Hope Franklin, Negro colonization seemed as important to Lincoln as emancipation. In 1862, Franklin notes, Lincoln called a group of prominent free Negroes to the White House and urged them to support colonization, telling them, "Your race suffers greatly, many of them by living among us, while ours suffers from your presence. If this is admitted, it affords a reason why we should be separated."

In spite of his unquestioned greatness, Abraham Lincoln was a man of his times and limited by some of the less worthy thinking of his times. This is demonstrated both by his reliance upon the concept of race in his analysis of the American dilemma and by his involvement in a plan of purging the nation of blacks as a means of healing the badly shattered ideals of democratic federalism. Although benign, his motive was no less a product of fantasy. It envisaged an attempt to relieve an inevitable suffering that marked the growing pains of the youthful body politic by an operation which would have amounted to the severing of a healthy and indispensable member.

Yet, like its twin, the illusion of secession, the fantasy of a benign amputation that would rid the country of black men to the benefit of a nation's health not only persists; today, in the form of neo-Garveyism, it fascinates black men no less than it once hypnotized whites. Both fantasies become operative whenever the nation grows weary of the struggle toward the ideal of American democratic equality. Both would use the black man as a scapegoat to achieve a national catharsis, and both would, by way of curing the patient, destroy him.

What is ultimately intriguing about the fantasy of "getting shut" of the Negro American is the fact that no one who entertains it seems ever to have considered what the nation would have become had Africans *not* been brought to the New World, and had their descendants not played such a complex and confounding role in the creation of American history and culture. Nor do they appear to have considered with any seriousness the effect upon the nation of having any of the schemes for exporting blacks succeed beyond settling some fifteen thousand or so in Liberia.

We are reminded that Daniel Patrick Moynihan, who has recently aggravated our social confusion over the racial issue while allegedly attempting to clarify it, is co-author of a work which insists that the American melting pot didn't melt because our white ethnic groups have resisted all assimilative forces that appear to threaten their identities. The problem here is that few Americans know who and what they really are. That is why few of these groups—or at least few of the children of these groups—have been able to resist the movies, television, baseball, jazz, football, drum-majoretting, rock, comic strips, radio commercials, soap operas, book clubs, slang, or any of a thousand other expressions and carriers of our pluralistic and easily available popular culture. And it is here precisely that ethnic resistance is least effective. On this level the melting pot did indeed melt, creating such deceptive metamorphoses and blending of identities, values, and life-styles that most American whites are culturally part Negro American without even realizing it.

If we can resist for a moment the temptation to view everything having to do with Negro Americans in terms of their racially imposed status, we become aware of the fact that for all the harsh reality of the social and economic injustices visited upon them, these injustices have failed to keep Negroes clear of the cultural mainstream; Negro Americans are in fact one of its major tributaries. If we can cease approaching American social reality in terms of such false concepts as white and nonwhite, black culture and white culture, and think of these apparently unthinkable matters in the realistic manner of Western pioneers confronting the unknown prairie, perhaps we can begin to imagine what the United States would have been, or not been, had there been no blacks to give it—if I may be so bold as to say—color.

For one thing, the American nation is in a sense the product of the American language, a colloquial speech that began emerging long before the British colonials and Africans were transformed into Americans. It is a language that evolved from the king's English but, basing itself upon the realities of the American land and colonial institutions—or lack of institutions, began quite early as a vernacular revolt against the signs, symbols, manners, and authority of the mother country. It is a language that began by merging the sounds of many tongues, brought together in the struggle of diverse regions. And whether it is admitted or not, much of the sound of that language is derived from the timbre of the African voice and the listening habits of the African ear. So there is a *de'z* and *do'z* of slave speech sounding beneath our most polished Harvard accents, and if there is such a thing as a Yale accent, there is a Negro wail in it—doubtlessly introduced there by Old Yalie John C. Calhoun, who probably got it from his mammy.

Whitman viewed the spoken idiom of Negro Americans as a source for a native grand opera. Its flexibility, its musicality, its rhythms, freewheeling diction, and metaphors, as projected in Negro American folklore, were absorbed by the creators of our great nineteenth-century literature even when the majority of blacks were still enslaved. Mark Twain celebrated it in the prose of *Huckleberry Finn;* without the presence of blacks, the book could not have been written. No Huck and Jim, no American novel as we know it. For not only is the black man a co-creator of the language that Mark Twain raised to the level of literary eloquence, but Jim's condition as American and Huck's commitment to freedom are at the moral center of the novel.

In other words, had there been no blacks, certain creative tensions arising from the cross-purposes of whites and blacks would also not have existed. Not only would there have been no Faulkner; there would have been no Stephen Crane, who found certain basic themes of his writing in the Civil War. Thus, also, there would have been no Hemingway, who took Crane as a source and guide. Without the presence of Negro American style, our jokes, our tall tales, even our sports would be lacking in the sudden turns, the shocks, the swift changes of pace (all jazz-shaped) that serve to remind us that the world is ever unexplored, and that while a complete mastery of life is mere illusion, the real secret of the game is to make life swing. It is its ability to articulate this tragic-comic attitude toward life that explains much of the mysterious power and attractiveness of that quality of Negro American style known as "soul." An expression of American diversity within unity, of blackness with whiteness, soul announces the presence of a creative struggle against the realities of existence.

Without the presence of blacks, our political history would have been otherwise. No slave economy, no Civil War; no violent destruction of the Reconstruction; no K.K.K. and no Jim Crow system. And without the disenfranchisement of black Americans and the manipulation of racial fears and prejudices, the disproportionate impact of white Southern politicians upon our domestic and foreign policies would have been impossible. Indeed, it is almost impossible to conceive of what our political system would have become without the snarl of forces—cultural, racial, religious—that make our nation what it is today.

Absent, too, would be the need for that tragic knowledge which we try ceaselessly to evade: that the true subject of democracy is not simply material well-being but the extension of the democratic process in the direction of perfecting itself. And that the most obvious test and clue to that perfection is the inclusion—*not* assimilation—of the black man.

Since the beginning of the nation, white Americans have suffered from a deep inner uncertainty as to who they really are. One of the ways that has been used to simplify the answer has been to seize upon the presence of black Americans and use them as a marker, a symbol of limits, a metaphor for the "outsider." Many whites could look at the social position of blacks and feel that color formed an easy and reliable gauge for determining to what extent one was or was not American. Perhaps that is why one of the first epithets that many European immigrants learned when they got off the boat was the term "nigger"—it made them feel instantly American. But this is tricky magic. Despite his racial difference and social status, something indisputably American about Negroes not only raised doubts about the white man's value system but aroused the troubling suspicion that whatever else the true American is, he is also somehow black.

Materially, psychologically, and culturally, part of the nation's heritage is Negro American, and whatever it becomes will be shaped in part by the Negro's presence. Which is fortunate, for today it is the black American who puts pressure upon the nation to live up to its ideals. It is he who gives creative tension to our struggle for justice and for the elimination of those factors, social and psychological, which make for slums and shaky suburban communities. It is he who insists that we purify the American language by demanding that there be a closer correlation between the meaning of words and reality, between ideal and conduct, our assertions and our actions. Without the black American, something irrepressibly hopeful and creative would go out of the American spirit, and the nation might well succumb to the moral slobbism that has ever threatened its existence from within.

When we look objectively at how the dry bones of the nation were hung together, it seems obvious that some one of the many groups that compose the United States had to suffer the fate of being allowed no easy escape from experiencing the harsh realities of the human condition as they were to exist under even so fortunate a democracy as ours. It would seem that some one group had to be stripped of the possibility of escaping such tragic knowledge by taking sanctuary in moral equivocation, racial chauvinism, or the advantage of superior social status. There is no point in complaining over the past or apologizing for one's fate. But for blacks, there are no hiding places down here, not in suburbia or in penthouse, neither in country nor in city. They are an American people who are geared to what *is* and who yet are driven by a sense of what it is possible for human life to be in this society. The nation could not survive being deprived of their presence because, by the irony implicit in the dynamics of American democracy, they symbolize both its most stringent testing and the possibility of its greatest human freedom.

THE POOR WHITE MUSICIAN
James Weldon Johnson

James Weldon Johnson (1871–1938) produced, in his classic The Autobiography of an Ex-Colored Man *(1912, published anonymously),
one of the most rich and extended inquiries into race and American identity. A Floridian educated at Atlanta University, Johnson achieved distinction in a remarkable variety of endeavors. A diplomat and the first
African-American head of the National Association for the Advancement
of Colored People, he also composed hit Broadway shows and wrote the
"Negro national anthem," "Lift Ev'ry Voice and Sing." Johnson's varied
poetry often drew on folk roots and on history, nowhere more eloquently
than in* God's Trombones *(1927). "The Poor White Musician (1915),"
a part of Johnson's significant journalistic writing, brings together his concerns with power, nation, and race.*

Perhaps nothing should astonish us during these days of war, when
the world seems to be up side down; but the following letter written
to *The Globe* is in a tone so unusual and unexpected that we reproduce
it in full:

> Editor of the *Globe,* Sir—Why does society prefer the Negro
> musician? is a question which is not infrequently discussed by
> white musicians; yes, I dare say, by artists. The Negro musician
> is to-day engaged at most of the functions given by society,
> especially its dances. Why this preference should be given to
> the Negro "so-called" musician, who hasn't the slightest con-
> ception of music, rather than to the Caucasian musician, who
> has spent well nigh a fortune—aside from numerous years of
> painstaking study—is incomprehensible.
>
> Surely it isn't because of the oft-refuted contention that rag-
> time music demands the Negro musician, for the white musi-
> cian has proven time and again that he can render a ragtime
> selection better than the Negro. Why should a famous dancing
> couple prefer a Negro orchestra for their dancing exhibitions?
> Even the New York hotels are now beginning to discard the

white musician for the Negro. It will not be long before the poor white musician will be obliged to blacken his face to make a livelihood or starve.

EUGENE DE BUERIS
New York, September 8.

Was a more pitiful wail ever uttered? And is it not difficult to grasp that fact that it is a white man and not a Negro uttering the wail?

The writer is evidently a New York musician, and he cannot understand why the Negro musicians of this city are making competition so strong for their white professional brothers. Some persons not acquainted with the facts might jump to the conclusion that the colored men worked cheaper than the whites, but it is certain that Mr. De Bueris would have been glad to make that charge in his letter, if such were the case.

On this point let us relate an amusing incident which happened a few days ago. A society lady called up on the telephone a man who makes a business of supplying musicians, and asked the price for a band of ten men. The man she called up is a colored man and supplies colored musicians, but as his office is on Broadway, such a thought seems not to have been anywhere near the lady's mind. He told her what ten men would cost for an evening. She was amazed and said to him, "Why I can get colored musicians for that price!"

The fact is, colored musicians charge more than white musicians; so we can see that after all there is some excuse for the bewilderment of Mr. De Bueris. Let us see if we can't enlighten him a bit.

When he refers to the colored players as "so-called musicians" he may think he is slurring them, but, instead, he is slurring the white society people, and hotel and cafe proprietors who prefer Negro musicians. But Mr. De Bueris is all wrong in belittling the musical ability of these men. They may not have spent "as many fortunes or as many years of painstaking study" as the white musicians, but what has that to do with natural musical ability? Nothing. It only goes to show that white men need to spend fortunes and years of study in order to play music as well, or almost as well, as Negroes do naturally. Let Mr. De Bueris think of what would happen to the white musicians if the colored men spent fortunes and years in study, and let him be thankful.

There are good and sufficient reasons why Negro musicians are preferred at social affairs. Modern music and modern dancing are both Negro creations.

Since ragtime has swept the world and become universally known as American music, there have been attempts to rob the Negro of the credit of originating it; but this is in accord with an old habit of the white race; as soon as anything is recognized as great, they set about to claim credit for it. In this manner they have attempted to rob the Negro of the credit of originating the plantation stories and songs. We all remember how after the Russo-Japanese war attempts were made to classify the Japanese as white. In the same way, scholars have "doubted" that the Zulus are real Negroes. Had Jack Johnson continued as champion, somebody would have tried to prove that he was not a real Negro. By this method, the white race has gathered to itself credit for originating nearly all the great and good things in the world. It has taken credit for what has been accomplished by the ancient Egyptians, the East Indians and the Arabs, by the simple process of declaring those black people to be white.

The truth is, the pure white race has not originated a single one of the great, fundamental intellectual achievements which have raised man in the scale of civilization.

The alphabet, the art of letters, of poetry, of music, of sculpture, of painting, of the drama, of architecture; numbers, the science of mathematics, of astronomy, of philosophy, of logic, of physics, of chemistry; the use of metals and the principles of mechanics were all invented or discovered by darker and, what are, in many cases, considered inferior races. The pure white race did not originate even the religion it uses.

But all of this is another story; let us get back to the "poor white musician."

Not only is modern American music a Negro creation but the modern dances are also. The dance steps which society debutantes are now learning and those which are the latest thing on the stage have been known among Negroes for years. Then it is only natural that when it comes for modern dancing, the Negro musician should be the real thing.

In a way, Mr. De Bueris is right when he says that white musicians can play ragtime as well as Negro musicians; that is, white musicians can play exactly what is put down on the paper. But Negro musicians are able to put into the music something that can't be put on the paper; a certain abandon which seems to enter in the blood of the dancers, and that is the answer to Mr. De Bueris' question, that is the secret, that is why Negro musicians are preferred.

And let us add a word to the Negro musician upon efficiency in his work. He cannot afford to run along merely upon his great natural gift.

This letter written to *The Globe* shows that the white musicians feel his competition, and that means that they will stop at nothing to put him out of business. Let the Negro musician improve and develop himself. He may not be able to spend a fortune, but he can, by some slight sacrifices, put in his spare time on painstaking study. It is only in this way that he can continue to hold his own.

VANILLA NIGHTMARES

Adrian Piper

Artist Adrian Piper (1948–) also teaches philosophy at Wellesley College. Political and moral issues animate both her art and her philosophy. Piper's work insistently questions the assumption of race. Her own appearance as a light-skinned woman of African-American heritage is the subject of such works as "Paleface: Political Self Portrait #2," and her video "Cornered." Her "My Calling (Card) #1" (1986) is a text to be given to those making racist remarks in her presence, believing her to be white. It concludes, "I regret any discomfort my presence is causing you, just as I am sure you regret the discomfort your racism is causing me." In her Vanilla Nightmares *series, begun in 1986, Piper draws in charcoal over* New York Times *articles on race relations and advertisements for lavish consumption. The Black presences she imposes set the images of white American normalcy and comfort in startling contexts.*

Vanilla Nightmares #3 (1986), charcoal on newspaper, 14" x 22"

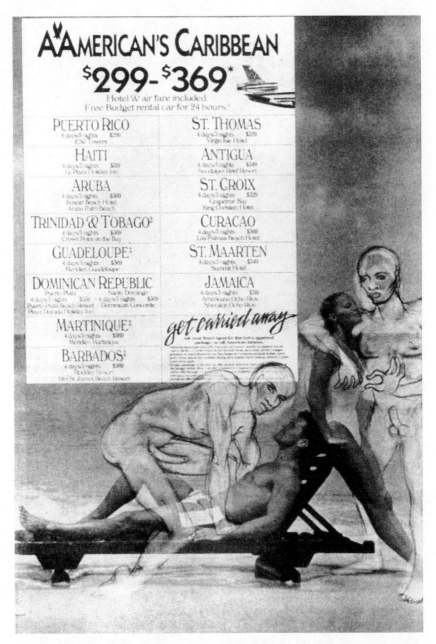

Vanilla Nightmares #6 (1986), charcoal and crayon on newspaper, 14" x 22"

Vanilla Nightmares #18 (1986), charcoal on newspaper, 14" x 22"

Vanilla Nightmares #19 (1988), charcoal on newspaper, 22" x 28"

ON BEING "WHITE" . . . AND OTHER LIES

James Baldwin

*James Baldwin (1924–1987) was the greatest expert on white conscious-
ness in the twentieth century United States. Born in what he described
as the "southern community" of Harlem, Baldwin published six novels,
including his brilliant treatment of fathers, sons, and religion in* Go Tell
It on the Mountain *(1953), and* Giovanni's Room *(1956), a work
concentrating on white, gay characters. Baldwin's early essays, collected
in* Notes of a Native Son *(1955),* Nobody Knows My Name
(1961), and The Fire Next Time *(1963), are works of remarkable
range, lucidity, and compassion. But his scandalously underappreciated
essays, generously sampled in* The Price of the Ticket *(1985), push
Baldwin's arguments regarding race and the meaning of America, racism,
homophobia, and the "male prison," and whiteness and the immigrant
experience to unprecedented levels of insight. "On Being 'White' . . .
and Other Lies," published originally in the popular African-American
magazine* Essence *in 1984, is a dramatic reminder that "becoming
American" meant learning to be white in a new way for European immigrants.*

The crisis of leadership in the white community is remarkable—and
terrifying—because there is, in fact, no white community.

This may seem an enormous statement—and it is. I'm willing to
be challenged. I'm also willing to attempt to spell it out.

My frame of reference is, of course, America, or that portion of
the North American continent that calls itself America. And this
means I am speaking, essentially, of the European vision of the
world—or more precisely, perhaps, the European vision of the universe. It is a vision as remarkable for what it pretends to include as for
what it remorselessly diminishes, demolishes or leaves totally out of
account.

There is, for example—at least, in principle—an Irish community:
here, there, anywhere, or, more precisely, Belfast, Dublin and Boston.

There is a German community: both sides of Berlin, Bavaria and Yorkville. There is an Italian community: Rome, Naples, the Bank of the Holy Ghost and Mulberry Street. And there is a Jewish community, stretching from Jerusalem to California to New York. There are English communities. There are French communities. There are Swiss consortiums. There are Poles: in Warsaw (where they would like us to be friends) and in Chicago (where because they are white we are enemies). There are, for that matter, Indian restaurants and Turkish baths. There is the underworld—the poor (to say nothing of those who intend to become rich) are always with us—but this does not describe a community. It bears terrifying witness to what happened to everyone who got here, and paid the price of the ticket. The price was to become "white." No one was white before he/she came to America. It took generations, and a vast amount of coercion, before this became a white country.

It is probable that it is the Jewish community—or more accurately, perhaps, its remnants—that in America has paid the highest and most extraordinary price for becoming white. For the Jews came here from countries where they were not white, and they came here, in part, *because* they were not white; and incontestably—in the eyes of the Black American (and not only in those eyes) American Jews have opted to become white, and this is how they operate. It was ironical to hear, for example, former Israeli prime minister Menachem Begin declare some time ago that "the Jewish people bow only to God" while knowing that the state of Israel is sustained by a blank check from Washington. Without further pursuing the implication of this mutual act of faith, one is nevertheless aware that the Black presence, here, can scarcely hope—at least, not yet—to halt the slaughter in South Africa.

And there is a reason for that.

America became white—the people who, as they claim, "settled" the country became white—because of the necessity of denying the Black presence, and justifying the Black subjugation. No community can be based on such a principle—or, in other words, no community can be established on so genocidal a lie. White men—from Norway, for example, where they were *Norwegians*—became white: by slaughtering the cattle, poisoning the wells, torching the houses, massacring Native Americans, raping Black women.

This moral erosion has made it quite impossible for those who think of themselves as white in this country to have any moral authority at all—privately, or publicly. The multitudinous bulk of them sit, stunned, before their TV sets, swallowing garbage that they know to be garbage, and—in a profound and unconscious effort to justify this torpor that disguises a profound and bitter panic—pay a vast amount of attention to athletics: even though they know that the football player (the Son of the Republic, *their* sons!) is merely another aspect of the money-making scheme. They are either relieved or embittered by the presence of the Black boy on the team. I do not know if they remember how long and hard they fought to keep him off it. I know that they do not dare have any notion of the price Black people (mothers and fathers) paid and pay. They do not want to know the meaning, or face the shame, of what they compelled—out of what they took as the necessity of being white—Joe Louis or Jackie Robinson or Cassius Clay (aka Muhammad Ali) to pay. I know that they, themselves, would not have liked to pay it.

There has never been a labor movement in this country, the proof being the absence of a Black presence in the so-called father-to-son unions. There are, perhaps, some niggers in the window; but Blacks have no power in the labor unions.

Just so does the white community, as a means of keeping itself white, elect, as they imagine, their political (!) representatives. No nation in the world, including England, is represented by so stunning a pantheon of the relentlessly mediocre. I will not name names—I will leave that to you.

But this cowardice, this necessity of justifying a totally false identity and of justifying what must be called a genocidal history, has placed everyone now living into the hands of the most ignorant and powerful people the world has ever seen: And how did they get that way?

By deciding that they were white. By opting for safety instead of life. By persuading themselves that a Black child's life meant nothing compared with a white child's life. By abandoning their children to the things white men could buy. By informing their children that Black women, Black men and Black children had no human integrity that those who call themselves white were bound to respect. And in this debasement and definition of Black people, they debased and defamed themselves.

And have brought humanity to the edge of oblivion: because they think they are white. Because they think they are white, they do not dare confront the ravage and the lie of their history. Because they think they are white, they cannot allow themselves to be tormented by the suspicion that all men are brothers. Because they think they are white, they are looking for, or bombing into existence, stable populations, cheerful natives and cheap labor. Because they think they are white, they believe, as even no child believes, in the dream of safety. Because they think they are white, however vociferous they may be and however multitudinous, they are as speechless as Lot's wife—looking backward, changed into a pillar of salt.

However—! White being, absolutely, a moral choice (for there *are* no white people), the crisis of leadership for those of us whose identity has been forged, or branded, as Black is nothing new. We—who were not Black before we got here either, who were defined as Black by the slave trade—have paid for the crisis of leadership in the white community for a very long time, and have resoundingly, even when we face the worst about ourselves, survived, and triumphed over it. If we had not survived and triumphed, there would not be a Black American alive.

And the fact that we are still here—even in suffering, darkness, danger, endlessly defined by those who do not dare define, or even confront, themselves—is the key to the crisis in white leadership. The past informs us of various kinds of people—criminals, adventurers and saints, to say nothing, of course, of popes—but it is the Black condition, and only that, which informs us concerning white people. It is a terrible paradox, but those who believed that they could control and define Black people divested themselves of the power to control and define themselves.

THE WHITE WITCH
James Weldon Johnson

Included in the James Weldon Johnson (see p. 168) collection Saint Peter
Relates an Incident *(1935), "The White Witch" illustrates the ways
in which the finest African-American evocations of whiteness cut across
the lines staked out by the division of this collection into parts. On one
level Johnson's poem clearly is concerned with the image of white womanhood as a lure and a threat to Black men. But critics have also persuasively
read "The White Witch" as personifying and warning against the power
and appeal of European and U.S. imperialism.*

O brothers mine, take care! Take care!
The great white witch rides out tonight,
Trust not your prowess nor your strength;
Your only safety lies in flight;
For in her glance there is a snare,
And in her smile there is a blight.

The great white witch you have not seen?
Then, younger brothers mine, forsooth,
Like nursery children you have looked
For ancient hag and snaggle-tooth;
But no, not so; the witch appears
In all the glowing charms of youth.

Her lips are like carnations red,
Her face like new-born lilies fair,
Her eyes like ocean waters blue,
She moves with subtle grace and air,
And all about her head there floats
The golden glory of her hair.

But though she always thus appears
In form of youth and mood of mirth,

Unnumbered centuries are hers,
The infant planets saw her birth;
The child of throbbing Life is she,
Twin sister to the greedy earth.

And back behind those smiling lips,
And down within those laughing eyes,
And underneath the soft caress
Of hand and voice and purring sighs,
The shadow of the panther lurks,
The spirit of the vampire lies.

For I have seen the great white witch,
And she has led me to her lair,
And I have kissed her red, red lips
And cruel face so white and fair;
Around me she has twined her arms,
And bound me with her yellow hair.

I felt those red lips burn and sear
My body like a living coal;
Obeyed the power of those eyes
As the needle trembles to the pole;
And did not care although I felt
The strength go ebbing from my soul.

Oh! she has seen your strong young limbs,
And heard your laughter loud and gay,
And in your voices she has caught
The echo of a far-off day,
When man was closer to the earth;
And she has marked you for her prey.

She feels the old Antæan strength
In you, the great dynamic beat
Of primal passions, and she sees

In you the last besieged retreat
Of love relentless, lusty, fierce,
Love pain-ecstatic, cruel-sweet.

O, brothers mine, take care! Take care!
The great white witch rides out tonight.
O, younger brothers mine, beware!
Look not upon her beauty bright;
For in her glance there is a snare,
And in her smile there is a blight.

THE SOULS OF WHITE FOLK
W.E.B. Du Bois

In the wake of the carnage of World War One, a conflict which he had portrayed as originating in European desires for empire, W.E.B. Du Bois (see p. 29) attempted to place the souls of white people in a context far broader than that of the national history of the United States. In this chapter from his Darkwater *(1920), Du Bois situates a distinctive "American" whiteness within a context of European expansion, past and present.*

High in the tower, where I sit above the loud complaining of the human sea, I know many souls that toss and whirl and pass, but none there are that intrigue me more than the Souls of White Folk.

Of them I am singularly clairvoyant. I see in and through them. I view them from unusual points of vantage. Not as a foreigner do I come, for I am native, not foreign, bone of their thought and flesh of their language. Mine is not the knowledge of the traveler or the colonial composite of dear memories, words and wonder. Nor yet is my knowledge that which servants have of masters, or mass of class, or capitalist of artisan. Rather I see these souls undressed and from the back and side. I see the working of their entrails. I know their thoughts and they know that I know. This knowledge makes them now embarrassed, now furious. They deny my right to live and be and call me misbirth! My word is to them mere bitterness and my soul, pessimism. And yet as they preach and strut and shout and threaten, crouching as they clutch at rags of facts and fancies to hide their nakedness, they go twisting, flying by my tired eyes and I see them ever stripped,—ugly, human.

The discovery of personal whiteness among the world's peoples is a very modern thing,—a nineteenth and twentieth century matter, indeed. The ancient world would have laughed at such a distinction. The Middle Age regarded skin color with mild curiosity; and even up into the eighteenth century we were hammering our national manikins into one, great, Universal Man, with fine frenzy which ignored color and race even more than birth. Today we have changed all that, and the world in a sudden, emotional conversion has discovered that it is white and by that token, wonderful!

This assumption that of all the hues of God whiteness alone is inherently and obviously better than brownness or tan leads to curious acts; even the sweeter souls of the dominant world as they discourse with me on weather, weal, and woe are continually playing above their actual words an obligato of tune and tone, saying:

"My poor, un-white thing! Weep not nor rage. I know, too well, that the curse of God lies heavy on you. Why? That is not for me to say, but be brave! Do your work in your lowly sphere, praying the good Lord that into heaven above, where all is love, you may, one day, be born—white!"

I do not laugh. I am quite straight-faced as I ask soberly:

"But what on earth is whiteness that one should so desire it?" Then always, somehow, some way, silently but clearly, I am given to understand that whiteness is the ownership of the earth forever and ever, Amen!

Now what is the effect on a man or a nation when it comes passionately to believe such an extraordinary dictum as this? That nations are coming to believe it is manifest daily. Wave on wave, each with increasing virulence, is dashing this new religion of whiteness on the shores of our time. Its first effects are funny: the strut of the Southerner, the arrogance of the Englishman amuck, the whoop of the hoodlum who vicariously leads your mob. Next it appears dampening generous enthusiasm in what we once counted glorious; to free the slave is discovered to be tolerable only in so far as it freed his master! Do we sense somnolent writhings in black Africa or angry groans in India or triumphant banzais in Japan? "To your tents, O Israel!" These nations are not white!

After the more comic manifestations and the chilling of generous enthusiasm come subtler, darker deeds. Everything considered, the title to the universe claimed by White Folk is faulty. It ought, at least, to look plausible. How easy, then, by emphasis and omission to make children believe that every great soul the world ever saw was a white man's soul; that every great thought the world ever knew was a white man's thought; that every great deed the world ever did was a white man's deed; that every great dream the world ever sang was a white man's dream. In fine, that if from the world were dropped everything that could not fairly be attributed to White Folk, the world would, if anything, be even greater, truer, better than now. And if all this be a lie, is it not a lie in a great cause?

Here it is that the comedy verges to tragedy. The first minor note is struck, all unconsciously, by those worthy souls in whom consciousness of high descent brings burning desire to spread the gift abroad,—the obligation of nobility to the ignoble. Such sense of duty assumes two things: a real possession of the heritage and its frank appreciation by the humble-born. So long, then, as humble black folk, voluble with thanks, receive barrels of old clothes from lordly and generous whites, there is much mental peace and moral satisfaction. But when the black man begins to dispute the white man's title to certain alleged bequests of the Fathers in wage and position, authority and training; and when his attitude toward charity is sullen anger rather than humble jollity; when he insists on his human right to swagger and swear and waste,—then the spell is suddenly broken and the philanthropist is ready to believe that Negroes are impudent, that the South is right, and that Japan wants to fight America.

After this the descent to Hell is easy. On the pale, white faces which the great billows whirl upward to my tower I see again and again, often and still more often, a writing of human hatred, a deep and passionate hatred, vast by the very vagueness of its expressions. Down through the green waters, on the bottom of the world, where men move to and fro, I have seen a man—an educated gentleman— grow livid with anger because a little, silent, black woman was sitting by herself in a Pullman car. He was a white man. I have seen a great, grown man curse a little child, who had wandered into the wrong waiting-room, searching for its mother: "Here, you damned black——" He was white. In Central Park I have seen the upper lip of a quiet, peaceful man curl back in a tigerish snarl of rage because black folk rode by in a motor car. He was a white man. We have seen, you and I, city after city drunk and furious with ungovernable lust of blood; mad with murder, destroying, killing, and cursing; torturing human victims because somebody accused of crime happened to be of the same color as the mob's innocent victims and because that color was not white! We have seen,—Merciful God! in these wild days and in the name of Civilization, Justice, and Motherhood,—what have we not seen, right here in America, of orgy, cruelty, barbarism, and murder done to men and women of Negro descent.

Up through the foam of green and weltering waters wells this great mass of hatred, in wilder, fiercer violence, until I look down and know that today to the millions of my people no misfortune could happen,—of death and pestilence, failure and defeat—that would not make the hearts of millions of their fellows beat with fierce, vindictive joy! Do you doubt it? Ask your own soul what it would say if the next census were to report that half of black America was dead and the other half dying.

Unfortunate? Unfortunate. But where is the misfortune? Mine? Am I, in my blackness, the sole sufferer? I suffer. And yet, somehow, above the suffering, above the shackled anger that beats the bars, above the hurt that crazes there surges in me a vast pity,—pity for a people imprisoned and enthralled, hampered and made miserable for such a cause, for such a phantasy!

Conceive this nation, of all human peoples, engaged in a crusade to make the "World Safe for Democracy"! Can you imagine the United States protesting against Turkish atrocities in Armenia, while the Turks are silent about mobs in Chicago and St. Louis; what is Louvain compared with Memphis, Waco, Washington, Dyersburg, and Estill Springs? In short, what is the black man but America's Belgium, and how could America condemn in Germany that which she commits, just as brutally, within her own borders?

A true and worthy ideal frees and uplifts a people; a false ideal imprisons and lowers. Say to men, earnestly and repeatedly: "Honesty is best, knowledge is power; do unto others as you would be done by." Say this and act it and the nation must move toward it, if not to it. But say to a people: "The one virtue is to be white," and the people rush to the inevitable conclusion, "Kill the 'nigger'!"

Is not this the record of present America? Is not this its headlong progress? Are we not coming more and more, day by day, to making the statement "I am white," the one fundamental tenet of our practical morality? Only when this basic, iron rule is involved is our defense of right nation-wide and prompt. Murder may swagger, theft may rule and prostitution may flourish and the nation gives but spasmodic, intermittent and lukewarm attention. But let the murderer be black or the thief brown or the violator of womanhood have a drop of Negro blood, and the righteousness of the indignation sweeps the world. Nor would this fact make the indignation less justifiable did not we all know that it was blackness that was condemned and not crime.

In the awful cataclysm of World War, where from beating, slandering, and murdering us the white world turned temporarily aside to kill each other, we of the Darker Peoples looked on in mild amaze.

Among some of us, I doubt not, this sudden descent of Europe into hell brought unbounded surprise; to others, over wide area, it brought the *Schaden Freude* of the bitterly hurt; but most of us, I judge, looked on silently and sorrowfully, in sober thought, seeing sadly the prophecy of our own souls.

Here is a civilization that has boasted much. Neither Roman nor Arab, Greek nor Egyptian, Persian nor Mongol ever took himself and his own perfectness with such disconcerting seriousness as the modern white man. We whose shame, humiliation, and deep insult his aggrandizement so often involved were never deceived. We looked at him clearly, with world-old eyes, and saw simply a human thing, weak and pitiable and cruel, even as we are and were.

These super-men and world-mastering demi-gods listened, however, to no low tongues of ours, even when we pointed silently to their feet of clay. Perhaps we, as folk of simpler soul and more primitive type, have been most struck in the welter of recent years by the utter failure of white religion. We have curled our lips in something like contempt as we have witnessed glib apology and weary explanation. Nothing of the sort deceived us. A nation's religion is its life, and as such white Christianity is a miserable failure.

Nor would we be unfair to this criticism: We know that we, too, have failed, as you have, and have rejected many a Buddha, even as you have denied Christ; but we acknowledge our human frailty, while you, claiming super-humanity, scoff endlessly at our shortcomings.

The number of white individuals who are practising with even reasonable approximation the democracy and unselfishness of Jesus Christ is so small and unimportant as to be fit subject for jest in Sunday supplements and in *Punch, Life, Le Rire,* and *Fliegende Blätter.* In her foreign mission work the extraordinary self-deception of white religion is epitomized: solemnly the white world sends five million dollars worth of missionary propaganda to Africa each year and in the same twelve months adds twenty-five million dollars worth of the vilest gin manufactured. Peace to the augurs of Rome!

We may, however, grant without argument that religious ideals have always far outrun their very human devotees. Let us, then, turn to more mundane matters of honor and fairness. The world today is trade. The world has turned shopkeeper; history is economic history; living is earning a living. Is it necessary to ask how much of high emprise and honorable conduct has been found here? Something, to be sure. The establishment of world credit systems is built on splendid and realizable faith in fellow-men. But it is, after all, so low and elementary a step that sometimes it looks merely like honor among thieves, for the revelations of highway robbery and low cheating in the business world and in all its great modern centers have raised in the hearts of all true men in our day an exceeding great cry for revolution in our basic methods and conceptions of industry and commerce.

We do not, for a moment, forget the robbery of other times and races when trade was a most uncertain gamble; but was there not a certain honesty and frankness in the evil that argued a saner morality? There are more merchants today, surer deliveries, and wider well-being, but are there not, also, bigger thieves, deeper injustice, and more calloused selfishness in well-being? Be that as it may,—certainly the nicer sense of honor that has risen ever and again in groups of forward-thinking men has been curiously and broadly blunted. Consider our chiefest industry,—fighting. Laboriously the Middle Ages built its rules of fairness—equal armament, equal notice, equal conditions. What do we see today? Machine-guns against assegais; conquest sugared with religion; mutilation and rape masquerading as culture,—all this, with vast applause at the superiority of white over black soldiers!

War is horrible! This the dark world knows to its awful cost. But has it just become horrible, in these last days, when under essentially equal conditions, equal armament, and equal waste of wealth white men are fighting white men, with surgeons and nurses hovering near?

Think of the wars through which we have lived in the last decade: in German Africa, in British Nigeria, in French and Spanish Morocco, in China, in Persia, in the Balkans, in Tripoli, in Mexico, and in a dozen lesser places—were not these horrible, too? Mind you, there were for most of these wars no Red Cross funds.

Behold little Belgium and her pitiable plight, but has the world forgotten Congo? What Belgium now suffers is not half, not even a tenth, of what she has done to black Congo since Stanley's great dream of 1880. Down the dark forests of inmost Africa sailed this modern Sir Galahad, in the name of "the noble-minded men of several nations," to introduce commerce and civilization. What came of it? "Rubber and murder, slavery in its worst form," wrote Glave in 1895.

Harris declares that King Leopold's régime meant the death of twelve million natives, "but what we who were behind the scenes felt most keenly was the fact that the real catastrophe in the Congo was desolation and murder in the larger sense. The invasion of family life, the ruthless destruction of every social barrier, the shattering of every tribal law, the introduction of criminal practices which struck the chiefs of the people dumb with horror—in a word, a veritable avalanche of filth and immorality overwhelmed the Congo tribes."

Yet the fields of Belgium laughed, the cities were gay, art and science flourished; the groans that helped to nourish this civilization fell on deaf ears because the world round about was doing the same sort of thing elsewhere on its own account.

As we saw the dead dimly through rifts of battle-smoke and heard faintly the cursings and accusations of blood brothers, we darker men said: This is not Europe gone mad; this is not aberration nor insanity; this *is* Europe; this seeming Terrible is the real soul of white culture—back of all culture,—stripped and visible today. This is where the world has arrived,—these dark and awful depths and not the shining and ineffable heights of which it boasted. Here is whither the might and energy of modern humanity has really gone.

But may not the world cry back at us and ask: "What better thing have you to show? What have you done or would do better than this if you had today the world rule? Paint with all riot of hateful colors the thin skin of European culture,—is it not better than any culture that arose in Africa or Asia?"

It is. Of this there is no doubt and never has been; but why is it better? Is it better because Europeans are better, nobler, greater, and more gifted than other folk? It is not. Europe has never produced and never will in our day bring forth a single human soul who cannot be matched and over-matched in every line of human endeavor by Asia and Africa. Run the gamut, if you will, and let us have the Europeans who in sober truth over-match Nefertari, Mohammed, Rameses and Askia, Confucius, Buddha, and Jesus Christ. If we could scan the calendar of thousands of lesser men, in like comparison, the result would be the same; but we cannot do this because of the deliberately educated ignorance of white schools by which they remember Napoleon and forget Sonni Ali.

The greatness of Europe has lain in the width of the stage on which she has played her part, the strength of the foundations on which she has builded, and a natural, human ability no whit greater (if as great) than that of other days and races. In other words, the deeper reasons for the triumph of European civilization lie quite outside and beyond Europe,—back in the universal struggles of all mankind.

Why, then, is Europe great? Because of the foundations which the mighty past have furnished her to build upon: the iron trade of ancient, black Africa, the religion and empire-building of yellow Asia, the art and science of the "dago" Mediterranean shore, east, south, and west, as well as north. And where she has builded securely upon this great past and learned from it she has gone forward to greater and more splendid human triumph; but where she has ignored this past and forgotten and sneered at it, she has shown the cloven hoof of poor, crucified humanity,—she has played, like other empires gone, the world fool!

If, then, European triumphs in culture have been greater, so, too, may her failures have been greater. How great a failure and a failure in what does the World War betoken? Was it national jealousy of the sort of the seventeenth century? But Europe has done more to break down national barriers than any preceding culture. Was it fear of the balance of power in Europe? Hardly, save in the half-Asiatic problems of the Balkans. What, then, does Hauptmann mean when he says: "Our jealous enemies forged an iron ring about our breasts and we knew our breasts had to expand,—that we had to split asunder this ring or else we had to cease breathing. But Germany will not cease to breathe and so it came to pass that the iron ring was forced apart."

Whither is this expansion? What is that breath of life, thought to be so indispensable to a great European nation? Manifestly it is expansion overseas; it is colonial aggrandizement which explains, and alone adequately explains, the World War. How many of us today fully realize the current theory of colonial expansion, of the relation of Europe which is white, to the world which is black and brown and yellow? Bluntly put, that theory is this: It is the duty of white Europe to divide up the darker world and administer it for Europe's good.

This Europe has largely done. The European world is using black and brown men for all the uses which men know. Slowly but surely white culture is evolving the theory that "darkies" are born beasts of burden for white folk. It were silly to think otherwise, cries the cultured world, with stronger and shriller accord. The supporting arguments grow and twist themselves in the mouths of merchant, scientist, soldier, traveler, writer, and missionary: Darker peoples are dark in mind as well as in body; of dark, uncertain, and imperfect descent; of frailer, cheaper stuff; they are cowards in the face of mausers and maxims; they have no feelings, aspirations, and loves; they are fools, illogical idiots,—"half-devil and half-child."

Such as they are civilization must, naturally, raise them, but soberly and in limited ways. They are not simply dark white men. They are not "men" in the sense that Europeans are men. To the very limited extent of their shallow capacities lift them to be useful to whites, to raise cotton, gather rubber, fetch ivory, dig diamonds,—and let them be paid what men think they are worth—white men who know them to be well-nigh worthless.

Such degrading of men by men is as old as mankind and the invention of no one race or people. Ever have men striven to conceive of their victims as different from the victors, endlessly different, in soul and blood, strength and cunning, race and lineage. It has been left, however, to Europe and to modern days to discover the eternal world-wide mark of meanness,—color!

Such is the silent revolution that has gripped modern European culture in the later nineteenth and twentieth centuries. Its zenith came in Boxer times: White supremacy was all but world-wide, Africa was dead, India conquered, Japan isolated, and China prostrate, while white America whetted her sword for mongrel Mexico and mulatto South America, lynching her own Negroes the while. Temporary halt in this program was made by little Japan and the white world immediately sensed the peril of such "yellow" presumption! What sort of a world would this be if yellow men must be treated "white"? Immediately the eventual overthrow of Japan became a subject of deep thought and intrigue, from St. Petersburg to San Francisco, from the Key of Heaven to the Little Brother of the Poor.

The using of men for the benefit of masters is no new invention of modern Europe. It is quite as old as the world. But Europe proposed to apply it on a scale and with an elaborateness of detail of which no former world ever dreamed. The imperial width of the thing,—the heaven-defying audacity—makes its modern newness.

The scheme of Europe was no sudden invention, but a way out of long-pressing difficulties. It is plain to modern white civilization that the subjection of the white working classes cannot much longer be maintained. Education, political power, and increased knowledge of the technique and meaning of the industrial process are destined to make a more and more equitable distribution of wealth in the near future. The day of the very rich is drawing to a close, so far as individual white nations are concerned. But there is a loophole. There is a chance for exploitation on an immense scale for inordinate profit, not simply to the very rich, but to the middle class and to the laborers.

This chance lies in the exploitation of darker peoples. It is here that the golden hand beckons. Here are no labor unions or votes or questioning onlookers or inconvenient consciences. These men may be used down to the very bone, and shot and maimed in "punitive" expeditions when they revolt. In these dark lands "industrial development" may repeat in exaggerated form every horror of the industrial history of Europe, from slavery and rape to disease and maiming, with only one test of success,—dividends!

This theory of human culture and its aims has worked itself through warp and woof of our daily thought with a thoroughness that few realize. Everything great, good, efficient, fair, and honorable is "white"; everything mean, bad, blundering, cheating, and dishonorable is "yellow"; a bad taste is "brown"; and the devil is "black." The changes of this theme are continually rung in picture and story, in newspaper heading and moving-picture, in sermon and school book, until, of course, the King can do no wrong,—a White Man is always right and a Black Man has no rights which a white man is bound to respect.

There must come the necessary despisings and hatreds of these savage half-men, this unclean *canaille* of the world—these dogs of men. All through the world this gospel is preaching. It has its literature, it has its priests, it has its secret propaganda and above all—it pays!

There's the rub,—it pays. Rubber, ivory, and palm-oil; tea, coffee, and cocoa; bananas, oranges, and other fruit; cotton, gold, and copper—they, and a hundred other things which dark and sweating bodies hand up to the white world from their pits of slime, pay and pay well, but of all that the world gets the black world gets only the pittance that the white world throws it disdainfully.

Small wonder, then, that in the practical world of things-that-be there is jealousy and strife for the possession of the labor of dark millions, for the right to bleed and exploit the colonies of the world where this golden stream may be had, not always for the asking, but surely for the whipping and shooting. It was this competition for the labor of yellow, brown, and black folks that was the cause of the World War. Other causes have been glibly given and other contributing causes there doubtless were, but they were subsidiary and subordinate to this vast quest of the dark world's wealth and toil.

Colonies, we call them, these places where "niggers" are cheap and the earth is rich; they are those outlands where like a swarm of hungry locusts white masters may settle to be served as kings, wield the lash of slave-drivers, rape girls and wives, grow as rich as Croesus and send homeward a golden stream. They belt the earth, these places, but they cluster in the tropics, with its darkened peoples: in Hong Kong and Anam, in Borneo and Rhodesia, in Sierra Leone and Nigeria, in Panama and Havana—these are the El Dorados toward which the world powers stretch itching palms.

Germany, at last one and united and secure on land, looked across the seas and seeing England with sources of wealth insuring a luxury and power which Germany could not hope to rival by the slower processes of exploiting her own peasants and working-men, especially with these workers half in revolt, immediately built her navy and entered into a desperate competition for possession of colonies of darker peoples. To South America, to China, to Africa, to Asia Minor, she turned like a hound quivering on the leash, impatient, suspicious, irritable, with blood-shot eyes and dripping fangs, ready for the awful word. England and France crouched watchfully over their bones, growling and wary, but gnawing industriously, while the blood of the dark world whetted their greedy appetites. In the background, shut out from the highway to the seven seas, sat Russia and Austria, snarling and snapping at each other and at the last Mediterranean gate to the El Dorado, where the Sick Man enjoyed bad health, and where millions of serfs in the Balkans, Russia, and Asia offered a feast to greed well-nigh as great as Africa.

The fateful day came. It had to come. The cause of war is preparation for war; and of all that Europe has done in a century there is nothing that has equaled in energy, thought, and time her preparation for wholesale murder. The only adequate cause of this preparation was conquest and conquest, not in Europe, but primarily among the darker peoples of Asia and Africa; conquest, not for assimilation and uplift, but for commerce and degradation. For this, and this mainly, did Europe gird herself at frightful cost for war.

The red day dawned when the tinder was lighted in the Balkans and Austro-Hungary seized a bit which brought her a step nearer to the world's highway; she seized one bit and poised herself for another. Then came that curious chorus of challenges, those leaping suspicions, raking all causes for distrust and rivalry and hatred, but saying little of the real and greatest cause.

Each nation felt its deep interests involved. But how? Not, surely, in the death of Ferdinand the Warlike; not, surely, in the old, half-forgotten *revanche* for Alsace-Lorraine; not even in the neutrality of Belgium. No! But in the possession of land overseas, in the right to colonies, the chance to levy endless tribute on the darker world,—on coolies in China, on starving peasants in India, on black savages in Africa, on dying South Sea Islanders, on Indians of the Amazon—all this and nothing more.

Even the broken reed on which we had rested high hopes of eternal peace,—the guild of the laborers—the front of that very important movement for human justice on which we had builded most, even this flew like a straw before the breath of king and kaiser. Indeed, the flying had been foreshadowed when in Germany and America "international" Socialists had all but read yellow and black men out of the kingdom of industrial justice. Subtly had they been bribed, but effectively: Were they not lordly whites and should they not share in the spoils of rape? High wages in the United States and England might be the skilfully manipulated result of slavery in Africa and of peonage in Asia.

With the dog-in-the-manger theory of trade, with the determination to reap inordinate profits and to exploit the weakest to the utmost there came a new imperialism,—the rage for one's own nation to own the earth or, at least, a large enough portion of it to insure as big profits as the next nation. Where sections could not be owned by one dominant nation there came a policy of "open door," but the "door" was open to "white people only." As to the darkest and weakest of peoples there was but one unanimity in Europe,—that which Herr Dernberg of the German Colonial Office called the agreement with England to maintain white "prestige" in Africa,—the doctrine of the divine right of white people to steal.

Thus the world market most wildly and desperately sought today is the market where labor is cheapest and most helpless and profit is most abundant. This labor is kept cheap and helpless because the white world despises "darkies." If one has the temerity to suggest that these workingmen may walk the way of white workingmen and climb by votes and self-assertion and education to the rank of men, he is howled out of court. They cannot do it and if they could, they shall not, for they are the enemies of the white race and the whites shall rule forever and forever and everywhere. Thus the hatred and despising of human beings from whom Europe wishes to extort her luxuries has led to such jealousy and bickering between European nations that they have fallen afoul of each other and have fought like crazed beasts. Such is the fruit of human hatred.

But what of the darker world that watches? Most men belong to this world. With Negro and Negroid, East Indian, Chinese, and Japanese they form two-thirds of the population of the world. A belief in humanity is a belief in colored men. If the uplift of mankind must be done by men, then the destinies of this world will rest ultimately in the hands of darker nations.

What, then, is this dark world thinking? It is thinking that as wild and awful as this shameful war was, *it is nothing to compare with that fight for freedom which black and brown and yellow men must and will make unless their oppression and humiliation and insult at the hands of the White World cease. The Dark World is going to submit to its present treatment just as long as it must and not one moment longer.*

Let me say this again and emphasize it and leave no room for mistaken meaning: The World War was primarily the jealous and avaricious struggle for the largest share in exploiting darker races. As such it is and must be but the prelude to the armed and indignant protest of these despised and raped peoples. Today Japan is hammering on the door of justice, China is raising her half-manacled hands to knock next, India is writhing for the freedom to knock, Egypt is sullenly muttering, the Negroes of South and West Africa, of the West Indies, and of the United States are just awakening to their shameful slavery. Is, then, this war the end of wars? Can it be the end, so long as sits enthroned, even in the souls of those who cry peace, the despising and robbing of darker peoples? If Europe hugs this delusion, then this is not the end of world war,—it is but the beginning!

We see Europe's greatest sin precisely where we found Africa's and Asia's,—in human hatred, the despising of men; with this difference, however: Europe has the awful lesson of the past before her, has the splendid results of widened areas of tolerance, sympathy, and love among men, and she faces a greater, an infinitely greater, world of men than any preceding civilization ever faced.

It is curious to see America, the United States, looking on herself, first, as a sort of natural peace-maker, then as a moral protagonist in this terrible time. No nation is less fitted for this rôle. For two or more centuries America has marched proudly in the van of human hatred,—making bonfires of human flesh and laughing at them hideously, and making the insulting of millions more than a matter of dislike,—rather a great religion, a world war-cry: Up white, down black; to your tents, O white folk, and world war with black and parti-colored mongrel beasts!

Instead of standing as a great example of the success of democracy and the possibility of human brotherhood America has taken her place as an awful example of its pitfalls and failures, so far as black and brown and yellow peoples are concerned. And this, too, in spite of the fact that there has been no actual failure; the Indian is not dying out, the Japanese and Chinese have not menaced the land, and the experiment of Negro suffrage has resulted in the uplift of twelve million people at a rate probably unparalleled in history. But what of this? America, Land of Democracy, wanted to believe in the failure of democracy so far as darker peoples were concerned. Absolutely without excuse she established a caste system, rushed into preparation for war, and conquered tropical colonies. She stands today shoulder to shoulder with Europe in Europe's worst sin against civilization. She aspires to sit among the great nations who arbitrate the fate of "lesser breeds without the law" and she is at times heartily ashamed even of the large number of "new" white people whom her democracy has admitted to place and power. Against this surging forward of Irish and German, of Russian Jew, Slav and "dago" her social bars have not availed, but against Negroes she can and does take her unflinching and immovable stand, backed by this new public policy of Europe. She trains her immigrants to this despising of "niggers" from the day of their landing, and they carry and send the news back to the submerged classes in the fatherlands.

All this I see and hear up in my tower, above the thunder of the seven seas. From my narrowed windows I stare into the night that looms beneath the cloud-swept stars. Eastward and westward storms are breaking,—great, ugly whirlwinds of hatred and blood and cruelty. I will not believe them inevitable. I will not believe that all that was must be, that all the shameful drama of the past must be done again today before the sunlight sweeps the silver seas.

If I cry amid this roar of elemental forces, must my cry be in vain, because it is but a cry,—a small and human cry amid Promethean gloom?

Back beyond the world and swept by these wild, white faces of the awful dead, why will this Soul of White Folk,—this modern Prometheus,—hang bound by his own binding, tethered by a fable of the past? I hear his mighty cry reverberating through the world, "I am white!" Well and good, O Prometheus, divine thief! Is not the world wide enough for two colors, for many little shinings of the sun? Why, then, devour your own vitals if I answer even as proudly, "I am black!"

PART IV
SOME WHITE FOLKS

The ways of white folks, I mean some white folks. . . .

—LANGSTON HUGHES

Some white folks have gone crazy from being white (Not all, but some).

—LANGSTON HUGHES

All white folk are not scoundrels or murderers. They are, as I am, painfully human.

—W.E.B. DU BOIS

In its quest for nonconformity, hip/beat maleness took seminal cues from urban Black masculinity. Thus having fitted itself through Black maleness, hipsterism came to question the manhood of the conformist.

—TRACY D. MORGAN

Blackness enables the exoticist to stick a middle finger up at all that whiteness that shackles him with its judgmental eyes. The more outrage whites show toward his actions, the more he can relish in the freedom of his own form of revenge, his own desire to make what he regards as truly human eyes, white eyes, slip into oblivion . . . the "blacker" the other, the more self-deceiving the exoticist's sense of escaping the judgmental eyes of human subjects.

—LEWIS GORDON

What, by the way, is one to make of a white youngster who, with a transistor radio screaming a Stevie Wonder tune glued to his ear, shouts racial epithets at black youngsters trying to swim at a public beach . . . ?

—RALPH ELLISON

The "paper tiger" hero, James Bond, offering the whites a triumphant image of themselves, is saying what many whites want desperately to hear reaffirmed: I am still the White Man, lord of the land, licensed to kill, and the world is still an empire at my feet. James Bond feeds on that secret little anxiety, the psychological white backlash, felt in some degree by most whites alive. It is exasperating to see little brown men and little yellow men from the mysterious Orient, and the opaque black men of Africa (to say nothing of these impudent American Negroes!) who come to the UN and talk smart to us, who are scurrying all over our globe in their strange mode of dress—much as if they were new, unpleasant arrivals from another planet.

—ELDRIDGE CLEAVER

From the very class of poor white men, comes the man who stands to-day with his hand across the helm of the nation. He fails to catch the watchword of the hour, and throws himself, the incarnation of meanness, across the pathway of the nation. My objection to Andrew Johnson is not that he has been a poor white man; my objection is that he keeps "poor whits" all the way through.

—FRANCES E. W. HARPER

. . . you could take two white guys from the same place—one would carry his whiteness like a loaded stick, ready to

bop everybody else on the head with it;
and the other would just simply be
white . . . and let it go at that. I liked
those two white kids; they were white,
but as my Aunt Fanny used to say, they
couldn't help that.

—CHESTER B. HIMES

The young white jazz musicians at least
had to face the black American head-on
and with only a very literal drum beat.
And they could not help but do this with
some sense of rebellion or separateness
from the rest of white America, since
white America could have no understanding of what they were doing, except
perhaps in the terms that [Paul] White-
man and the others succeeded in doing
it, which was not at all—that is, explaining a bird by comparing it with an air-
plane.

—AMIRI BARAKA

JEFFERSON DAVIS
AS A REPRESENTATIVE
OF CIVILIZATION

W.E.B. Du Bois

The first African-American commencement orator for a Harvard University graduating class was W.E.B. Du Bois. (see pps. 29 and 184). Du Bois's 1890 address, with the First Lady of the United States in attendance, featured a remarkable choice of topics. Allotted ten minutes (and choosing, as was his custom, to speak less), Du Bois used his time to discuss the Confederate president Jefferson Davis. Concentrating not on "the man but the type of civilization he represented," Du Bois delivered an oration which, according to a reporter for The Nation, *handled his "hazardous subject" with "almost contemptuous fairness."*

Jefferson Davis was a typical Teutonic Hero; the history of civilization during the last millennium has been the development of the idea of the Strong Man of which he was the embodiment. The Anglo-Saxon loves a soldier—Jefferson Davis was an Anglo-Saxon, Jefferson Davis was a soldier. There was not a phase in that familiarly strange life that would not have graced a mediaeval romance: from the fiery and impetuous young lieutenant who stole as his bride the daughter of a ruler-elect of the land, to the cool and ambitious politician in the Senate hall. So boldly and surely did that cadaverous figure with the thin nervous lips and flashing eye, write the first line of the new page of American history, that the historian of the future must ever see back of the war of Secession, the strong arm of one imperious man, who defied disease, trampled on precedent, would not be defeated, and never surrendered. A soldier and a lover, a statesman and a ruler; passionate, ambitious and indomitable; bold reckless guardian of a peoples' All—judged by the whole standard of Teutonic civilization, there is something noble in the figure of Jefferson Davis; and judged by every canon of human justice, there is something fundamentally incomplete about that standard.

I wish to consider not the man, but the type of civilization which

his life represented: its foundation is the idea of the strong man—
Individualism coupled with the rule of might—and it is this idea that
has made the logic of even modern history, the cool logic of the
Club. It made a naturally brave and generous man, Jefferson Davis—
now advancing civilization by murdering Indians, now hero of a
national disgrace called by courtesy, the Mexican War; and finally, as
the crowning absurdity, the peculiar champion of a people fighting to
be free in order that another people should not be free. Whenever this
idea has for a moment, escaped from the individual realm, it has
found an even more secure foothold in the policy and philosophy of
the State. The Strong Man and his mighty Right Arm has become the
Strong Nation with its armies. Under whatever guise, however, a Jefferson Davis may appear as man, as race, or as nation, his life can only
logically mean this: the advance of a part of the world at the expense
of the whole; the overweening sense of the I, and the consequent
forgetting of the Thou. It has thus happened, that advance in civilization has always been handicapped by shortsighted national selfishness.
The vital principle of division of labor has been stifled not only in
industry, but also in civilization; so as to render it well nigh impossible
for a new race to introduce a new idea into the world except by
means of the cudgel. To say that a nation is in the way of civilization
is a contradiction in terms, and a system of human culture whose
principle is the rise of one race on the ruins of another is a farce and a
lie. Yet this is the type of civilization which Jefferson Davis represented: it represents a field for stalwart manhood and heroic character,
and at the same time for moral obtuseness and refined brutality. These
striking contradictions of character always arise when a people seemingly become convinced that the object of the world is not civilization, but Teutonic civilization. Such a type is not wholly evil or
fruitless: the world has needed and will need its Jefferson Davises; but
such a type is incomplete and never can serve its best purpose until
checked by its complementary ideas. Whence shall these come?

To the most casual observer, it must have occurred that the Rod of
Empire has in these days, turned towards the South. In every South-
ern country, however destined to play a future part in the world—in
Southern North America, South America, Australia, and Africa—a

new nation has a more or less firm foothold. This circumstance, has, however, attracted but incidental notice, hitherto; for wherever the Negro people have touched civilization their rise has been singularly unromantic and unscientific. Through the glamour of history, the rise of a nation has ever been typified by the Strong Man crushing out an effete civilization. That brutality buried aught else beside Rome when it descended golden haired and drunk from the blue north has scarcely entered human imagination. Not as the muscular warrior came the Negro, but as the cringing slave. The Teutonic met civilization and crushed it—the Negro met civilization and was crushed by it. The one was the hero the world has ever worshipped, who gained unthought of triumphs and made unthought of mistakes; the other was the personification of dogged patience bending to the inevitable, and waiting. In the history of this people, we seek in vain the elements of Teutonic deification of Self, and Roman brute force, but we do find an idea of submission apart from cowardice, laziness or stupidity, such as the world never saw before. This is the race which by its very presence must play a part in the world of tomorrow; and this is the race whose rise, I contend, has practically illustrated an idea which is at once the check and complement of the Teutonic Strong Man. It is the doctrine of the Submissive Man—given to the world by strange coincidence, by the race of whose rights, Jefferson Davis had not heard.

What then is the change made in the conception of civilization, by adding to the idea of the Strong Man, that of the Submissive Man? It is this: the submission of the strength of the Strong to the advance of all—not in mere aimless sacrifice, but recognizing the fact that, "To no one type of mind is it given to discern the totality of Truth," that civilization cannot afford to lose the contribution of the very least of nations for its full development: that not only the assertion of the I, but also the submission to the Thou is the highest individualism.

The Teuton stands today as the champion of the idea of Personal Assertion: the Negro as the peculiar embodiment of the idea of Personal Submission: either, alone, tends to an abnormal development— towards Despotism on the one hand which the world has just cause to fear, and yet covertly admires, or towards slavery on the other which the world despises and which yet is not wholly despicable. No matter how great and striking the Teutonic type of impetuous manhood may be, it must receive the cool purposeful "Ich Dien" of the African for its round and full development. In the rise of Negro people and development of this idea, you whose nation was founded on the loftiest ideals, and who many times forgot those ideals with a strange forgetfulness, have more than a sentimental interest, more than a sentimental duty. You owe a debt to humanity for this Ethiopia of the Outstretched Arm, who has made her beauty, patience, and her grandeur, law.

ON AARON HENRY
Charles M. Payne

In his massive and remarkable history of civil rights organizing in Missis-sippi, I've Got the Light of Freedom (1995), Northwestern Univer-sity professor Charles M. Payne (1948–) devotes considerable attention to the ways in which African-American protest leader Aaron Henry main-tained relationships with even hostile whites. He argues that Henry's abil-ity to maintain very cordial personal relations with people who were his political enemies may have softened, temporarily, the response of white leadership to his defiance. The drama and complexity of those relations are suggested by the excerpt which follows.

Consider the complexity of Aaron Henry's relations with white people. Henry once ordered by mail a copy of *Black Monday*, the famous racist tract of the Citizens' Council. Late one evening, the book was hand-delivered to him by Robert Patterson, founder of the council. Patterson was afraid that a mailed copy might fall into the wrong hands, and some of Henry's people might misunderstand why Henry would be reading Council literature. It was the same "Tut" Patterson who as a youngster had been Henry's best friend growing up in Clarksdale. Apparently, enough of the memory of that friendship survived that the head of the Council cared a little about the reputation of the head of the NAACP. Myrlie Evers, who tells that story, says there is nothing unusual about it; one could find simi-lar stories in small towns across the south.

If, as was suggested earlier, Henry seemed to have an especially acute sense of white folks, perhaps it was because his early life could provide the material for a textbook on the complexities of interracial relations in the Delta. Part of his education came when he worked as night clerk at a Clarksdale motor inn. "I saw white people do things that I had been told were done only by Negroes, I heard prominent white men who stood staunchly with the system tell me to stand up and be a man, although I'm sure their advice did not mean for me to consider myself their equal." The owner of the motel encouraged him to go to college and helped him learn to do simultaneous equations, in itself an enormous breech of the racial norms, yet the owner himself was a firm believer in the existing racial system. On the other hand, some white men thought it so insulting to have to hand their money to a nigger clerk that they refused to do it; others took personal pleasure in publicly degrading Henry in front of their friends. He found that the very poorest whites, contrary to their redneck image, were often willing to get along with Blacks. When he returned home from the service, the registrar refused three times to let him register. He was able to get a white veteran to help him register. His first business partner was white, and the two of them always maintained a generally egalitarian relationship, with his partner willing to stick out his neck a little in Henry's defense when Henry was accused of being a communist. Henry knew white people who pretended to be friendly to Blacks because it was good business and others who acted more racist than they felt because they were in situations where that was expedient. Aaron Henry had seen white people from a variety of angles; he had seen them change for the better and for the worse. It is not a background that easily lends itself to thinking that race, in and of itself, is determinative. The rich, complex experience with whites that Henry had is very much a generational experience. With each succeeding cohort, urbanization, the changes in the structure of work, the increasing tendency of younger Blacks to keep white contacts to a minimum, meant that fewer Blacks had the complexity of interracial experience Henry had been exposed to.

ON HERMAN MELVILLE
Toni Morrison

In a 1988 Michigan Quarterly Review *article anticipating parts of the argument of her* Playing in the Dark, *Toni Morrison (see p. 155) considered Herman Melville's work. She described a writer who grappled far more seriously with racial identity, including and especially whiteness, than did many of the critics who praised his work as universal and transcendent. Melville was, in this sense, kept "under lock and key" by critics. More liberating readings of his work have recently been opened by Morrison, Carolyn Karcher, Michael Rogin, and the African-American writers Sterling Stuckey and Joshua Leslie.*

It only seems that the canon of American literature is "naturally" or "inevitably" "white." In fact it is studiously so. In fact these absences of vital presences in Young American literature may be the insistent fruit of the scholarship rather than the text. Perhaps some of these writers, although under current house arrest, have much more to say than has been realized. Perhaps some were not so much transcending politics, or escaping blackness, as they were transforming it into intelligible, accessible, yet artistic modes of discourse. To ignore this possibility by never questioning the strategies of transformation is to disenfranchise the writer, diminish the text and render the bulk of the literature aesthetically and historically incoherent—an exorbitant price for cultural (white-male) purity, and, I believe, a spendthrift one. The re-examination of founding literature of the United States for the unspeakable unspoken may reveal those texts to have deeper and other meanings, deeper and other power, deeper and other significances.

One such writer, in particular, it has been almost impossible to keep under lock and key is Herman Melville.

Among several astute scholars, Michael Rogin has done one of the most exhaustive studies of how deeply Melville's social thought is woven into his writing. He calls our attention to the connection Melville made between American slavery and American freedom, how heightened the one rendered the other. And he has provided evidence of the impact on the work of Melville's family, milieu, and, most importantly, the raging, all-encompassing conflict of the time: slavery. He has reminded us that it was Melville's father-in-law who had, as judge, decided the case that made the Fugitive Slave Law law, and that "other evidence in *Moby Dick* also suggests the impact of Shaw's ruling on the climax of Melville's tale. Melville conceived the final confrontation between Ahab and the white whale some time in the first half of 1851. He may well have written his last chapters only after returning from a trip to New York in June. [Judge Shaw's decision was handed down in April, 1851.] When New York anti-slavery leaders William Seward and John van Buren wrote public letters protesting the *Sims* ruling, the New York *Herald* responded. Its attack on "The Anti-Slavery Agitators" began: "Did you ever see a whale? Did you ever see a mighty whale struggling?" . . .

Rogin also traces the chronology of the whale from its "birth in a state of nature" to its final end as commodity. Central to his argument is that Melville in *Moby Dick* was being allegorically and insistently political in his choice of the whale. But within his chronology, one singular whale transcends all others, goes beyond nature, adventure, politics and commodity to an abstraction. What is this abstraction? This "wicked idea"? Interpretation has been varied. It has been viewed as an allegory of the state in which Ahab is Calhoun, or Daniel Webster; an allegory of capitalism and corruption, God and man, the individual and fate, and most commonly, the single allegorical meaning of the white whale is understood to be brute, indifferent Nature, and Ahab the madman who challenges that Nature.

But let us consider, again, the principal actor, Ahab, created by an author who calls himself Typee, signed himself Tawney, identified himself as Ishmael, and who had written several books before *Moby Dick* criticizing missionary forays into various paradises.

Ahab loses sight of the commercial value of his ship's voyage, its point, and pursues an idea in order to destroy it. His intention, revenge, "an audacious, immitigable and supernatural revenge," develops stature—maturity—when we realize that he is not a man mourning his lost leg or a scar on his face. However intense and dislocating his fever and recovery had been after his encounter with the white whale, however satisfactorily "male" this vengeance is read, the vanity of it is almost adolescent. But if the whale is more than blind, indifferent Nature unsubduable by masculine aggression, if it is as much its adjective as it is its noun, we can consider the possibility that Melville's "truth" was his recognition of the moment in America when whiteness became ideology. And if the white whale is the ideology of race, what Ahab has lost to it is personal dismemberment and family and society and his own place as a human in the world. The trauma of racism is, for the racist and the victim, the severe fragmentation of the self, and has always seemed to me a cause (not a symptom) of psychosis—strangely of no interest to psychiatry. Ahab, then, is navigating between an idea of civilization that he renounces and an idea of savagery he must annihilate, because the two cannot co-exist. The former is based on the latter. What is terrible in its complexity is that the idea of savagery is not the missionary one: it is white racial ideology that is savage and if, indeed, a white, nineteenth-century, American male took on not abolition, not the amelioration of racist institutions or their laws, but the very concept of whiteness as an inhuman idea, he would be very alone, very desperate, and very doomed. Madness would be the only appropriate description of such audacity, and "he heaves me," the most succinct and appropriate description of that obsession.

I would not like to be understood to argue that Melville was engaged in some simple and simple-minded black/white didacticism, or that he was satanizing white people. Nothing like that. What I am suggesting is that he was overwhelmed by the philosophical and metaphysical inconsistencies of an extraordinary and unprecedented idea that had its fullest manifestation in his own time in his own country, and that that idea was the successful assertion of whiteness as ideology.

On the *Pequod* the multiracial, mainly foreign, proletariat is at work to produce a commodity, but it is diverted and converted from that labor to Ahab's more significant intellectual quest. We leave whale as commerce and confront whale as metaphor. With that interpretation in place, two of the most famous chapters of the book become luminous in a completely new way. One is Chapter 9, The

Sermon. In Father Mapple's thrilling rendition of Jonah's trials, emphasis is given to the purpose of Jonah's salvation. He is saved from the fish's belly for one single purpose, "To preach the Truth to the face of Falsehood! That was it!" Only then the reward "Delight"— which strongly calls to mind Ahab's lonely necessity. "Delight is to him . . . who against the proud gods and commodores of this earth, ever stand forth his own inexorable self. . . . Delight is to him whose strong arms yet support him, when the ship of this base treacherous world has gone down beneath him. Delight is to him who gives no quarter in the truth and kills, burns, and destroys all *sin* though he pluck it out from under the robes of Senators and Judges. Delight— top-gallant delight is to him who acknowledges no law or lord, but the Lord his God, and is only a *patriot to heaven*" [italics mine]. No one, I think, has denied that the sermon is designed to be prophetic, but it seems unremarked what the nature of the sin is—the sin that must be destroyed, regardless. Nature? A sin? The terms do not apply. Capitalism? Perhaps. Capitalism fed greed, lent itself inexorably to corruption, but probably was not in and of itself sinful to Melville. Sin suggests a moral outrage within the bounds of man to repair. The concept of racial superiority would fit seamlessly. It is difficult to read those words ("destruction of sin," "patriot to heaven") and not hear in them the description of a different Ahab. Not an adolescent male in adult clothing, a maniacal egocentric, or the "exotic plant" that V. S. Parrington thought Melville was. Not even a morally fine liberal voice adjusting, balancing, compromising with racial institutions. But another Ahab: the only white male American heroic enough to try to slay the monster that was devouring the world as he knew it.

Another chapter that seems freshly lit by this reading is Chapter 42, The Whiteness of the Whale. Melville points to the do-or-die significance of his effort to say something unsayable in this chapter. "I almost despair," he writes, "of putting it in a comprehensive form. It was the whiteness of the whale that above all things appalled me. But how can I hope to explain myself here; and yet in some dim, random way, explain myself I must, *else all these chapters might be naught*" [italics mine]. The language of this chapter ranges between benevolent, beautiful images of whiteness and whiteness as sinister and shocking. After dissecting the ineffable, he concludes: "Therefore . . . symbolize whatever grand or gracious he will by whiteness, no man can deny that in its profoundest *idealized significance* it calls up a peculiar apparition to the soul." I stress "idealized significance" to emphasize and make clear (if such clarity needs stating) that Melville is not exploring white *people,* but whiteness idealized. Then, after informing the reader of his "hope to light upon some chance clue to conduct us to the hidden course we seek," he tries to nail it. To provide the key to the "hidden course." His struggle to do so is gigantic. He cannot. Nor can we. But in nonfigurative language, he identifies the imaginative tools needed to solve the problem: "subtlety appeals to subtlety, and without imagination no man can follow another into these halls." And his final observation reverberates with personal trauma. "This visible [colored] world seems formed in love, the invisible [white] spheres were formed in fright." The necessity for whiteness as privileged "natural" state, the invention of it, was indeed formed in fright.

"Slavery," writes Rogin, "confirmed Melville's isolation, decisively established in *Moby Dick,* from the dominant consciousness of his time." I differ on this point and submit that Melville's hostility and repugnance for slavery would have found company. There were many white Americans of his acquaintance who felt repelled by slavery, wrote journalism about it, spoke about it, legislated on it and were active in abolishing it. His attitude to slavery alone would not have condemned him to the almost autistic separation visited upon him. And if he felt convinced that blacks were worthy of being treated like whites, or that capitalism was dangerous—he had company or could have found it. But to question the very notion of white progress, the very idea of racial superiority, of whiteness as privileged place in the evolutionary ladder of humankind, and to meditate on the fraudulent, self-destroying philosophy of that superiority, to "pluck it out from under the robes of Senators and Judges," to drag the "judge himself to the bar,"—that was dangerous, solitary, radical work. Especially then. Especially now. To be "only a patriot to heaven" is no mean aspiration in Young America for a writer—or the captain of a whaling ship.

wasn't in his own bed by the furnace. There was a light in Mattie's room, so Michael knocked softly. Mattie said, "Who's that?" And Michael poked his head in, and here were Luther and Mattie in bed together!

Of course, Anne condoned them. "It's so simple and natural for Negroes to make love." But Mattie, after all, was forty if she was a day. And Luther was only a kid. Besides Anne thought that Luther had been ever so much nicer when he first came than he was now. But from so many nights at the Savoy, he had become a marvellous dancer, and he was teaching Anne the Lindy Hop to Cab Calloway's records. Besides, her picture of "The Boy on the Block" wasn't anywhere near done. And he did take pretty good care of the furnace. So they kept him. At least, Anne kept him, although Michael said he was getting a little bored with the same Negro always in the way.

For Luther had grown a bit familiar lately. He smoked up all their cigarettes, drank their wine, told jokes on them to their friends, and sometimes even came upstairs singing and walking about the house when the Carraways had guests in who didn't share their enthusiasm for Negroes, natural or otherwise.

Luther and Mattie together were a pair. They quite frankly lived with one another now. Well, let that go. Anne and Michael prided themselves on being different; artists, you know, and liberal-minded people—maybe a little scatter-brained, but then (secretly, they felt) that came from genius. They were not ordinary people, bothering about the liberties of others. Certainly, the last thing they would do would be to interfere with the delightful simplicity of Negroes.

But Mattie must be giving Luther money and buying him clothes. He was really dressing awfully well. And on her Thursday afternoons off she would come back loaded down with packages. As far as the Carraways could tell, they were all for Luther.

And sometimes there were quarrels drifting up from the basement. And often, all too often, Mattie had moods. Then Luther would have moods. And it was pretty awful having two dark and glowering people around the house. Anne couldn't paint and Michael couldn't play.

One day, when she hadn't seen Luther for three days, Anne called downstairs and asked him if he wouldn't please come up and take off his shirt and get on the box. The picture was almost done. Luther came dragging his feet upstairs and humming:

> "Before I'd be a slave
> I'd be buried in ma grave
> And go home to my Jesus
> And be free."

And that afternoon he let the furnace go almost out.

That was the state of things when Michael's mother (whom Anne had never liked) arrived from Kansas City to pay them a visit. At once neither Mattie nor Luther liked her either. She was a mannish old lady, big and tall, and inclined to be bossy. Mattie, however, did spruce up her service, cooked delicious things, and treated Mrs. Carraway with a great deal more respect than she did Anne.

"I never play with servants," Mrs. Carraway had said to Michael, and Mattie must have heard her.

But Luther, he was worse than ever. Not that he did anything wrong, Anne thought, but the way he did things! For instance, he didn't need to sing now all the time, especially since Mrs. Carraway had said she didn't like singing. And certainly not songs like "You Rascal, You."

But all things end! With the Carraways and Luther it happened like this: One forenoon, quite without a shirt (for he expected to pose) Luther came sauntering through the library to change the flowers in the vase. He carried red roses. Mrs. Carraway was reading her morning scripture from the Health and Life.

"Oh good morning," said Luther. "How long are you gonna stay in this house?"

"I never liked familiar Negroes," said Mrs. Carraway, over her nose glasses.

"Huh!" said Luther. "That's too bad! I never liked poor white folks."

Mrs. Carraway screamed, a short loud, dignified scream. Michael came running in bathrobe and pyjamas. Mrs. Carraway grew tall. There was a scene. Luther talked. Michael talked. Anne appeared.

"Never, never, never," said Mrs. Carraway, "have I suffered such impudence from servants—and a nigger servant—in my own son's house."

"Mother, Mother, Mother," said Michael. "Be calm. I'll discharge him." He turned on the nonchalant Luther. "Go!" he said, pointing toward the door. "Go, go!"

"Michael," Anne cried, "I haven't finished 'The Slave on the Block.'" Her husband looked nonplussed. For a moment he breathed deeply.

"Either he goes or I go," said Mrs. Carraway, firm as a rock.

"He goes," said Michael with strength from his mother.

"Oh!" cried Anne. She looked at Luther. His black arms were full of roses he had brought to put in the vases. He had on no shirt. "Oh!" His body was ebony.

"Don't worry 'bout me!" said Luther. "I'll go."

"Yes, we'll go," boomed Mattie from the doorway, who had come up from below, fat and belligerent. "We've stood enough foolery from you white folks! Yes, we'll go. Come on, Luther."

What could she mean, "stood enough"? What had they done to them, Anne and Michael wondered. They had tried to be kind. "Oh!"

"Sneaking around knocking on our door at night," Mattie went on. "Yes, we'll go. Pay us! Pay us! Pay us!" So she remembered the time they had come for Luther at night. That was it.

"I'll pay you," said Michael. He followed Mattie out.

Anne looked at her black boy.

"Good-bye," Luther said. "You fix the vases."

He handed her his armful of roses, glanced impudently at old Mrs. Carraway and grinned—grinned that wide, beautiful, white-toothed grin that made Anne say when she first saw him, "He looks like the jungle." Grinned, and disappeared in the dark hall, with no shirt on his back.

"Oh," Anne moaned distressfully, "my 'Boy on the Block'!"

"Huh!" snorted Mrs. Carraway.

JOHN BROWN
Jacob Lawrence

When asked for whom he intended to vote in one lackluster presidential election, James Baldwin answered, "John Brown." Brown, the white abolitionist revolutionary executed after leading an ill-fated 1859 raid on the federal arsenal at Harpers Ferry, Virginia, has been the subject of a large body of African-American tributes, including Countee Cullen's wrenching "A Negro Mother's Lullaby" (1942) and W.E.B. Du Bois's 1909 biography. The great historian Benjamin Quarles gathered many of these tributes in Blacks on John Brown. *Jacob Lawrence (1917–), the most renowned living artist from the United States, memorialized Brown in an impressive 1941 series of gouaches. Lawrence, born in New Jersey and trained as a painter by Charles Alston while living in Harlem, made common people, especially African Americans on the job and on the move, the subject of vibrant and monumental art. His depictions of Brown, like those by Cullen, draw strongly on Christian images of martyrdom. The selections which follow are numbers 6, 20, 21, and 22 in the* John Brown *series. The originals are in color. They are used here through the courtesy of the artist and Francine Seders Gallery of Seattle. Photograph © The Detroit Institute of Arts. Gift of Mr. and Mrs. Milton Lowenthal.*

John Brown Series #6 (1941), gouache on white wove paper, 14" x 20"

John Brown Series #20 (1941), gouache on white wove paper, 20" x 14"

John Brown Series #21 (1941), gouache on white wove paper, 14" x 20"

John Brown Series #22 (1941), gouache on white wove paper, 14" x 20"

PART V

WHITE WOMEN, WHITE MEN

Because she knew the black community, Miz Minnie also had plenty of information about the white one. Blanche wondered if people who hired domestic help had any idea how much their employees learned about them while fixing their meals, making their beds, and emptying their trash. Did it ever occur to the kind of women for whom she worked that they and their lives were often topics of conversation and sometimes objects of ridicule or pity among the help's friends and families?

—Barbara Neely

I speak out of direct and particular anger at an academic conference, and a white woman says, "Tell me how you feel but don't say it too harshly or I cannot hear you."

—Audre Lorde

I wheel my two-year-old daughter in a shopping cart through a supermarket in Eastchester in 1967, and a little white girl riding past in her mother's cart calls out excitedly, "Oh look, Mommy, a baby maid!" And your mother shushes; but she does not correct you. And so fifteen years later, at a conference on racism, you can still find that story humorous. But I hear your laughter is full of terror and disease.

—Audre Lorde

But it 'pears dat Miss Libbie heard 'bout de gwines on Mars Jeems's plantation, en she des 'lowed she could n' trus' herse'f wid no sech a man dat he mought git useter 'busin' his niggers dat he'd 'mence ter 'buse his wife atter he got useter habbin' her roun' de house.

—CHARLES W. CHESNUTT, CHARACTER IN *THE CONJURE WOMAN*

I do not believe that white women are dewdrops just exhaled from the skies.

—FRANCES E. W. HARPER

Gazing on the prosex possibilities of a world beat without the Third World, feminist discourses have, ultimately, given Madonna a body politic to deconstruct (and a racial aesthetic to exploit) because they do, in fact, take race as their referential starting point—only they position whiteness as the origin of all theories postmodern, if not to the very idea of theory itself.

—JACKIE GOLDSBY

GOING TO MEET THE MAN
James Baldwin

James Baldwin (see p. 177) published his splendid collection of short fiction, Going to Meet the Man, *in 1965. In the title story, reprinted here, Baldwin accounts for the ferocity of racist reaction to civil rights protest by tracing the movement of white terror across generations and from public to private realms. The connections among white supremacy, the learning of manhood, and the lives of white women are tellingly made. Graphically linking whiteness and sexual violence, Baldwin also offers arresting insights into the ways in which the music of African-American protest was heard by whites and conveys the role of complicity in terror and bonding whites together. "They were soldiers fighting a war," he writes, "but their relationship to each other was that of accomplices to a crime. They had to keep their mouths shut." Like the selections by Ellison and Cuthbert in Part VI, "Going to Meet the Man" is an African-American account of racial violence told largely from the point of view of a white character strongly defined in terms of gender as well as race.*

"What's the matter?" she asked.

"I don't know," he said, trying to laugh, "I guess I'm tired."

"You've been working too hard," she said. "I keep telling you."

"Well, goddammit, woman," he said, "it's not my fault!" He tried again; he wretchedly failed again. Then he just lay there, silent, angry, and helpless. Excitement filled him like a tooth-ache, but it refused to enter his flesh. He stroked her breast. This was his wife. He could not ask her to do just a little thing for him, just to help him out, just for a little while, the way he could ask a nigger girl to do it. He lay there, and he sighed. The image of a black girl caused a distant excitement in him, like a far-away light; but, again, the excitement was more like pain; instead of forcing him to act, it made action impossible.

"Go to sleep," she said, gently, "you got a hard day tomorrow."

"Yeah," he said, and rolled over on his side, facing her, one hand still on one breast. "Goddamn the niggers. The black stinking coons.

You'd think they'd learn. Wouldn't you think they'd learn? I mean, *wouldn't* you?"

"They going to be out there tomorrow," she said, and took his hand away, "get some sleep."

He lay there, one hand between his legs, staring at the frail sanctuary of his wife. A faint light came from the shutters; the moon was full. Two dogs, far away, were barking at each other, back and forth, insistently, as though they were agreeing to make an appointment. He heard a car coming north on the road and he half sat up, his hand reaching for his holster, which was on a chair near the bed, on top of his pants. The lights hit the shutters and seemed to travel across the room and then went out. The sound of the car slipped away, he heard it hit gravel, then heard it no more. Some liver-lipped students, probably, heading back to that college—but coming from where? His watch said it was two in the morning. They could be coming from anywhere, from out of state most likely, and they would be at the court-house tomorrow. The niggers were getting ready. Well, they would be ready, too.

He moaned. He wanted to let whatever was in him out; but it wouldn't come out. Goddamn! he said aloud, and turned again, on his side, away from Grace, staring at the shutters. He was a big, healthy man and he had never had any trouble sleeping. And he wasn't old enough yet to have any trouble getting it up—he was only forty-two. And he was a good man, a God-fearing man, he had tried to do his duty all his life, and he had been a deputy sheriff for several years. Nothing had ever bothered him before, certainly not getting it up. Sometimes, sure, like any other man, he knew that he wanted a little more spice than Grace could give him and he would drive over yonder and pick up a black piece or arrest her, it came to the same thing, but he couldn't do that now, no more. There was no telling what might happen once your ass was in the air. And they were low enough to kill a man then, too, everyone of them, or the girl herself might do it, right while she was making believe you made her feel so good. The niggers. What had the good Lord Almighty had in mind when he made the niggers? Well. They were pretty good at that, all right. Damn. Damn. Goddamn.

This wasn't helping him to sleep. He turned again, toward Grace again, and moved close to her warm body. He felt something he had never felt before. He felt that he would like to hold her, hold her, hold her, and be buried in her like a child and never have to get up in the morning again and go downtown to face those faces, good Christ, they were ugly! and never have to enter that jail house again and smell that smell and hear that singing; never again feel that filthy, kinky, greasy hair under his hand, never again watch those black breasts leap against the leaping cattle prod, never hear those moans again or watch that blood run down or the fat lips split or the sealed eyes struggle open. They were animals, they were no better than animals, what could be done with people like that? Here they had been in a civilized country for years and they still lived like animals. Their houses were dark, with oil cloth or cardboard in the windows, the smell was enough to make you puke your guts out, and there they sat, a whole tribe, pumping out kids, it looked like, every damn five minutes, and laughing and talking and playing music like they didn't have a care in the world, and he reckoned they didn't, neither, and coming to the door, into the sunlight, just standing there, just looking foolish, not thinking of anything but just getting back to what they were doing, saying, Yes suh, Mr. Jesse. I surely will, Mr. Jesse. Fine weather, Mr. Jesse. Why, I thank you, Mr. Jesse. He had worked for a mail-order house for a while and it had been his job to collect the payments for the stuff they bought. They were too dumb to know that they were being cheated blind, but that was no skin off his ass—he was just sup-posed to do his job. They would be late—they didn't have the sense to put money aside; but it was easy to scare them, and he never really had any trouble. Hell, they all liked him, the kids used to smile when he came to the door. He gave them candy, sometimes, or chewing gum, and rubbed their rough bullet heads—maybe the candy should have been poisoned. Those kids were grown now. He had had trouble with one of them today.

"There was this nigger today," he said; and stopped; his voice sounded peculiar. He touched Grace. "You awake?" he asked. She mumbled something, impatiently, she was probably telling him to go to sleep. It was all right. He knew that he was not alone.

"What a funny time," he said, "to be thinking about a thing like that—you listening?" She mumbled something again. He rolled over on his back. "This nigger's one of the ringleaders. We had trouble with him before. We must have had him out there at the work farm three or four times. Well, Big Jim C. and some of the boys really had to whip that nigger's ass today." He looked over at Grace; he could not tell whether she was listening or not; and he was afraid to ask again. "They had this line you know, to register"—he laughed, but she did not—"and they wouldn't stay where Big Jim C. wanted them, no, they had to start blocking traffic all around the court house so couldn't nothing or nobody get through, and Big Jim C. told them to disperse and they wouldn't move, they just kept up that singing, and Big Jim C. figured that the others would move if this nigger would move, him being the ring-leader, but he wouldn't move and he wouldn't let the others move, so they had to beat him and a couple of the others and they threw them in the wagon—but *I* didn't see this nigger till I got to the jail. They were still singing and I was supposed to make them stop. Well, I couldn't make them stop for me but I knew he could make them stop. He was lying on the ground jerking and moaning, they had threw him in a cell by himself, and blood was coming out his ears from where Big Jim C. and his boys had whipped him. Wouldn't you think they'd learn? I put the prod to him and he jerked some more and he kind of screamed—but he didn't have much voice left. "You make them stop that singing," I said to him, "you hear me? You make them stop that singing." He acted like he didn't hear me and I put it to him again, under his arms, and he just rolled around on the floor and blood started coming from his mouth. He'd pissed his pants already." He paused. His mouth felt dry and his throat was as rough as sandpaper; as he talked, he began to hurt all over with that peculiar excitement which refused to be released. "You all are going to stop your singing, I said to him, and you are going to stop coming down to the court house and disrupting traffic and molesting the people and keeping us from our duties and keeping doctors from getting to sick white women and getting all them Northerners in this town to give our town a bad name—!" As he said this, he kept prodding the boy, sweat pouring from beneath the helmet he had not yet taken off. The boy rolled around in his own dirt and water and blood and tried to scream again as the prod hit his testicles, but the scream did not come out, only a kind of rattle and a moan. He stopped. He was not supposed to kill the nigger. The cell was filled with a terrible odor. The boy was still. "You hear me?" he called. "You had enough?" The singing went on. "You had enough?" His foot leapt out, he had not known it was going to, and caught the boy flush on the jaw. *Jesus,* he thought, *this ain't no nigger, this is a goddamn bull,* and he screamed again, "You had enough? You going to make them stop that singing now?"

But the boy was out. And now he was shaking worse than the boy had been shaking. He was glad no one could see him. At the same time, he felt very close to a very peculiar, particular joy; something deep in him and deep in his memory was stirred, but whatever was in his memory eluded him. He took off his helmet. He walked to the cell door.

"White man," said the boy, from the floor, behind him.

He stopped. For some reason, he grabbed his privates.

"You remember Old Julia?"

The boy said, from the floor, with his mouth full of blood, and one eye, barely open, glaring like the eye of a cat in the dark, "My grandmother's name was Mrs. Julia Blossom. *Mrs.* Julia Blossom. You going to call our women by their right names yet.—And those kids ain't going to stop singing. We going to keep on singing until every one of you miserable white mothers go stark raving out of your minds." Then he closed the one eye; he spat blood; his head fell back against the floor.

He looked down at the boy, whom he had been seeing, off and on, for more than a year, and suddenly remembered him: Old Julia had been one of his mail-order customers, a nice old woman. He had not seen her for years, he supposed that she must be dead.

He had walked into the yard, the boy had been sitting in a swing. He had smiled at the boy, and asked, "Old Julia home?"

The boy looked at him for a long time before he answered. "Don't no Old Julia live here."

"This is her house. I know her. She's lived here for years."

The boy shook his head. "You might know a Old Julia someplace else, white man. But don't nobody by that name live here."

He watched the boy; the boy watched him. The boy certainly wasn't more than ten. *White man*. He didn't have time to be fooling around with some crazy kid. He yelled, "Hey! Old Julia!"

But only silence answered him. The expression on the boy's face did not change. The sun beat down on them both, still and silent; he had the feeling that he had been caught up in a nightmare, a nightmare dreamed by a child; perhaps one of the nightmares he himself had dreamed as a child. It had that feeling—everything familiar, without undergoing any other change, had been subtly and hideously displaced: the trees, the sun, the patches of grass in the yard, the leaning porch and the weary porch steps and the card-board in the windows and the black hole of the door which looked like the entrance to a cave, and the eyes of the pickaninny, all, all, were charged with malevolence. *White man*. He looked at the boy. "She's gone out?"

The boy said nothing.

"Well," he said, "tell her I passed by and I'll pass by next week." He started to go; he stopped. "You want some chewing gum?"

The boy got down from the swing and started for the house. He said, "I don't want nothing you got, white man." He walked into the house and closed the door behind him.

Now the boy looked as though he were dead. Jesse wanted to go over to him and pick him up and pistol whip him until the boy's head burst open like a melon. He began to tremble with what he believed was rage, sweat, both cold and hot, raced down his body, the singing filled him as though it were a weird, uncontrollable, monstrous howling rumbling up from the depths of his own belly, he felt an icy fear rise in him and raise him up, and he shouted, he howled, "You lucky we *pump* some white blood into you every once in a while—your women! Here's what I got for all the black bitches in the world—!" Then he was, abruptly, almost too weak to stand; to his bewilderment, his horror, beneath his own fingers, he felt himself violently stiffen—with no warning at all; he dropped his hands and he stared at the boy and he left the cell.

"All that singing they do," he said. "All that singing." He could not remember the first time he had heard it; he had been hearing it all his life. It was the sound with which he was most familiar—though it was also the sound of which he had been least conscious—and it had always contained an obscure comfort. They were singing to God. They were singing for mercy and they hoped to go to heaven, and he had even sometimes felt, when looking into the eyes of some of the old women, a few of the very old men, that they were singing for mercy for his soul, too. Of course he had never thought of their heaven or of what God was, or could be, for them; God was the same for everyone, he supposed, and heaven was where good people went—he supposed. He had never thought much about what it meant to be a good person. He tried to be a good person and treat everybody right: it wasn't his fault if the niggers had taken it into their heads to fight against God and go against the rules laid down in the Bible for everyone to read! Any preacher would tell you that. He was only doing his duty: protecting white people from the niggers and the niggers from themselves. And there were still lots of good niggers around—he had to remember that; they weren't all like that boy this afternoon; and the good niggers must be mighty sad to see what was happening to their people. They would thank him when this was over. In that way they had, the best of them, not quite looking him in the eye, in a low voice, with a little smile: We surely thanks you, Mr. Jesse. From the bottom of our hearts, we thanks you. He smiled. They hadn't all gone crazy. This trouble would pass.—He knew that the young people had changed some of the words to the songs. He had scarcely listened to the words before and he did not listen to them now; but he knew that the words were different; he could hear that much. He did not know if the faces were different, he had never, before this trouble began, watched them as they sang, but he certainly did not like what he saw now. They hated him, and this hatred was blacker than their hearts, blacker than their skins, redder than their blood, and harder, by far, than his club. Each day, each night, he felt worn out, aching, with their smell in his nostrils and filling his lungs, as though he were drowning—drowning in niggers; and it was all to be done again when he awoke. It would never end. It would never end. Perhaps this was what the singing had meant all along. They had not been singing black folks into heaven, they had been singing white folks into hell.

Everyone felt this black suspicion in many ways, but no one knew how to express it. Men much older than he, who had been responsible for law and order much longer than he, were now much quieter than they had been, and the tone of their jokes, in a way that he could not quite put his finger on, had changed. These men were his models, they had been friends to his father, and they had taught him what it meant to be a man. He looked to them for courage now. It wasn't that he didn't know that what he was doing was right—he knew that, nobody had to tell him that; it was only that he missed the ease of former years. But they didn't have much time to hang out with each other these days. They tended to stay close to their families every free minute because nobody knew what might happen next. Explosions rocked the night of their tranquil town. Each time each man wondered silently if perhaps this time the dynamite had not fallen into the wrong hands. They thought that they knew where all the guns were; but they could not possibly know every move that was made in that secret place where the darkies lived. From time to time it was suggested that they form a posse and search the home of every nigger, but they hadn't done it yet. For one thing, this might have brought the bastards from the North down on their backs; for another, although the niggers were scattered throughout the town—down in the hollow near the railroad tracks, way west near the mills, up on the hill, the well-off ones, and some out near the college—nothing seemed to happen in one part of town without the niggers immediately knowing it in the other. This meant that they could not take them by surprise. They rarely mentioned it, but they *knew* that some of the niggers had guns. It stood to reason, as they said, since, after all, some of them had been in the Army. There were niggers in the Army right now and God knows they wouldn't have had any trouble stealing this half-assed government blind—the whole world was doing it, look at the European countries and all those countries in Africa. They made jokes about it—bitter jokes; and they cursed the government in Washington, which had betrayed them; but they had not yet formed a posse. Now, if their town had been laid out like some towns in the

North, where all the niggers lived together in one locality, they could have gone down and set fire to the houses and brought about peace that way. If the niggers had all lived in one place, they could have kept the fire in one place. But the way this town was laid out, the fire could hardly be controlled. It would spread all over town—and the niggers would probably be helping it to spread. Still, from time to time, they spoke of doing it, anyway; so that now there was a real fear among them that somebody might go crazy and light the match.

They rarely mentioned anything not directly related to the war that they were fighting, but this had failed to establish between them the unspoken communication of soldiers during a war. Each man, in the thrilling silence which sped outward from their exchanges, their laughter, and their anecdotes, seemed wrestling, in various degrees of darkness, with a secret which he could not articulate to himself, and which, however directly it related to the war, related yet more surely to his privacy and his past. They could no longer be sure, after all, that they had all done the same things. They had never dreamed that their privacy could contain any element of terror, could threaten, that is, to reveal itself, to the scrutiny of a judgment day, while remaining unreadable and inaccessible to themselves; nor had they dreamed that the past, while certainly refusing to be forgotten, could yet so stubbornly refuse to be remembered. They felt themselves mysteriously set at naught, as no longer entering into the real concerns of other people—while here they were, out-numbered, fighting to save the civilized world. They had thought that people would care—people didn't care; not enough, anyway, to help them. It would have been a help, really, or at least a relief, even to have been forced to surrender. Thus they had lost, probably forever, their old and easy connection with each other. They were forced to depend on each other more and, at the same time, to trust each other less. Who could tell when one of them might not betray them all, for money, or for the ease of confession? But no one dared imagine what there might be to confess. They were soldiers fighting a war, but their relationship to each other was that of accomplices in a crime. They all had to keep their mouths shut.

I stepped in the river at Jordan.

Out of the darkness of the room, out of nowhere, the line came flying up at him, with the melody and the beat. He turned wordlessly toward his sleeping wife. *I stepped in the river at Jordan.* Where had he heard that song?

"Grace," he whispered. "You awake?"

She did not answer. If she was awake, she wanted him to sleep. Her breathing was slow and easy, her body slowly rose and fell.

I stepped in the river at Jordan.

The water came to my knees.

He began to sweat. He felt an overwhelming fear, which yet contained a curious and dreadful pleasure.

I stepped in the river at Jordan.

The water came to my waist.

It had been night, as it was now, he was in the car between his mother and his father, sleepy, his head in his mother's lap, sleepy, and yet full of excitement. The singing came from far away, across the dark fields. There were no lights anywhere. They had said good-bye to all the others and turned off on this dark dirt road. They were almost home.

I stepped in the river at Jordan,

The water came over my head,

I looked way over to the other side,

He was making up my dying bed!

"I guess they singing for him," his father said, seeming very weary and subdued now. "Even when they're sad, they sound like they just about to go and tear off a piece." He yawned and leaned across the boy and slapped his wife lightly on the shoulder, allowing his hand to rest there for a moment. "Don't they?"

"Don't talk that way," she said.

"Well, that's what we going to do," he said, "you can make up your mind to that." He started whistling. "You see? When I begin to feel it, I gets kind of musical, too."

Oh, Lord! Come on and ease my troubling mind!

He had a black friend, his age, eight, who lived nearby. His name was Otis. They wrestled together in the dirt. Now the thought of

Otis made him sick. He began to shiver. His mother put her arm around him.

"He's tired," she said.

"We'll be home soon," said his father. He began to whistle again.

"We didn't see Otis this morning," Jesse said. He did not know why he said this. His voice, in the darkness of the car, sounded small and accusing.

"You haven't seen Otis for a couple of mornings," his mother said.

That was true. But he was only concerned about *this* morning.

"No," said his father, "I reckon Otis's folks was afraid to let him show himself this morning."

"But Otis didn't do nothing!" Now his voice sounded questioning.

"Otis *can't* do nothing," said his father, "he's too little." The car lights picked up their wooden house, which now solemnly approached them, the lights falling around it like yellow dust. Their dog, chained to a tree, began to bark.

"We just want to make sure Otis *don't* do nothing," said his father, and stopped the car. He looked down at Jesse. "And you tell him what your Daddy said, you hear?"

"Yes sir," he said.

His father switched off the lights. The dog moaned and pranced, but they ignored him and went inside. He could not sleep. He lay awake, hearing the night sounds, the dog yawning and moaning outside, the sawing of the crickets, the cry of the owl, dogs barking far away, then no sounds at all, just the heavy, endless buzzing of the night. The darkness pressed on his eyelids like a scratchy blanket. He turned, he turned again. He wanted to call his mother, but he knew his father would not like this. He was terribly afraid. Then he heard his father's voice in the other room, low, with a joke in it; but this did not help him, it frightened him more, he knew what was going to happen. He put his head under the blanket, then pushed his head out again, for fear, staring at the dark window. He heard his mother's moan, his father's sigh; he gritted his teeth. Then their bed began to rock. His father's breathing seemed to fill the world.

That morning, before the sun had gathered all its strength, men and women, some flushed and some pale with excitement, came with news. Jesse's father seemed to know what the news was before the first jalopy stopped in the yard, and he ran out, crying, "They got him, then? They got him?"

The first jalopy held eight people, three men and two women and three children. The children were sitting on the laps of the grown-ups. Jesse knew two of them, the two boys; they shyly and uncomfortably greeted each other. He did not know the girl.

"Yes, they got him," said one of the women, the older one, who wore a wide hat and a fancy, faded blue dress. "They found him early this morning."

"How far had he got?" Jesse's father asked.

"He hadn't got no further than Harkness," one of the men said. "Look like he got lost up there in all them trees—or maybe he just got so scared he couldn't move." They all laughed.

"Yes, and you know it's near a graveyard, too," said the younger woman, and they laughed again.

"Is that where they got him now?" asked Jesse's father.

By this time there were three cars piled behind the first one, with everyone looking excited and shining, and Jesse noticed that they were carrying food. It was like a Fourth of July picnic.

"Yeah, that's where he is," said one of the men, "declare, Jesse, you going to keep us here all day long, answering your damn fool questions. Come on, we ain't got no time to waste."

"Don't bother putting up no food," cried a woman from one of the other cars, "we got enough. Just come on."

"Why, thank you," said Jesse's father, "we be right along, then."

"I better get a sweater for the boy," said his mother, "in case it turns cold."

Jesse watched his mother's thin legs cross the yard. He knew that she also wanted to comb her hair a little and maybe put on a better dress, the dress she wore to church. His father guessed this, too, for he yelled behind her, "Now don't you go trying to turn yourself into no movie star. You just come on." But he laughed as he said this, and winked at the men; his wife was younger and prettier than most of the other women. He clapped Jesse on the head and started pulling him toward the car. "You all go on," he said, "I'll be right behind you. Jesse, you go tie up that there dog while I get this car started."

The cars sputtered and coughed and shook; the caravan began to move; bright dust filled the air. As soon as he was tied up, the dog began to bark. Jesse's mother came out of the house, carrying a jacket for his father and a sweater for Jesse. She had put a ribbon in her hair and had an old shawl around her shoulders.

"Put these in the car, son," she said, and handed everything to him. She bent down and stroked the dog, looked to see if there was water in his bowl, then went back up the three porch steps and closed the door.

"Come on," said his father, "ain't nothing in there for nobody to steal." He was sitting in the car, which trembled and belched. The last car of the caravan had disappeared but the sound of singing floated behind them.

Jesse got into the car, sitting close to his father, loving the smell of the car, and the trembling, and the bright day, and the sense of going on a great and unexpected journey. His mother got in and closed the door and the car began to move. Not until then did he ask, "Where are we going? Are we going on a picnic?"

He had a feeling that he knew where they were going, but he was not sure.

"That's right," his father said, "we're going on a picnic. You won't ever forget *this* picnic—!"

"Are we," he asked, after a moment, "going to see the bad nigger—the one that knocked down old Miss Standish?"

"Well, I reckon," said his mother, "that we *might* see him."

He started to ask, *Will a lot of niggers be there? Will Otis be there?*— but he did not ask his question, to which, in a strange and uncomfortable way, he already knew the answer. Their friends, in the other cars, stretched up the road as far as he could see; other cars had joined them; there were cars behind them. They were singing. The sun seemed, suddenly very hot, and he was, at once very happy and a little afraid. He did not quite understand what was happening, and he did not know what to ask—he had no one to ask. He had grown accustomed, for the solution of such mysteries, to go to Otis. He felt that Otis knew everything. But he could not ask Otis about this. Anyway, he had not seen Otis for two days; he had not seen a black face anywhere for more than two days; and he now realized, as they began chugging up the long hill which eventually led to Harkness, that there were no black faces on the road this morning, no black people anywhere. From the houses in which they lived, all along the road, no smoke curled, no life stirred—maybe one or two chickens were to be seen, that was all. There was no one at the windows, no one in the yard, no one sitting on the porches, and the doors were closed. He had come this road many a time and seen women washing in the yard (there were no clothes on the clotheslines) men working in the fields, children playing in the dust; black men passed them on the road other mornings, other days, on foot, or in wagons, sometimes in cars, tipping their hats, smiling, joking, their teeth a solid white against their skin, their eyes as warm as the sun, the blackness of their skin like dull fire against the white of the blue or the grey of their torn clothes. They passed the nigger church—dead-white, desolate, locked up; and the graveyard, where no one knelt or walked, and he saw no flowers. He wanted to ask, *Where are they? Where are they all?* But he did not dare. As the hill grew steeper, the sun grew colder. He looked at his mother and his father. They looked straight ahead, seeming to be listening to the singing which echoed and echoed in this graveyard silence. They were strangers to him now. They were looking at something he could not see. His father's lips had a strange, cruel curve, he wet his lips from time to time, and swallowed. He was terribly aware of his father's tongue, it was as though he had never seen it before. And his father's body suddenly seemed immense, bigger than a mountain. His eyes, which were grey-green, looked yellow in the sunlight; or at least there was a light in them which he had never seen before. His mother patted her hair and adjusted the ribbon, leaning forward to look into the car mirror. "You look all right," said his father, and laughed. "When that nigger looks at you, he's going to swear he threw his life away for nothing. Wouldn't be surprised if he don't come back to haunt you." And he laughed again.

The singing now slowly began to cease; and he realized that they were nearing their destination. They had reached a straight, narrow, pebbly road, with trees on either side. The sunlight filtered down on them from a great height, as though they were under-water; and the branches of the trees scraped against the cars with a tearing sound. To the right of them, and beneath them, invisible now, lay the town; and to the left, miles of trees which led to the high mountain range which his ancestors had crossed in order to settle in this valley. Now, all was silent, except for the bumping of the tires against the rocky road, the sputtering of motors, and the sound of a crying child. And they seemed to move more slowly. They were beginning to climb again. He watched the cars ahead as they toiled patiently upward, disappearing into the sunlight of the clearing. Presently, he felt their vehicle also rise, heard his father's changed breathing, the sunlight hit his face, the trees moved away from them, and they were there. As their car crossed the clearing, he looked around. There seemed to be millions, there were certainly hundreds of people in the clearing, staring toward something he could not see. There was a fire. He could not see the flames, but he smelled the smoke. Then they were on the other side of the clearing, among the trees again. His father drove off the road and parked the car behind a great many other cars. He looked down at Jesse.

"You all right?" he asked.

"Yes sir," he said.

"Well, come on, then," his father said. He reached over and opened the door on his mother's side. His mother stepped out first. They followed her into the clearing. At first he was aware only of confusion, of his mother and father greeting and being greeted, himself being handled, hugged, and patted, and told how much he had grown. The wind blew the smoke from the fire across the clearing into his eyes and nose. He could not see over the backs of the people in front of him. The sounds of laughing and cursing and wrath—and something else—rolled in waves from the front of the mob to the back. Those in front expressed their delight at what they saw, and this delight rolled backward, wave upon wave, across the clearing, more acrid than the smoke. His father reached down suddenly and sat Jesse on his shoulders.

Now he saw the fire—of twigs and boxes, piled high; flames made pale orange and yellow and thin as a veil under the steadier light of the sun; grey-blue smoke rolled upward and poured over their heads. Beyond the shifting curtain of fire and smoke, he made out first only a length of gleaming chain, attached to a great limb of the tree; then he saw that this chain bound two black hands together at the wrist, dirty yellow palm facing dirty yellow palm. The smoke poured up; the hands dropped out of sight; a cry went up from the crowd. Then the hands slowly came into view again, pulled upward by the chain. This time he saw the kinky, sweating, bloody head—he had never before seen a head with so much hair on it, hair so black and so tangled that it seemed like another jungle. The head was hanging. He saw the forehead, flat and high, with a kind of arrow of hair in the center, like he had, like his father had; they called it a widow's peak; and the mangled eye brows, the wide nose, the closed eyes, and the glinting eye lashes and the hanging lips, all streaming with blood and sweat. His hands were straight above his head. All his weight pulled downward from his hands; and he was a big man, a bigger man than his father, and black as an African jungle Cat, and naked. Jesse pulled upward; his father's hands held him firmly by the ankles. He wanted to say something, he did not know what, but nothing he said could have been heard, for now the crowd roared again as a man stepped forward and put more wood on the fire. The flames leapt up. He thought he heard the hanging man scream, but he was not sure. Sweat was pouring from the hair in his armpits, poured down his sides, over his chest, into his navel and his groin. He was lowered again; he was raised again. Now Jesse knew that he heard him scream. The head went back, the mouth wide open, blood bubbling from the mouth; the veins of the neck jumped out; Jesse clung to his father's neck in terror as the cry rolled over the crowd. The cry of all the people rose to answer the dying man's cry. He wanted death to come quickly. They wanted to make death wait: and it was they who held death, now, on a leash which they lengthened little by little. *What did he do?* Jesse wondered. *What did the man do? What did he do?*—but he could not ask his father. He was seated on his father's shoulders, but his father was far away. There were two older men, friends of his father's, raising and lowering the chain; everyone, indiscriminately, seemed to be responsible for the fire. There was no hair left on the nigger's privates, and the eyes, now, were wide open, as white as the eyes of a clown or a doll. The smoke now carried a terrible odor across the clearing, the odor of something burning which was both sweet and rotten.

He turned his head a little and saw the field of faces. He watched his mother's face. Her eyes were very bright, her mouth was open: she was more beautiful than he had ever seen her, and more strange. He began to feel a joy he had never felt before. He watched the hanging, gleaming body, the most beautiful and terrible object he had ever seen till then. One of his father's friends reached up and in his hands he held a knife: and Jesse wished that he had been that man. It was a long, bright knife and the sun seemed to catch it, to play with it, to caress it—it was brighter than the fire. And a wave of laughter swept the crowd. Jesse felt his father's hands on his ankles slip and tighten. The man with the knife walked toward the crowd, smiling slightly; as though this were a signal, silence fell; he heard his mother cough. Then the man with the knife walked up to the hanging body. He turned and smiled again. Now there was a silence all over the field. The hanging head looked up. It seemed fully conscious now, as though the fire had burned out terror and pain. The man with the knife took the nigger's privates in his hand, one hand, still smiling, as though he were weighing them. In the cradle of the one white hand, the nigger's privates seemed as remote as meat being weighed in the scales; but seemed heavier, too, much heavier, and Jesse felt his scrotum tighten; and huge, huge, much bigger than his father's, flaccid, hairless, the largest thing he had ever seen till then, and the blackest. The white hand stretched them, cradled them, caressed them. Then the dying man's eyes looked straight into Jesse's eyes—it could not have been as long as a second, but it seemed longer than a year. Then Jesse screamed, and the crowd screamed as the knife flashed, first up, then down, cutting the dreadful thing away, and the blood came roaring down. Then the crowd rushed forward, tearing at the body with

their hands, with knives, with rocks, with stones, howling and cursing. Jesse's head, of its own weight, fell downward toward his father's
head. Someone stepped forward and drenched the body with kerosene.
Where the man had been, a great sheet of flame appeared. Jesse's
father lowered him to the ground.

"Well, I told you," said his father, "you wasn't never going to forget *this* picnic." His father's face was full of sweat, his eyes were very
peaceful. At that moment Jesse loved his father more than he had ever
loved him. He felt that his father had carried him through a mighty
test, had revealed to him a great secret which would be the key to his
life forever.

"I reckon," he said. "I reckon."

Jesse's father took him by the hand and, with his mother a little
behind them, talking and laughing with the other women, they
walked through the crowd, across the clearing. The black body was
on the ground, the chain which had held it was being rolled up by
one of his father's friends. Whatever the fire had left undone, the
hands and the knives and the stones of the people had accomplished.
The head was caved in, one eye was torn out, one ear was hanging.
But one had to look carefully to realize this, for it was, now, merely a
black charred object on the black, charred ground. He lay spread-
eagled with what had been a wound between what had been his legs.

"They going to leave him here, then?" Jesse whispered.

"Yeah," said his father, "they'll come and get him by and by. I
reckon we better get over there and get some of that food before it's
all gone."

"I reckon," he muttered now to himself, "I reckon." Grace stirred
and touched him on the thigh: the moonlight covered her like glory.
Something bubbled up in him, his nature again returned to him. He
thought of the boy in the cell; he thought of the man in the fire; he
thought of the knife and grabbed himself and stroked himself and a
terrible sound, something between a high laugh and a howl, came out
of him and dragged his sleeping wife up on one elbow. She stared at
him in a moonlight which had now grown cold as ice. He thought of
the morning and grabbed her, laughing and crying, crying and laughing, and he whispered, as he stroked her, as he took her, "Come on,

sugar, I'm going to do you like a nigger, just like a nigger, come on, sugar, and love me just like you'd love a nigger." He thought of the morning as he labored and she moaned, thought of morning as he labored harder than he ever had before, and before his labors had ended, he heard the first cock crow and the dogs begin to bark, and the sound of tires on the gravel road.

MRS. AULD

Frederick Douglass

Born a slave in Maryland, Frederick Douglass (1818–1895) became the leading American abolitionist orator, a best-selling author, and the editor of the North Star. *His accomplishments defy listing. In his* Narrative of the Life of Frederick Douglass *(1845), Douglass described his life as a slave, the reclamation of his humanity through physical resistance, and his lonely joy after escaping to the North. Eager to recruit white women to abolitionism, and himself active in the women's rights movement, Douglass offered the following classic account of the destructive impact of slavery on slaveholding women. In it, he describes his new mistress from the perspective of a slave just moved to Baltimore. Sophia Auld is "a woman of the kindest heart and the finest feelings" who must learn to suppress all that.*

My new mistress proved to be all she appeared when I first met her at the door,—a woman of the kindest heart and finest feelings. She had never had a slave under her control previously to myself, and prior to her marriage she had been dependent upon her own industry for a living. She was by trade a weaver; and by constant application to her business, she had been in a good degree preserved from the blighting and dehumanizing effects of slavery. I was utterly astonished at her goodness. I scarcely knew how to behave towards her. She was entirely unlike any other white woman I had ever seen. I could not approach her as I was accustomed to approach other white ladies. My early instruction was all out of place. The crouching servility, usually so acceptable a quality in a slave, did not answer when manifested toward her. Her favor was not gained by it; she seemed to be disturbed by it. She did not deem it impudent or unmannerly for a slave to look her in the face. The meanest slave was put fully at ease in her presence, and none left without feeling better for having seen her. Her face was made of heavenly smiles, and her voice of tranquil music.

But, alas! this kind heart had but a short time to remain such. The fatal poison of irresponsible power was already in her hands, and soon commenced its infernal work. That cheerful eye, under the influence of slavery, soon became red with rage; that voice, made all of sweet accord, changed to one of harsh and horrid discord; and that angelic face gave place to that of a demon.

Very soon after I went to live with Mr. and Mrs. Auld, she very kindly commenced to teach me the A, B, C. After I had learned this, she assisted me in learning to spell words of three or four letters. Just at this point of my progress, Mr. Auld found out what was going on, and at once forbade Mrs. Auld to instruct me further, telling her, among other things, that it was unlawful, as well as unsafe, to teach a slave to read. To use his own words, further, he said, "If you give a nigger an inch, he will take an ell. A nigger should know nothing but to obey his master—to do as he is told to do. Learning would *spoil* the best nigger in the world. Now," said he, "if you teach that nigger (speaking of myself) how to read, there would be no keeping him. It would forever unfit him to be a slave. He would at once become unmanageable, and of no value to his master. As to himself, it could do him no good, but a great deal of harm. It would make him discontented and unhappy." These words sank deep into my heart, stirred up sentiments within that lay slumbering, and called into existence an entirely new train of thought. It was a new and special revelation, explaining dark and mysterious things, with which my youthful understanding had struggled, but struggled in vain. I now understood what had been to me a most perplexing difficulty—to wit, the white man's power to enslave the black man. It was a grand achievement, and I prized it highly. From that moment, I understood the pathway from slavery to freedom. It was just what I wanted, and I got it at a time when I the least expected it. Whilst I was saddened by the thought of losing the aid of my kind mistress, I was gladdened by the invaluable instruction which, by the merest accident, I had gained from my master. Though conscious of the difficulty of learning without a teacher, I set out with high hope, and a fixed purpose, at whatever cost of trouble, to learn how to read. The very decided manner with which he spoke, and strove to impress his wife with the evil consequences of giving me instruction, served to convince me that he was deeply sensible of the truths he was uttering. It gave me the best assurance that I might rely with the utmost confidence on the results which, he said, would flow from teaching me to read. What he most dreaded, that I most desired. What he most loved, that I most hated. That which to him was a great evil, to be carefully shunned, was to me a great good, to be diligently sought; and the argument which he so warmly urged, against my learning to read, only served to inspire me with a desire and determination to learn. In learning to read, I owe almost as much to the bitter opposition of my master, as to the kindly aid of my mistress. I acknowledge the benefit of both.

I had resided but a short time in Baltimore before I observed a marked difference, in the treatment of slaves, from that which I had witnessed in the country. A city slave is almost a freeman, compared with a slave on the plantation. He is much better fed and clothed, and enjoys privileges altogether unknown to the slave on the plantation. There is a vestige of decency, a sense of shame, that does much to curb and check those outbreaks of atrocious cruelty so commonly enacted upon the plantation. He is a desperate slaveholder, who will shock the humanity of his non-slaveholding neighbors with the cries of his lacerated slave. Few are willing to incur the odium attaching to the reputation of being a cruel master; and above all things, they would not be known as not giving a slave enough to eat. Every city slaveholder is anxious to have it known of him, that he feeds his slaves well; and it is due to them to say, that most of them do give their slaves enough to eat. There are, however, some painful exceptions to this rule. Directly opposite to us, on Philpot Street, lived Mr. Thomas Hamilton. He owned two slaves. Their names were Henrietta and Mary. Henrietta was about twenty-two years of age, Mary was about fourteen; and of all the mangled and emaciated creatures I ever looked upon, these two were the most so. His heart must be harder than stone, that could look upon these unmoved. The head, neck, and shoulders of Mary were literally cut to pieces. I have frequently felt her head, and found it nearly covered with festering sores, caused by the lash of her cruel mistress. I do not know that her master ever whipped her, but I have been an eye-witness to the cruelty of Mrs. Hamilton. I used to be in Mr. Hamilton's house nearly every day. Mrs.

Hamilton used to sit in a large chair in the middle of the room, with a heavy cowskin always by her side, and scarce an hour passed during the day but was marked by the blood of one of these slaves. The girls seldom passed her without her saying, "Move faster, you *black gip!*" at the same time giving them a blow with the cowskin over the head or shoulders, often drawing the blood. She would then say, "Take that, you *black gip!*"—continuing, "If you don't move faster, I'll move you!" Added to the cruel lashings to which these slaves were subjected, they were kept nearly half-starved. They seldom knew what it was to eat a full meal. I have seen Mary contending with the pigs for the offal thrown into the street. So much was Mary kicked and cut to pieces, that she was oftener called *"pecked"* than by her name.

THE JEALOUS MISTRESS
Harriet Jacobs

Harriet Jacobs (c. 1813–1897), the author of the first major autobiography by a female former slave in the United States, was born in Edenton, North Carolina. After escaping to the North, she published Incidents in the Life of a Slave Girl *(1861), describing her harrowing captivity. Jacobs's portrayal of Mrs. Flint, and of "the jealous mistress" generally, acutely focused on questions of sexuality. Jacobs, like Frederick Douglass, makes clear that the suffering of slaveholding women was far from ennobling.*

I would ten thousand times rather that my children should be the half-starved paupers of Ireland than to be the most pampered among the slaves of America. I would rather drudge out my life on a cotton plantation, till the grave opened to give me rest, than to live with an unprincipled master and a jealous mistress. The felon's home in a penitentiary is preferable. He may repent, and turn from the error of his ways, and so find peace; but it is not so with a favorite slave. She is not allowed to have any pride of character. It is deemed a crime in her to wish to be virtuous.

Mrs. Flint possessed the key to her husband's character before I was born. She might have used this knowledge to counsel and to screen the young and the innocent among her slaves; but for them she had no sympathy. They were the objects of her constant suspicion and malevolence. She watched her husband with unceasing vigilance; but he was well practised in means to evade it. What he could not find opportunity to say in words he manifested in signs. He invented more than were ever thought of in a deaf and dumb asylum. I let them pass, as if I did not understand what he meant; and many were the curses and threats bestowed on me for my stupidity. One day he caught me teaching myself to write. He frowned, as if he was not well pleased; but I suppose he came to the conclusion that such an accomplishment might help to advance his favorite scheme. Before long, notes were often slipped into my hand. I would return them, saying, "I can't read

them, sir." "Can't you?" he replied; "then I must read them to you."
He always finished the reading by asking, "Do you understand?"
Sometimes he would complain of the heat of the tea room, and order
his supper to be placed on a small table in the piazza. He would seat
himself there with a well-satisfied smile, and tell me to stand by and
brush away the flies. He would eat very slowly, pausing between the
mouthfuls. These intervals were employed in describing the happiness
I was so foolishly throwing away, and in threatening me with the
penalty that finally awaited my stubborn disobedience. He boasted
much of the forbearance he had exercised towards me, and reminded
me that there was a limit to his patience. When I succeeded in avoid-
ing opportunities for him to talk to me at home, I was ordered to
come to his office, to do some errand. When there, I was obliged to
stand and listen to such language as he saw fit to address to me. Sometimes I so openly expressed my contempt for him that he would
become violently enraged, and I wondered why he did not strike me.
Circumstanced as he was, he probably thought it was better policy to
be forbearing. But the state of things grew worse and worse daily. In
desperation I told him that I must and would apply to my grandmother for protection. He threatened me with death, and worse than
death, if I made any complaint to her. Strange to say, I did not despair.
I was naturally of a buoyant disposition, and always I had a hope of
somehow getting out of his clutches. Like many a poor, simple slave
before me, I trusted that some threads of joy would yet be woven into
my dark destiny.

I had entered my sixteenth year, and every day it became more
apparent that my presence was intolerable to Mrs. Flint. Angry words
frequently passed between her and her husband. He had never punished me himself, and he would not allow any body else to punish
me. In that respect, she was never satisfied; but, in her angry moods
no terms were too vile for her to bestow upon me. Yet I, whom she
detested so bitterly, had far more pity for her than he had, whose duty
it was to make her life happy. I never wronged her, or wished to
wrong her; and one word of kindness from her would have brought
me to her feet.

After repeated quarrels between the doctor and his wife, he announced his intention to take his youngest daughter, then four years old, to sleep in his apartment. It was necessary that a servant should sleep in the same room, to be on hand if the child stirred. I was selected for that office, and informed for what purpose that arrangement had been made. By managing to keep within sight of people, as much as possible, during the day time, I had hitherto succeeded in eluding my master, though a razor was often held to my throat to force me to change this line of policy. At night I slept by the side of my great aunt, where I felt safe. He was too prudent to come into her room. She was an old woman, and had been in the family many years. Moreover, as a married man, and a professional man, he deemed it necessary to save appearances in some degree. But he resolved to remove the obstacle in the way of his scheme; and he thought he had planned it so that he should evade suspicion. He was well aware how much I prized my refuge by the side of my old aunt, and he determined to dispossess me of it. The first night the doctor had the little child in his room alone. The next morning, I was ordered to take my station as nurse the following night. A kind Providence interposed in my favor. During the day Mrs. Flint heard of this new arrangement, and a storm followed. I rejoiced to hear it rage.

After a while my mistress sent for me to come to her room. Her first question was, "Did you know you were to sleep in the doctor's room?"

"Yes, ma'am."

"Who told you?"

"My master."

"Will you answer truly all the questions I ask?"

"Yes, ma'am."

"Tell me, then, as you hope to be forgiven, are you innocent of what I have accused you?"

"I am."

She handed me a Bible, and said, "Lay your hand on your heart, kiss this holy book, and swear before God that you tell me the truth."

I took the oath she required, and I did it with a clear conscience.

"You have taken God's holy word to testify your innocence," said she. "If you have deceived me, beware! Now take this stool, sit down, look me directly in the face, and tell me all that has passed between your master and you."

I did as she ordered. As I went on with my account her color changed frequently, she wept, and sometimes groaned. She spoke in tones so sad, that I was touched by her grief. The tears came to my eyes; but I was soon convinced that her emotions arose from anger and wounded pride. She felt that her marriage vows were desecrated, her dignity insulted; but she had no compassion for the poor victim of her husband's perfidy. She pitied herself as a martyr; but she was incapable of feeling for the condition of shame and misery in which her unfortunate, helpless slave was placed.

Yet perhaps she had some touch of feeling for me; for when the conference was ended, she spoke kindly, and promised to protect me. I should have been much comforted by this assurance if I could have had confidence in it; but my experiences in slavery had filled me with distrust. She was not a very refined woman, and had not much control over her passions. I was an object of her jealousy, and, consequently, of her hatred; and I knew I could not expect kindness or confidence from her under the circumstances in which I was placed. I could not blame her. Slaveholders' wives feel as other women would under similar circumstances. The fire of her temper kindled from small sparks, and now the flame became so intense that the doctor was obliged to give up his intended arrangement.

I knew I had ignited the torch, and I expected to suffer for it afterwards; but I felt too thankful to my mistress for the timely aid she rendered me to care much about that. She now took me to sleep in a room adjoining her own. There I was an object of her especial care, though not of her especial comfort, for she spent many a sleepless night to watch over me. Sometimes I woke up, and found her bending over me. At other times she whispered in my ear, as though it was her husband who was speaking to me, and listened to hear what I would answer. If she startled me, on such occasions, she would glide stealthily away; and the next morning she would tell me I had been talking in my sleep, and ask who I was talking to. At last, I began to be fearful for my life. It had been often threatened; and you can imagine, better than I can describe, what an unpleasant sensation it must pro-

duce to wake up in the dead of night and find a jealous woman bending over you. Terrible as this experience was, I had fears that it would
give place to one more terrible.

My mistress grew weary of her vigils; they did not prove satisfac-
tory. She changed her tactics. She now tried the trick of accusing my
master of crime, in my presence, and gave my name as the author of
the accusation. To my utter astonishment, he replied, "I don't believe
it; but if she did acknowledge it, you tortured her into exposing me."
Tortured into exposing him! Truly, Satan had no difficulty in distinguishing the color of his soul! I understood his object in making this
false representation. It was to show me that I gained nothing by seeking the protection of my mistress; that the power was still all in his
own hands. I pitied Mrs. Flint. She was a second wife, many years the
junior of her husband; and the hoary-headed miscreant was enough
to try the patience of a wiser and better woman. She was completely
foiled, and knew not how to proceed. She would gladly have had me
flogged for my supposed false oath; but, as I have already stated, the
doctor never allowed any one to whip me. The old sinner was politic.
The application of the lash might have led to remarks that would have
exposed him in the eyes of his children and grandchildren. How often
did I rejoice that I lived in a town where all the inhabitants knew each
other! If I had been on a remote plantation, or lost among the multi-
tude of a crowded city, I should not be a living woman at this day.

The secrets of slavery are concealed like those of the Inquisition.
My master was, to my knowledge, the father of eleven slaves. But did
the mothers dare to tell who was the father of their children? Did the
other slaves dare to allude to it, except in whispers among themselves?
No, indeed! They knew too well the terrible consequences.

My grandmother could not avoid seeing things which excited her
suspicions. She was uneasy about me, and tried various ways to buy
me; but the never-changing answer was always repeated: "Linda does
not belong to *me*. She is my daughter's property, and I have no legal
right to sell her." The conscientious man! He was too scrupulous
to *sell* me; but he had no scruples whatever about committing a
much greater wrong against the helpless young girl placed under his
guardianship, as his daughter's property. Sometimes my persecutor

would ask me whether I would like to be sold. I told him I would rather be sold to any body than to lead such a life as I did. On such occasions he would assume the air of a very injured individual, and reproach me for my ingratitude. "Did I not take you into the house, and make you the companion of my own children?" he would say. "Have I ever treated you like a negro? I have never allowed you to be punished, not even to please your mistress. And this is the recompense I get, you ungrateful girl!" I answered that he had reasons of his own for screening me from punishment, and that the course he pursued made my mistress hate me and persecute me. If I wept, he would say, "Poor child! Don't cry! don't cry! I will make peace for you with your mistress. Only let me arrange matters in my own way. Poor, foolish girl! you don't know what is for your own good. I would cherish you. I would make a lady of you. Now go, and think of all I have promised you."

I did think of it.

Reader, I draw no imaginary pictures of southern homes. I am telling you the plain truth. Yet when victims make their escape from this wild beast of Slavery, northerners consent to act the part of bloodhounds, and hunt the poor fugitive back into his den, "full of dead men's bones, and all uncleanness." Nay, more, they are not only willing, but proud, to give their daughters in marriage to slaveholders. The poor girls have romantic notions of a sunny clime, and of the flowering vines that all the year round shade a happy home. To what disappointments are they destined! The young wife soon learns that the husband in whose hands she has placed her happiness pays no regard to his marriage vows. Children of every shade of complexion play with her own fair babies, and too well she knows that they are born unto him of his own household. Jealousy and hatred enter the flowery home, and it is ravaged of its loveliness.

WIMODAUGHSIS
Anna Julia Cooper

Anna Julia Cooper (1858?–1964) championed the rights of African-American women in the late nineteenth century, pioneering in Black feminist thought. Born a slave in North Carolina, Cooper received a master's degree from Oberlin College and, in her sixties, a doctorate in French from the University of Paris. A teacher and university administrator, Cooper helped to organize the National Conference of Colorado Women in 1895 and attended the first Pan-African Conference in 1900 in London. In 1892 Cooper published A Voice from the South by a Black Woman of the South, *a collection of essays which demonstrates her depth of insight into the social and political dynamics of her time. In addition to stunning observations about the complex intersections of race and gender in Black women's lives, Cooper offers sharp analyses of the motivations behind white women's actions in women's organizations. In the brief passages which follow, she alludes to a controversy over color bars in Wimodaughsis, a women's organization taking its name from the first letters of the words* wives, mothers, daughters, *and* sisters. *Cooper explains why those excluding African-American applicants for membership ought to be in a renamed organization acknowledging the centrality of whiteness to their identities as women.*

Pandora's box is opened in the ideal harmony of this modern Eden without an Adam when a colored lady, a teacher in one of our schools, applies for admission to its privileges and opportunities.

The Kentucky secretary, a lady zealous in good works and one who, I can't help imagining, belongs to that estimable class who daily thank the Lord that He made the earth that they may have the job of superintending its rotations, and who really would like to help "elevate" the colored people (in her own way of course and so long as they understand their places) is filled with grief and horror that any persons of Negro extraction should aspire to learn type-writing or languages or to enjoy any other advantages offered in the sacred halls of Wimodaughsis. Indeed, she had not calculated that there were any wives, mothers, daughters, and sisters, except white ones; and she is really convinced that *Whimodaughsis* would sound just as well, and then it need mean just *white mothers, daughters and sisters.* In fact, so far as there is anything in a name, nothing would be lost by omitting for the sake of euphony, from this unique mosaic, the letters that represent wives. *Whiwimodaughsis* might be a little startling, and on the whole wives would better yield to white; since clearly all women are not wives, while surely all wives are daughters. The daughters therefore could represent the wives and this immaculate assembly for propagating liberal and progressive ideas and disseminating a broad and humanizing culture might be spared the painful possibility of the sight of a black man coming in the future to escort from an evening class this solitary cream-colored applicant.

THE CASE STATED

Ida B. Wells-Barnett

Ida B. Wells-Barnett (1862–1931), the child of Mississippi slaves, attended Fisk University, where she began her career in journalism. At twenty-seven, she became editor and part owner of the Memphis Free Speech. *Her crusading articles tested whether such speech was possible in Memphis. After Wells exposed the fraudulence of charges against three Black businessmen lynched in the city in 1892, a mob destroyed the offices of the* Free Speech. *Wells could not remain in Memphis but continued her career at the* New York Age. *Her short studies of lynchings, especially* Southern Horrors *(1892) and* A Red Record *(1895), are so meticulous in journalistic detail that the force of Wells's historical analysis of lynchings and gender relations in the South can be overlooked. The initial pages of* A Red Record, *reprinted below, are perhaps her most extended treatment of the broad meaning of sexual violence and of white Southern males' claims to chivalry.*

The student of American sociology will find the year 1894 marked by a pronounced awakening of the public conscience to a system of anarchy and outlawry which had grown during a series of ten years to be so common, that scenes of unusual brutality failed to have any visible effect upon the humane sentiments of the people of our land.

Beginning with the emancipation of the Negro, the inevitable result of unbridled power exercised for two and a half centuries, by the white man over the Negro, began to show itself in acts of conscienceless outlawry. During the slave regime, the Southern white man owned the Negro body and soul. It was to his interest to dwarf the soul and preserve the body. Vested with unlimited power over his slave, to subject him to any and all kinds of physical punishment, the white man was still restrained from such punishment as tended to injure the slave by abating his physical powers and thereby reducing his financial worth. While slaves were scourged mercilessly, and in countless cases inhumanly treated in other respects, still the white owner rarely permitted his anger to go so far as to take a life, which would entail upon him a loss of several hundred dollars. The slave was rarely killed, he was too valuable; it was easier and quite as effective, for discipline or revenge, to sell him "Down South."

But Emancipation came and the vested interests of the white man in the Negro's body were lost. The white man had no right to scourge the emancipated Negro, still less has he a right to kill him. But the Southern white people had been educated so long in that school of practice, in which might makes right, that they disdained to draw strict lines of action in dealing with the Negro. In slave times the Negro was kept subservient and submissive by the frequency and severity of the scourging, but, with freedom, a new system of intimidation came into vogue; the Negro was not only whipped and scourged; he was killed.

Not all nor nearly all of the murders done by white men, during the past thirty years in the South, have come to light, but the statistics as gathered and preserved by white men, and which have not been questioned, show that during these years more than ten thousand Negroes have been killed in cold blood, without the formality of judicial trial and legal execution. And yet, as evidence of the absolute impunity with which the white man dares to kill a Negro, the same record shows that during all these years, and for all these murders only three white men have been tried, convicted, and executed. As no white man has been lynched for the murder of colored people, these three executions are the only instances of the death penalty being visited upon white men for murdering Negroes.

Naturally enough the commission of these crimes began to tell upon the public conscience, and the Southern white man, as a tribute to the nineteenth century civilization, was in a manner compelled to give excuses for his barbarism. His excuses have adapted themselves to the emergency, and are aptly outlined by that greatest of all Negroes, Frederick Douglass, in an article of recent date, in which he shows that there have been three distinct eras of Southern barbarism, to account for which three distinct excuses have been made.

The first excuse given to the civilized world for the murder of unoffending Negroes was the necessity of the white man to repress and stamp out alleged "race riots." For years immediately succeeding the war there was an appalling slaughter of colored people, and the wires usually conveyed to northern people and the world the intelligence, first, that an insurrection was being planned by Negroes, which, a few hours later, would prove to have been vigorously resisted by white men, and controlled with a resulting loss of several killed and wounded. It was always a remarkable feature in these insurrections and riots that only Negroes were killed during the rioting, and that all the white men escaped unharmed.

From 1865 to 1872, hundreds of colored men and women were mercilessly murdered and the almost invariable reason assigned was that they met their death by being alleged participants in an insurrection or riot. But this story at last wore itself out. No insurrection ever materialized; no Negro rioter was ever apprehended and proven guilty, and no dynamite ever recorded the black man's protest against oppression and wrong. It was too much to ask thoughtful people to believe this transparent story, and the southern white people at last made up their minds that some other excuse must be had.

Then came the second excuse, which had its birth during the turbulent times of reconstruction. By an amendment to the Constitution the Negro was given the right of franchise, and, theoretically at least, his ballot became his invaluable emblem of citizenship. In a government "of the people, for the people, and of the people," the Negro's vote became an important factor in all matters of state and national politics. But this did not last long. The southern white man would not consider that the Negro had any right which a white man was bound to respect, and the idea of a republican form of government in the southern states grew into general contempt. It was maintained that "This is a white man's government," and regardless of numbers the white man should rule. "No Negro domination" became the new legend on the sanguinary banner of the sunny South, and under it rode the Ku Klux Klan, the Regulators, and the lawless mobs, which for any cause chose to murder one man or a dozen as suited their purpose best. It was a long, gory campaign; the blood chills and the heart almost loses faith in Christianity when one thinks of Yazoo, Hamburg, Edgefield, Copiah, and the countless massacres of defenseless

Negroes, whose only crime was the attempt to exercise their right to vote.

But it was a bootless strife for colored people. The government which had made the Negro a citizen found itself unable to protect him. It gave him the right to vote, but denied him the protection which should have maintained that right. Scourged from his home; hunted through the swamps; hung by midnight raiders, and openly murdered in the light of day, the Negro clung to his right of franchise with a heroism which would have wrung admiration from the hearts of savages. He believed that in that small white ballot there was a subtle something which stood for manhood as well as citizenship, and thousands of brave black men went to their graves, exemplifying the one by dying for the other.

The white man's victory soon became complete by fraud, violence, intimidation and murder. The franchise vouchsafed to the Negro grew to be a "barren ideality," and regardless of numbers, the colored people found themselves voiceless in the councils of those whose duty it was to rule. With no longer the fear of "Negro Domination" before their eyes, the white man's second excuse became valueless. With the Southern governments all subverted and the Negro actually eliminated from all participation in state and national elections, there could be no longer an excuse for killing Negroes to prevent "Negro Domination."

Brutality still continued; Negroes were whipped, scourged, exiled, shot and hung whenever and wherever it pleased the white man so to treat them, and as the civilized world with increasing persistency held the white people of the South to account for its outlawry, the murderers invented the third excuse—that Negroes had to be killed to avenge their assaults upon women. There could be framed no possible excuse more harmful to the Negro and more unanswerable if true in its sufficiency for the white man.

Humanity abhors the assailant of womanhood, and this charge upon the Negro at once placed him beyond the pale of human sympathy. With such unanimity, earnestness and apparent candor was this charge made and reiterated that the world has accepted the story that

the Negro is a monster which the Southern white man has painted
him. And to-day, the Christian world feels, that while lynching is a
crime, and lawlessness and anarchy the certain precursors of a nation's
fall, it can not by word or deed, extend sympathy or help to a race of
outlaws, who might mistake their plea for justice and deem it an
excuse for their continued wrongs.

The Negro has suffered much and is willing to suffer more. He
recognizes that the wrongs of two centuries can not be righted in a
day, and he tries to bear his burden with patience for to-day and be
hopeful for to-morrow. But there comes a time when the veriest
worm will turn, and the Negro feels to-day that after all the work
he has done, all the sacrifices he has made, and all the suffering he
has endured, if he did not, now, defend his name and manhood from
this vile accusation, he would be unworthy even of the contempt of
mankind. It is to this charge he now feels he must make answer.

If the Southern people in defense of their lawlessness, would tell
the truth and admit that colored men and women are lynched for
almost any offense, from murder to a misdemeanor, there would not
now be the necessity for this defense. But when they intentionally,
maliciously and constantly belie the record and bolster up these false-
hoods by the words of legislators, preachers, governors and bishops,
then the Negro must give to the world his side of the awful story.

A word as to the charge itself. In considering the third reason
assigned by the Southern white people for the butchery of blacks, the
question must be asked, what the white man means when he charges
the black man with rape. Does he mean the crime which the statutes
of the civilized states describe as such? Not by any means. With
the Southern white man, any mesalliance existing between a white
woman and a colored man is a sufficient foundation for the charge of
rape. The Southern white man says that it is impossible for a voluntary alliance to exist between a white woman and a colored man, and
therefore, the fact of an alliance is a proof of force. In numerous
instances where colored men have been lynched on the charge of
rape, it was positively known at the time of lynching, and indisputably proven after the victim's death, that the relationship sustained
between the man and woman was voluntary and clandestine, and that

in no court of law could even the charge of assault have been success-fully maintained.

It was for the assertion of this fact, in the defense of her own race, that the writer hereof became an exile; her property destroyed and her return to her home forbidden under penalty of death, for writ-ing the following editorial which was printed in her paper, the Free Speech, in Memphis, Tenn., May 21, 1892:

"Eight Negroes lynched since last issue of the 'Free Speech' one at Little Rock, Ark., last Saturday morning where the citizens broke (?) into the penitentiary and got their man; three near Anniston, Ala., one near New Orleans; and three at Clarksville, Ga., the last three for killing a white man, and five on the same old racket—the new alarm about raping white women. The same programme of hanging, then shooting bullets into the lifeless bodies was carried out to the letter. Nobody in this section of the country believes the old threadbare lie that Negro men rape white women. If Southern white men are not careful, they will over-reach themselves and public sentiment will have a reaction; a conclusion will then be reached which will be very damaging to the moral reputation of their women."

But threats cannot suppress the truth, and while the Negro suffers the soul deformity, resultant from two and a half centuries of slavery, he is no more guilty of this vilest of all vile charges than the white man who would blacken his name.

During all the years of slavery, no such charge was ever made, not even during the dark days of the rebellion, when the white man, fol-lowing the fortunes of war went to do battle for the maintenance of slavery. While the master was away fighting to forge the fetters upon the slave, he left his wife and children with no protectors save the Negroes themselves. And yet during those years of trust and peril, no Negro proved recreant to his trust and no white man returned to a home that had been dispoiled.

Likewise during the period of alleged "insurrection," and alarm-ing "race riots," it never occurred to the white man, that his wife and children were in danger of assault. Nor in the Reconstruction era, when the hue and cry was against "Negro Domination," was there ever a thought that the domination would ever contaminate a fireside or strike to death the virtue of womanhood. It must appear strange indeed, to every thoughtful and candid man, that more than a quarter of a century elapsed before the Negro began to show signs of such infamous degeneration.

In his remarkable apology for lynching, Bishop Haygood, of Georgia, says: "No race, not the most savage, tolerates the rape of woman, but it may be said without reflection upon any other people that the Southern people are now and always have been most sensitive concerning the honor of their women—their mothers, wives, sisters and daughters." It is not the purpose of this defense to say one word against the white women of the South. Such need not be said, but it is their misfortune that the chivalrous white men of that section, in order to escape the deserved execration of the civilized world, should shield themselves by their cowardly and infamously false excuse, and call into question that very honor about which their distinguished priestly apologist claims they are most sensitive. To justify their own barbarism they assume a chivalry which they do not possess. True chivalry respects all womanhood, and no one who reads the record, as it is written in the faces of the million mulattoes in the South, will for a minute conceive that the southern white man had a very chivalrous regard for the honor due the women of his own race or respect for the womanhood which circumstances placed in his power. That chivalry which is "most sensitive concerning the honor of women" can hope for but little respect from the civilized world, when it confines itself entirely to the women who happen to be white. Virtue knows no color line, and the chivalry which depends upon complexion of skin and texture of hair can command no honest respect.

When emancipation came to the Negroes, there arose in the northern part of the United States an almost divine sentiment among the noblest, purest and best white women of the North, who felt called to a mission to educate and Christianize the millions of southern ex-slaves. From every nook and corner of the North, brave young white women answered that call and left their cultured homes, their happy associations and their lives of ease, and with heroic determination went to the South to carry light and truth to the benighted blacks. It was a heroism no less than that which calls for volunteers for

India, Africa and the Isles of the sea. To educate their unfortunate charges; to teach them the Christian virtues and to inspire in them the moral sentiments manifest in their own lives, these young women braved dangers whose record reads more like fiction than fact. They became social outlaws in the South. The peculiar sensitiveness of the southern white men for women, never shed its protecting influence about them. No friendly word from their own race cheered them in their work; no hospitable doors gave them the companionship like that from which they had come. No chivalrous white man doffed his hat in honor or respect. They were "Nigger teachers"—unpardonable offenders in the social ethics of the South, and were insulted, persecuted and ostracised, not by Negroes, but by the white manhood which boasts of its chivalry toward women.

And yet these northern women worked on, year after year, unselfishly, with a heroism which amounted almost to martyrdom. Threading their way through dense forests, working in schoolhouse, in the cabin and in the church, thrown at all times and in all places among the unfortunate and lowly Negroes, whom they had come to find and to serve, these northern women, thousands and thousands of them, have spent more than a quarter of a century in giving to the colored people their splendid lessons for home and heart and soul. Without protection, save that which innocence gives to every good woman, they went about their work, fearing no assault and suffering none. Their chivalrous protectors were hundreds of miles away in their northern homes, and yet they never feared any "great dark faced mobs," they dared night or day to "go beyond their own roof trees." They never complained of assaults, and no mob was ever called into existence to avenge crimes against them. Before the world adjudges the Negro a moral monster, a vicious assailant of womanhood and a menace to the sacred precincts of home, the colored people ask the consideration of the silent record of gratitude, respect, protection and devotion of the millions of the race in the South, to the thousands of northern white women who have served as teachers and missionaries since the war.

The Negro may not have known what chivalry was, but he knew enough to preserve inviolate the womanhood of the South which was entrusted to his hands during the war. The finer sensibilities of his soul may have been crushed out by years of slavery, but his heart was full of gratitude to the white women of the North, who blessed his home and inspired his soul in all these years of freedom. Faithful to his trust in both of these instances, he should now have the impartial ear of the civilized world, when he dares to speak for himself as against the infamy wherewith he stands charged.

It is his regret, that, in his own defense, he must disclose to the world that degree of dehumanizing brutality which fixes upon America the blot of a national crime. Whatever faults and failings other nations may have in their dealings with their own subjects or with other people, no other civilized nation stands condemned before the world with a series of crimes so peculiarly national. It becomes a painful duty of the Negro to reproduce a record which shows that a large portion of the American people avow anarchy, condone murder and defy the contempt of civilization.

ON WHITE WOMEN WORKERS
Richard Wright

The Mississippi-born genius Richard Wright (1908–1960) famously explored the intersections of race, violence, and gender in such works as Native Son *(1940) and* Uncle Tom's Children *(1938). He also wrote, in* Savage Holiday *(1954), one of the finest African-American novels to focus exclusively on white characters. In* Black Boy *(1945), Wright drew on personal experiences extensively. The combination of compassion and fear, which shapes Wright's observations of white working women in the lines below from* Black Boy, *runs through much African-American writing on white females.*

One summer morning a white girl came late to work and rushed into the pantry where I was busy. She went into the women's room and changed her clothes; I heard the door open and a second later I was surprised to hear her voice:

"Richard, quick! Tie my apron!"

She was standing with her back to me and the strings of her apron dangled loose. There was a moment of indecision on my part, then I took the two loose strings and carried them around her body and brought them again to her back and tied them in a clumsy knot.

"Thanks a million," she said, grasping my hand for a split second, and was gone.

I continued my work, filled with all the possible meanings that that tiny, simple, human event could have meant to any Negro in the South where I had spent most of my hungry days.

I did not feel any admiration for the girls, nor any hate. My attitude was one of abiding and friendly wonder. For the most part I was silent with them, though I knew that I had a firmer grasp of life than most of them. As I worked I listened to their talk and perceived its puzzled, wandering, superficial fumbling with the problems and facts of life. There were many things they wondered about that I could have explained to them, but I never dared.

During my lunch hour, which I spent on a bench in a near-by park, the waitresses would come and sit beside me, talking at random, laughing, joking, smoking cigarettes. I learned about their tawdry dreams, their simple hopes, their home lives, their fear of feeling anything deeply, their sex problems, their husbands. They were an eager, restless, talkative, ignorant bunch, but casually kind and impersonal for all that. They knew nothing of hate and fear, and strove instinctively to avoid all passion.

I often wondered what they were trying to get out of life, but I never stumbled upon a clue, and I doubt if they themselves had any notion. They lived on the surface of their days; their smiles were surface smiles, and their tears were surface tears. Negroes lived a truer and deeper life than they, but I wished that Negroes, too, could live as thoughtlessly, serenely as they. The girls never talked of their feelings; none of them possessed the insight or the emotional equipment to understand themselves or others. How far apart in culture we stood! All my life I had done nothing but feel and cultivate my feelings; all their lives they had done nothing but strive for petty goals, the trivial material prizes of American life. We shared a common tongue, but my language was a different language from theirs.

It was in the psychological distance that separated the races that the deepest meaning of the problem of the Negro lay for me. For these poor, ignorant white girls to have understood my life would have meant nothing short of a vast revolution in theirs. And I was convinced that what they needed to make them complete and grown-up in their living was the inclusion in their personalities of a knowledge of lives such as I lived and suffered containedly.

HEALTH CARD

Alice Childress

Born into poverty in Charleston, South Carolina, Alice Childress (1920–1994) attended Fisk University. Long associated with the American Negro Theatre in Harlem, where she acted, performed, and directed, Childress also achieved stature as a playwright and as the author of the acclaimed 1973 novel A Hero Ain't Nothin' but a Sandwich. *Her fierce and funny* Like One of the Family *(1956) consists of stories recounted by a domestic worker to her friend Marge. Often, as in the selection below, Marge hears about the presumptions and the foibles of white employers, especially the mistress.*

Well, Marge, I started an extra job today. . . . Just wait, girl. Don't laugh yet. Just wait till I tell you. . . . The woman seems real nice. . . . Well, you know what I mean. . . . She was pretty nice, anyway. Shows me this and shows me that, but she was real cautious about loadin' on too much work the first morning. And she stopped short when she caught the light in my eye.

Comes the afternoon, I was busy waxin' woodwork when I notice her hoverin' over me kind of timid-like. She passed me once and smiled and then she turned and blushed a little. I put down the wax can and gave her an inquirin' look. The lady takes a deep breath and comes up with, "Do you live in Harlem, Mildred?"

Now you know I expected somethin' more than that after all the hesitatin'. I had already given her my address so I didn't quite get the idea behind the question. "Yes, Mrs. Jones," I answered, "that is where I live."

Well, she backed away and retired to the living room and I could hear her and the husband just a-buzzin'. A little later on I was in the kitchen washin' glasses. I looks up and there she was in the doorway, lookin' kind of strained around the gills. First she stuttered and then she stammered and after beatin' all around the bush she comes out with, "Do you have a health card, Mildred?"

That let the cat out of the bag. I thought real fast. Honey, my brain was runnin' on wheels. "Yes, Mrs. Jones," I says, "I have a health card." Now Marge, this is a lie. I do not have a health card. "I'll bring it tomorrow," I add real sweet-like.

She beams like a chromium platter and all you could see above her taffeta house coat is smile. "Mildred," she said, "I don't mean any offense, but one must be careful, mustn't one?"

Well, all she got from me was solid agreement. "Sure, I said, "indeed *one* must, and I am glad you are so understandin', 'cause I was just worryin' and studyin' on how I was goin' to ask you for yours, and of course you'll let me see one from your husband and one for each of the three children."

By that time she was the same color as the housecoat, which is green, but I continue on: "Since I have to handle laundry and make beds, you know . . ." She stops me right there and after excusin' herself she scurries from the room and has another conference with hubby.

Inside fifteen minutes she was back. "Mildred, you don't have to bring a health card. I am sure it will be all right."

I looked up real casual kind-of and said, "On second thought, you folks look real clean, too, so . . ." And then she smiled and I smiled and then she smiled again. . . . Oh, stop laughin' so loud, Marge, everybody on this bus is starin'.

WHITE MEN AS PERFORMERS IN THE LYNCHING RITUAL

Trudier Harris

Trudier Harris (1948–) is a professor of English at the University of North Carolina. Harris's From Mammies to Militants *(1982) examines the portrayals of a noteworthy group of experts on whiteness, domestic servants, in African-American literature. In the section of* Exorcising Blackness: Historical and Literary Lynching and Burning Rituals *(1984) reprinted below, Harris continues a rich African-American tradition, stretching from Harriet Jacobs to Calvin Hernton, of African-American analysis of white masculinity.*

The history of lynchings and burnings in this country is the history of racial control by a specific form of violence. Its effects were as psychologically pervasive as were the methods of intimidation which Gladys-Marie Fry discusses in *Nightriders in Black Folk History*. Fry explores how, under the cover of sheets and darkness, white men in the South used forms of intimidation ranging from beatings to lynchings in order to keep Blacks contained politically and socially during the years of Reconstruction. Mysterious and ghostly in their appearances before their victims, these white men conveyed to Blacks that there was always someone watching over their shoulders ready to punish them for the slightest offense or the least deviation from acceptable lines of action. Certain patterns of behavior, made into rituals by habit and custom, were outlined to black people by whites, and when one black individual dared to violate the restrictions, he or she was used as an example to reiterate to the entire race that the group would continually be held responsible for the actions of the individual. Thus an accusation of rape could lead not only to the accused black man being lynched and burned, but to the burning of black homes and the whipping or lynching of other black individuals as well.

The white male's function, ostensibly, was to protect his home and especially the white woman who was the center of it. That immediate reason for punishing black men when they came into questionable contact with white women had as its basis the larger reason informing almost all black and white relationships in this country: the white man's craving for power and mastery as indications of his ultimate superiority not only in assigning a place to his women, but especially in keeping black people, particularly black men, in the place he had assigned for them. The notion that the white man was really trying to prevent "mongrelization" of the white race is just that—a notion. No such concern for racial purity defined his actions with black women; consequently, his objections to miscegenation were designed to control the behavior of black males and white females without interfering with his own sexual preferences. No one stopped to consider that, during the years of the Civil War, when white men left their wives, daughters, and homes in the hands of black men, not a single instance of rape was reported. The issue, then, really boils down to one between white men and black men and the mythic conception the former have of the latter.

James Baldwin has long argued that the prevailing metaphor for understanding the white man's need to suppress the black man is that attached to sexual prowess. White men have originated and passed along to their women the myth of the black man's unusual ability in sexual intercourse. So long has the myth been a part of his culture and his psyche that the white man can no longer separate reality from the larger-than-life beliefs that his ancestors created. In his modern manifestation, then, the white man becomes a victim of his culture's imagination. Unlike any other victim of beliefs, however, he is the one in the American context who has most power to respond to his beliefs, whether they are real or not. When he acts to save his woman from the mad, rampaging, overly endowed black man, at one level he believes he is acting in the best interest of all. He sees himself as savior, father, keeper of the purity of his race. In this capacity, he must show his women that there is nothing to fear by capturing the source of that fear, then torturing and killing it. Thus, the white man attains kingly status by determining what is wrong with his society, ferreting it out, and reestablishing the order which was the norm before the disturbance.

At a deeper level, he is acting out his fear of sexual competition from the black man. By maintaining that sexual contact between black males and white females is taboo, he eliminates that mythic phallic symbol, which he himself has created, from competition with himself; for there is always the realistic possibility that if black men are so favorably endowed, white women may prefer them as sexual partners. To prevent that, the white man tells his women that coupling with a black man is tantamount to coupling with an ape or some other subhuman species. Despite the insistence on black subhumanity, however, the myth of black sexual superiority represents a potential competition that, in the folk imagination, is always detrimental to the white man. The stereotype about black male sexuality has proved so powerful that it has found its way into many black folktales where, instead of being denied, it is turned into a positive trait at the expense of the white male characters who appear in such folk narratives. Consider, for example, the following black folktale in which the length of the sexual organ is the key to freedom:

> Three men were sent to court: a white, a Negro and a Mexican. They got to court and the judge said, "If you have fifteen inches of length between you, I'll let you go." The judge called for the bailiff to measure the penises. So he measured the Negro's and it was seven and one-half inches long. Then he measured the Mexican's and it was five and one-half inches long. Next he measured the white man's and it was two inches long. That was fifteen inches. Therefore they were set free. When they got outside the court, they all started laughing and bragging. The Negro said, "You'd better be glad mine was seven and a half inches." The Mexican said, "You'd better be glad mine was five and a half inches." The white man looked at them and said, "Both of you better be glad that I was on hard."

The folk imagination turns the stereotype of the over-endowed black male into a positive thing and makes the white man's underendowment the butt of the joke. The exaggeration in the tale, which makes the white man the biggest braggart, serves to underscore how pathetically he has been slighted by nature. Through their humor, black folk have been able to use the stereotype of the black man's sexuality to their own advantage and to show that, as far as black men and white men are concerned, there will always be some kind of sexual measurement going on. By understanding how he is viewed in that larger white world, the black man is better prepared to deal with it. Thus the tale not only illustrates the necessity within the black folk community for understanding more about the oppressor than the oppressor understands about Blacks, but it also shows that that bestial quality so often attached to black male sexuality is made into a valuable asset for the white man as well as for the other characters in the tale.

As long as the potential sexual competition between black males and white males was suppressed historically, there was no need for any open jealousy on the part of the white man. The nature of the hunt and the kill, however, suggests that there was still a major factor of jealousy operative in the (sexual) power relationship between black males and white males. In simultaneously perpetuating and attempting to destroy the myth of black male sexuality, the white men involved in the lynchings and burnings spent an inordinate amount of time examining the genitals of the black men whom they were about to kill. Even as they castrated the black men, there was a suggestion of fondling, of envious caress. The many emotions involved at that moment perhaps led the white men to slash even more violently at what could not be theirs, but which, at some level, they very much desired (without the apish connotations, of course).

Many scholars have recognized that the inclusion of castration in the atrocities committed against black men by white men sprang from envy and sexual competition between them. Daryl Dance is one cultural analyst who refers to the "ritualistic castration" of black men for "familiarity" with white women, and who asserts that "the very nature of the lynch mob's punishment of Blacks—the sexual mutilation of the victim—suggests the white man's efforts to wrest from the Black man that symbol of manhood (that testament of superiority) which he so fears."

A desire to harness the finest qualities in one's enemies has long been recognized as a trait in man. For some warriors, eating the hearts of their most challenging enemies became a literal way of trying to transfer some of the opponent's courage to themselves. For white males involved in the lynchings and burnings of black males, there is a symbolic transfer of sexual power at the point of the executions. The black man is stripped of his prowess, but the very act of stripping brings symbolic power to the white man. His actions suggest that, subconsciously, he craves the very thing he is forced to destroy. Yet he destroys it as an indication of the political (sexual) power he has and takes it unto himself in the form of souvenirs as an indication of the kind of power he would like. In some historical accounts, the lynchers were reputed to have divided pieces of the black man's genitals among themselves. Again, James Baldwin is especially good in illustrating how sexual and political power are linked in lynchings.

The details involved in the process of stripping the black male of his sexuality suggest that the group of whites who usually attended such gatherings engaged in a communal orgiastic climax which made the sexual nature of the ritual explicit. There was initially tension involved in the pursuit of the assumed sexual offender; often the homes of other Blacks were rifled and general destruction preceded the capture of the black man. Tension increased in getting the offender from the place of capture to the place of execution, a process which might involve finding a suitable tree for the lynching or a territory large enough to accommodate all those wishing to view the lynching. Tension continued to mount as various members of the crowd gathered the implements necessary to carry out the ritualized punishment—rope, wood, tar and feathers if desired. The height of the tension was reached when the rope was actually around the offender's neck, and when the fire had been started. The climactic release began with the crackling of fire against flesh, with the gathering of souvenirs, and with the cries of the victim; it concluded in the yells of the crowd when they knew the victim was dead, yells which gave way to the silence of complete (sexual) purgation, the ultimate release from all tension.

From one perspective, then, there is an ironic reversal in that there is a communal rape of the black man by the crowd which executes him. They violate him by exposing the most private parts of his body and by forcing him, finally, into ultimate submission to them. Comparable to sexual snuff films, in which the victims participate against their wills, or without knowing what the end of the film will be, and provide pleasure without intending to do so, the lynched black man becomes a source of sexual pleasure to those who kill him. As Lillian Smith, a Southern white woman writing about the social and sexual mores of the South points out, "the lynched Negro becomes *not an object that must die* but a receptacle for every man's dammed-up hate, and a receptacle for every man's forbidden sex feelings." Killing the black man, therefore, provides a peculiar kind of satisfaction.

His death also enables white males to act out a fear of castration even as they are in the process of castrating the black man. Perhaps the worst fear any man can have is the fear that someone will cut off his penis; the white man, heir to that fear just as the black man is, designs as the peculiar punishment for black men that which all males fear most. His action simultaneously shows his kinship to the black man and denies the connection. He does to the black man what, in his worse nightmares, he perhaps imagines other adversaries doing to him; before he becomes victim, he victimizes.

Keep in mind, too, that it is the white man's tradition to call the black man *"boy."* If the black man is indeed a boy, then he can be easily controlled in everyday affairs. Calling him a boy suggests, as well, the strange lens through which the white man must view the black man sexually. "Boy," an effort at controlling language and thereby controlling the reality the language is designed to reflect, wipes out the symbolic, sexual implications of the black man as Man. So when the "boys" step out of their place by accosting white women or being accused of accosting them, the "men" must punish them accordingly.

FROM *BAD FAITH AND ANTIBLACK RACISM*

Lewis Gordon

Lewis Gordon (1962–) was educated in New York City public schools and, at the graduate level, at Yale University. He teaches philosophy at Brown University. Singularly successful at arguing the most difficult points and at reaching out toward a popular audience, Gordon has published Fanon and the Crisis of European Man *(1995) and* Bad Faith and Antiblack Racism *(1995), a study of the application of the work of Jean-Paul Sartre to the study of race in the United States. The highly concentrated insights in the passages reprinted here from* Bad Faith and Antiblack Racism *resonate with particular Sartrean concepts but also offer accessible and fresh rethinking of the place of white women in a racist order.*

Hence the white woman should not be regarded as the jewel of the antiblack racist. For hidden in her whiteness—like the secret blackness of milk, the secret abundance of blackness, the fertility that so outrages Manichaeism with its propensity to split apart and weaken the Light—is the antiblack racist's suspicion of her blackness. She stands as a white blackness, as a living contradiction of white supremacy. Out of her comes every white, placing a question mark on the notion of the purity of whiteness in the flesh. Unlike the black woman, out of whom only black children can be born, she can bear *both* white and black children. Because of this, the white woman ultimately stands on the same ontological level as slime in an antiblack world. She is regarded as a frightening substance that simultaneously attracts and repels.

Comparing consciousness to water, Sartre writes,

> Slime is the agony of water. It presents itself as a phenomenon in process of becoming; it does not have the permanence within change that water has but on the contrary represents an accomplished break in a change of state. This fixed instability

in the slimy discourages possession. . . . The slimy flees with a heavy flight which has the same relation to water as the unwieldy earthbound flight of the chicken as to that of the hawk. Even this flight can not be possessed because it denies itself as flight. It is already almost a solid permanence. Nothing testifies more clearly to its ambiguous character as a "substance in between two states" than the slowness with which the slimy melts into itself.

Being linked to the slimy in an antiblack world and thereby being able to stand as a "substance between two states" situates the white woman as an attracting being—like the simultaneous stickiness and slipperiness of slime—whose "nature" stands below the psychic and above nature:

> What comes back to us then as an objective quality [in our contact with slime] is a new *nature* which is neither material (and physical) nor psychic, but which transcends the opposition of the psychic and the physical, by revealing itself to us as the ontological expression of the entire world; that is, which offers itself as a rubric for classifying all the "thises" in the world, so that we have to deal with the material organizations or transcended transcendence. This means that the apprehension of the slimy as such has, by the same stroke, created for the in-itself of the world a particular mode of giving itself.

The entire web of legal structures built around the protection of the white woman amid the simultaneous deprecation and violation of her by "men" in the antiblack world is built upon her displacement. She both attracts and nauseates the antiblack with the "obscenity," under his gaze, of being a white hole. The antiblack glorifies the white woman because he distrusts her; he entombs her in an edifice of serious value so as to hide, even from herself, her propensity to make choices.

MADONNA: PLANTATION
MISTRESS OR SOUL SISTER

bell hooks

The idea of studying the popularity of Madonna has been grist for the mills of many critics of trends in scholarship on American culture. No writer has more precisely described what is at stake in such studies than bell hooks (see page 38). In her "Power to the Pussy" from Outlaw Culture *(1994) and in the essay reprinted below from* Black Looks *(1992), hooks locates Madonna's "transgressions" within limits firmly established by homophobia, sexism, and racism.*

Subversion is contextual, historical, and above all social. No matter how exciting the "destabilizing" potential of texts, bodily or otherwise, whether those texts are subversive or recuperative or both or neither cannot be determined by abstraction from actual social practice.

SUSAN BORDO

White women "stars" like Madonna, Sandra Bernhard, and many others publicly name their interest in, and appropriation of, black culture as yet another sign of their radical chic. Intimacy with that "nasty" blackness good white girls stay away from is what they seek. To white and other non-black consumers, this gives them a special flavor, an added spice. After all it is a very recent historical phenomenon for any white girl to be able to get some mileage out of flaunting her fascination and envy of blackness. The thing about envy is that it is always ready to destroy, erase, take-over, and consume the desired object. That's exactly what Madonna attempts to do when she appropriates and commodifies aspects of black culture. Needless to say this kind of fascination is a threat. It endangers. Perhaps that is why so many of the grown black women I spoke with about Madonna had no interest in her as a cultural icon and said things like, "The bitch can't even sing." It was only among young black females that I could find die-hard Madonna fans. Though I often admire and, yes at times, even envy Madonna because she has created a cultural space where she can invent and reinvent herself and receive public affirmation and material reward, I do not consider myself a Madonna fan.

Once I read an interview with Madonna where she talked about her envy of black culture, where she stated that she wanted to be black as a child. It is a sign of white privilege to be able to "see" blackness and black culture from a standpoint where only the rich culture of opposition black people have created in resistance marks and defines us. Such a perspective enables one to ignore white supremacist domination and the hurt it inflicts *via* oppression, exploitation, and everyday wounds and pains. White folks who do not see black pain never really understand the complexity of black pleasure. And it is no wonder then that when they attempt to imitate the joy in living which they see as the "essence" of soul and blackness, their cultural productions may have an air of sham and falseness that may titillate and even move white audiences yet leave many black folks cold.

Needless to say, if Madonna had to depend on masses of black women to maintain her status as cultural icon she would have been dethroned some time ago. Many of the black women I spoke with expressed intense disgust and hatred of Madonna. Most did not respond to my cautious attempts to suggest that underlying those negative feelings might lurk feelings of envy, and dare I say it, desire. No black woman I talked to declared that she wanted to "be Madonna." Yet we have only to look at the number of black women entertainers/stars (Tina Turner, Aretha Franklin, Donna Summer, Vanessa Williams, Yo-Yo, etc.) who gain greater cross-over recognition when they demonstrate that, like Madonna, they too, have a healthy dose of "blonde ambition." Clearly their careers have been influenced by Madonna's choices and strategies.

For masses of black women, the political reality that underlies Madonna's and our recognition that this is a society where "blondes" not only "have more fun" but where they are more likely to succeed in any endeavor is white supremacy and racism. We cannot see Madonna's change in hair color as being merely a question of aesthetic choice. I agree with Julie Burchill in her critical work *Girls on Film,* when she reminds us: "What does it say about racial purity that the best blondes have all been brunettes (Harlow, Monroe, Bardot)? I think it says that we are not as white as we think. I think it says that Pure is a Bore." I also know that it is the expressed desire of the non-blonde Other for those characteristics that are seen as the quintessential markers of racial aesthetic superiority that perpetuate and uphold white supremacy. In this sense Madonna has much in common with the masses of black women who suffer from internalized racism and are forever terrorized by a standard of beauty they feel they can never truly embody.

Like many black women who have stood outside the culture's fascination with the blonde beauty and who have only been able to reach it through imitation and artifice, Madonna often recalls that she was a working-class white-girl who saw herself as ugly, as outside the mainstream beauty standard. And indeed what some of us like about her is the way she deconstructs the myth of "natural" white girl beauty by exposing the extent to which it can be and is usually artificially constructed and maintained. She mocks the conventional racist defined beauty ideal even as she rigorously strives to embody it. Given her obsession with exposing the reality that the ideal female beauty in this society can be attained by artifice and social construction it should come as no surprise that many of her fans are gay men, and that the majority of non-white men, particularly black men, are among that group. Jennie Livingston's film *Paris Is Burning* suggests that many black gay men, especially queens/divas, are as equally driven as Madonna by "blonde ambition." Madonna never lets her audience forget that whatever "look" she acquires is attained by hard work—"it ain't natural." And as Burchill comments in her chapter "Homosexual Girls":

> I have a friend who drives a cab and looks like a Marlboro Man but at night is the second best Jean Harlow I have ever seen. He summed up the kind of film star he adores, brutally and brilliantly, when he said, "I like actresses who look as if they've spent hours putting themselves together—and even then they don't look right."

Certainly no one, not even die-hard Madonna fans, ever insists that her beauty is not attained by skillful artifice. And indeed, a major point of the documentary film *Truth or Dare: In Bed With Madonna* was to demonstrate the amount of work that goes into the construction of her image. Yet when the chips are down, the image Madonna most exploits is that of the quintessential "white girl." To maintain that image she must always position herself as an outsider in relation to black culture. It is that position of outsider that enables her to colonize and appropriate black experience for her own opportunistic ends even as she attempts to mask her acts of racist aggression as affirmation. And no other group sees that as clearly as black females in this society. For we have always known that the socially constructed image of innocent white womanhood relies on the continued production of the racist/sexist sexual myth that black women are not innocent and never can be. Since we are coded always as "fallen" women in the racist cultural iconography we can never, as can Madonna, publicly "work" the image of ourselves as innocent female daring to be bad. Mainstream culture always reads the black female body as sign of sexual experience. In part, many black women who are disgusted by Madonna's flaunting of sexual experience are enraged because the very image of sexual agency that she is able to project and affirm with material gain has been the stick this society has used to justify its continued beating and assault on the black female body. The vast majority of black women in the United States, more concerned with projecting images of respectability than with the idea of female sexual agency and transgression, do not often feel we have the "freedom" to act in rebellious ways in regards to sexuality without being punished. We have only to contrast the life story of Tina Turner with that of Madonna to see the different connotations "wild" sexual agency has when it is asserted by a black female. Being represented publicly as an active sexual being has only recently enabled Turner to gain control over her life and career. For years the public image of aggressive sexual agency Turner projected belied the degree to which she was sexually abused and exploited privately. She was also materially exploited. Madonna's career could not be all that it is if there were no Tina

Turner and yet, unlike her cohort Sandra Bernhard, Madonna never articulates the cultural debt she owes black females.

In her most recent appropriations of blackness, Madonna almost always imitates phallic black masculinity. Although I read many articles which talked about her appropriating male codes, no critic seems to have noticed her emphasis on black male experience. In his *Playboy* profile, "Playgirl of the Western World," Michael Kelly describes Madonna's crotch grabbing as "an eloquent visual put-down of male phallic pride." He points out that she worked with choreographer Vince Paterson to perfect the gesture. Even though Kelly tells readers that Madonna was consciously imitating Michael Jackson, he does not contextualize his interpretation of the gesture to include this act of appropriation from black male culture. And in that specific context the groin grabbing gesture is an assertion of pride and phallic domination that usually takes place in an all male context. Madonna's imitation of this gesture could just as easily be read as an expression of envy.

Throughout much of her autobiographical interviews runs a thread of expressed desire to possess the power she perceives men have. Madonna may hate the phallus, but she longs to possess its power. She is always first and foremost in competition with men to see who has the biggest penis. She longs to assert phallic power, and like every other group in this white supremacist society, she clearly sees black men as embodying a quality of maleness that eludes white men. Hence, they are often the group of men she most seeks to imitate, taunting white males with her own version of "black masculinity." When it comes to entertainment rivals, Madonna clearly perceives black male stars like Prince and Michael Jackson to be the standard against which she must measure herself and that she ultimately hopes to transcend.

Fascinated yet envious of black style, Madonna appropriates black culture in ways that mock and undermine, making her presentation one that upstages. This is most evident in the video "Like a Prayer." Though I read numerous articles that discussed public outrage at this video, none focused on the issue of race. No article called attention to the fact that Madonna flaunts her sexual agency by suggesting that she is breaking the ties that bind her as a white girl to white patriarchy, and establishing ties with black men. She, however, and not black men, does the choosing. The message is directed at white men. It suggests that they only labeled black men rapists for fear that white girls would choose black partners over them. Cultural critics commenting on the video did not seem at all interested in exploring the reasons Madonna chooses a black cultural backdrop for this video, i.e., black church and religious experience. Clearly, it was this backdrop that added to the video's controversy.

In her commentary in the *Washington Post,* "Madonna: Yuppie Goddess," Brooke Masters writes: "Most descriptions of the controversial video focus on its Catholic imagery: Madonna kisses a black saint, and develops Christ-like markings on her hands. However, the video is also a feminist fairy tale. Sleeping Beauty and Snow White waited for their princes to come along, Madonna finds her own man and wakes him up." Notice that this writer completely overlooks the issue of race and gender. That Madonna's chosen prince was a black man is in part what made the representation potentially shocking and provocative to a white supremacist audience. Yet her attempt to exploit and transgress traditional racial taboos was rarely commented on. Instead critics concentrated on whether or not she was violating taboos regarding religion and representation.

In the United States, Catholicism is most often seen as a religion that has little or no black followers and Madonna's video certainly perpetuates this stereotype with its juxtaposition of images of black non-Catholic representations with the image of the black saint. Given the importance of religious experience and liberation theology in black life, Madonna's use of this imagery seemed particularly offensive. For she made black characters act in complicity with her as she aggressively flaunted her critique of Catholic manners, her attack on organized religion. Yet, no black voices that I know of came forward in print calling attention to the fact that the realm of the sacred that is mocked in this film is black religious experience, or that this appropriative "use" of that experience was offensive to many black folk. Looking at the video with a group of students in my class on the pol-

itics of sexuality where we critically analyze the way race and representations of blackness are used to sell products, we discussed the way
in which black people in the video are caricatures reflecting stereotypes. They appear grotesque. The only role black females have in this
video is to catch (i.e., rescue) the "angelic" Madonna when she is
"falling." This is just a contemporary casting of the black female as
Mammy. Made to serve as supportive backdrop for Madonna's drama,
black characters in *Like a Prayer* remind one of those early Hollywood
depictions of singing black slaves in the great plantation movies or
those Shirley Temple films where Bojangles was trotted out to dance
with Miss Shirley and spice up her act. Audiences were not supposed
to be enamored of Bojangles, they were supposed to see just what a
special little old white girl Shirley really was. In her own way Madonna is a modern day Shirley Temple. Certainly her expressed affin-
ity with black culture enhances her value.

Eager to see the documentary *Truth or Dare* because it promised to
focus on Madonna's transgressive sexual persona, which I find interesting, I was angered by her visual representation of her domination
over not white men (certainly not over Warren Beatty or Alek
Keshishian), but people of color and white working-class women. I
was too angered by this to appreciate other aspects of the film I might
have enjoyed. In *Truth or Dare* Madonna clearly revealed that she can
only think of exerting power along very traditional, white supremacist, capitalistic, patriarchal lines. That she made people who were
dependent on her for their immediate livelihood submit to her will
was neither charming nor seductive to me or the other black folks
that I spoke with who saw the film. We thought it tragically ironic
that Madonna would choose as her dance partner a black male with
dyed blonde hair. Perhaps had he appeared less like a white-identified
black male consumed by "blonde ambition" he might have upstaged
her. Instead he was positioned as a mirror, into which Madonna and
her audience could look and see only a reflection of herself and the
worship of "whiteness" she embodies—that white supremacist culture wants everyone to embody. Madonna used her power to ensure
that he and the other non-white women and men who worked for
her, as well as some of the white subordinates, would all serve as the

backdrop to her white-girl-makes-good drama. Joking about the film with other black folks, we commented that Madonna must have searched long and hard to find a black female that was not a good dancer, one who would not deflect attention away from her. And it is telling that when the film directly reflects something other than a positive image of Madonna, the camera highlights the rage this black female dancer was suppressing. It surfaces when the "subordinates" have time off and are "relaxing."

As with most Madonna videos, when critics talk about this film they tend to ignore race. Yet no viewer can look at this film and not think about race and representation without engaging in forms of denial. After choosing a cast of characters from marginalized groups—non-white folks, heterosexual and gay, and gay white folks—Madonna publicly describes them as "emotional cripples." And of course in the context of the film this description seems borne out by the way they allow her to dominate, exploit, and humiliate them. Those Madonna fans who are determined to see her as politically progressive might ask themselves why it is she completely endorses those racist/sexist/classist stereotypes that almost always attempt to portray marginalized groups as "defective." Let's face it, by doing this, Madonna is not breaking with any white supremacist, patriarchal *status quo;* she is endorsing and perpetuating it.

Some of us do not find it hip or cute for Madonna to brag that she has a "fascistic side," a side well documented in the film. Well, we did not see any of her cute little fascism in action when it was Warren Beatty calling her out in the film. No, there the image of Madonna was the little woman who grins and bears it. No, her "somebody's got to be in charge side," as she names it, was most expressed in her interaction with those representatives from marginalized groups who are most often victimized by the powerful. Why is it there is little or no discussion of Madonna as racist or sexist in her relation to other women? Would audiences be charmed by some rich white male entertainer telling us he must "play father" and oversee the actions of the less powerful, especially women and men of color? So why did so many people find it cute when Madonna asserted that she dominates the inter-racial casts of gay and heterosexual folks in her film because they are crippled and she "like[s] to play mother." No, this was not a display of feminist power, this was the same old phallic nonsense with white pussy at the center. And many of us watching were not simply unmoved—we were outraged.

Perhaps it is a sign of a collective feeling of powerlessness that many black, non-white, and white viewers of this film who were disturbed by the display of racism, sexism, and heterosexism (yes, it's possible to hire gay people, support AIDS projects, and still be biased in the direction of phallic patriarchal heterosexuality) in *Truth or Dare* have said so little. Sometimes it is difficult to find words to make a critique when we find ourselves attracted by some aspect of a performer's act and disturbed by others, or when a performer shows more interest in promoting progressive social causes than is customary. We may see that performer as above critique. Or we may feel our critique will in no way intervene on the worship of them as a cultural icon.

To say nothing, however, is to be complicit with the very forces of domination that make "blonde ambition" necessary to Madonna's success. Tragically, all that is transgressive and potentially empowering to feminist women and men about Madonna's work may be undermined by all that it contains that is reactionary and in no way unconventional or new. It is often the conservative elements in her work converging with the *status quo* that has the most powerful impact. For example: Given the rampant homophobia in this society and the concomitant heterosexist voyeuristic obsession with gay lifestyles, to what extent does Madonna progressively seek to challenge this if she insists on primarily representing gays as in some way emotionally handicapped or defective? Or when Madonna responds to the critique that she exploits gay men by cavalierly stating: "What does exploitation mean? . . . In a revolution, some people have to get hurt. To get people to change, you have to turn the table over. Some dishes get broken."

I can only say this doesn't sound like liberation to me. Perhaps when Madonna explores those memories of her white working-class childhood in a troubled family in a way that enables her to understand intimately the politics of exploitation, domination, and submission,